China's Unruly Journalists

Despite operating in one of the most tightly controlled media environments in the world, Chinese journalists sometimes take extraordinary risks, braving the perils of job loss or imprisonment to report sensitive stories. As a result, a group of journalists stands at the forefront of some of China's most dramatic social and political changes.

This book is the first to systematically explore why some Chinese journalists decide to challenge Communist Party power holders and the censorship system. Based on 18 months of fieldwork, interviews with over 70 Chinese journalists and academics and analysis of nearly 20,000 Chinese newspaper articles, it investigates the motivation behind news workers who often brave the perils of challenging an authoritarian system. Rather than being driven by commercial pressures or financial inducements, the book suggests that many aggressive journalists push the limits of acceptable coverage because of their sense of public spirit and their professional role orientation. It argues that ultimately, these advocate journalists matter because they challenge specific policies and are changing China, one article at a time.

By investigating these path-breaking journalists, the book engages with literature across the social sciences on contentious politics and social movements, political communication, media theory and the sociology of professions. Therefore, it will be of great interest to students and scholars of Chinese Studies, Politics and Media Studies.

Jonathan Hassid is an Assistant Professor in political science at Iowa State University, USA.

Routledge Contemporary China Series

1 **Nationalism, Democracy and National Integration in China**
Leong Liew and Wang Shaoguang

2 **Hong Kong's Tortuous Democratization**
A comparative analysis
Ming Sing

3 **China's Business Reforms**
Institutional challenges in a globalised economy
Edited by Russell Smyth, On Kit Tam, Malcolm Warner and Cherrie Zhu

4 **Challenges for China's Development**
An enterprise perspective
Edited by David H. Brown and Alasdair MacBean

5 **New Crime in China**
Public order and human rights
Ron Keith and Zhiqiu Lin

6 **Non-Governmental Organizations in Contemporary China**
Paving the way to civil society?
Qiusha Ma

7 **Globalization and the Chinese City**
Fulong Wu

8 **The Politics of China's Accession to the World Trade Organization**
The dragon goes global
Hui Feng

9 **Narrating China**
Jia Pingwa and his fictional world
Yiyan Wang

10 **Sex, Science and Morality in China**
Joanne McMillan

11 **Politics in China Since 1949**
Legitimizing authoritarian rule
Robert Weatherley

12 **International Human Resource Management in Chinese Multinationals**
Jie Shen and Vincent Edwards

13 **Unemployment in China**
Economy, human resources and labour markets
Edited by Grace Lee and Malcolm Warner

14 **China and Africa**
Engagement and compromise
Ian Taylor

15 **Gender and Education in China**
Gender discourses and women's schooling in the early twentieth century
Paul J. Bailey

16 **SARS**
Reception and interpretation in three Chinese cities
Edited by Deborah Davis and Helen Siu

17 **Human Security and the Chinese State**
Historical transformations and the modern quest for sovereignty
Robert E. Bedeski

18 **Gender and Work in Urban China**
Women workers of the unlucky generation
Liu Jieyu

19 **China's State Enterprise Reform**
From Marx to the market
John Hassard, Jackie Sheehan, Meixiang Zhou, Jane Terpstra-Tong and Jonathan Morris

20 **Cultural Heritage Management in China**
Preserving the cities of the Pearl River Delta
Edited by Hilary du Cros and Yok-shiu F. Lee

21 **Paying for Progress**
Public finance, human welfare and inequality in China
Edited by Vivienne Shue and Christine Wong

22 **China's Foreign Trade Policy**
The new constituencies
Edited by Ka Zeng

23 **Hong Kong, China**
Learning to belong to a nation
Gordon Mathews, Tai-lok Lui, and Eric Kit-wai Ma

24 **China Turns to Multilateralism**
Foreign policy and regional security
Edited by Guoguang Wu and Helen Lansdowne

25 **Tourism and Tibetan Culture in Transition**
A place called Shangrila
Åshild Kolås

26 **China's Emerging Cities**
The making of new urbanism
Edited by Fulong Wu

27 **China-US Relations Transformed**
Perceptions and strategic interactions
Edited by Suisheng Zhao

28 **The Chinese Party-State in the 21st Century**
Adaptation and the reinvention of legitimacy
Edited by André Laliberté and Marc Lanteigne

29 **Political Change in Macao**
Sonny Shiu-Hing Lo

30 **China's Energy Geopolitics**
The Shanghai Cooperation Organization and Central Asia
Thrassy N. Marketos

31 **Regime Legitimacy in Contemporary China**
Institutional change and stability
Edited by Thomas Heberer and Gunter Schubert

32 **U.S.-China Relations**
China policy on Capitol Hill
Tao Xie

33 **Chinese Kinship**
Contemporary anthropological perspectives
Edited by Susanne Brandtstädter and Gonçalo D. Santos

34 **Politics and Government in Hong Kong**
Crisis under Chinese sovereignty
Edited by Ming Sing

35 **Rethinking Chinese Popular Culture**
Cannibalizations of the canon
Edited by Carlos Rojas and Eileen Cheng-yin Chow

36 **Institutional Balancing in the Asia Pacific**
Economic interdependence and China's rise
Kai He

37 **Rent Seeking in China**
Edited by Tak-Wing Ngo and Yongping Wu

38 **China, Xinjiang and Central Asia**
History, transition and crossborder interaction into the 21st century
Edited by Colin Mackerras and Michael Clarke

39 **Intellectual Property Rights in China**
Politics of piracy, trade and protection
Gordon Cheung

40 **Developing China**
Land, politics and social conditions
George C.S. Lin

41 **State and Society Responses to Social Welfare Needs in China**
Serving the people
Edited by Jonathan Schwartz and Shawn Shieh

42 **Gay and Lesbian Subculture in Urban China**
Loretta Wing Wah Ho

43 **The Politics of Heritage Tourism in China**
A view from Lijiang
Xiaobo Su and Peggy Teo

44 **Suicide and Justice**
A Chinese perspective
Wu Fei

45 **Management Training and Development in China**
Educating managers in a globalized economy
Edited by Malcolm Warner and Keith Goodall

46 **Patron-Client Politics and Elections in Hong Kong**
Bruce Kam-kwan Kwong

47 **Chinese Family Business and the Equal Inheritance System**
Unravelling the myth
Victor Zheng

48 **Reconciling State, Market and Civil Society in China**
The long march towards prosperity
Paolo Urio

49 **Innovation in China**
The Chinese software industry
Shang-Ling Jui

50 **Mobility, Migration and the Chinese Scientific Research System**
Koen Jonkers

51 **Chinese Film Stars**
Edited by Mary Farquhar and Yingjin Zhang

52 **Chinese Male Homosexualities**
Memba, Tongzhi and Golden Boy
Travis S.K. Kong

53 **Industrialisation and Rural Livelihoods in China**
Agricultural processing in Sichuan
Susanne Lingohr-Wolf

54 **Law, Policy and Practice on China's Periphery**
Selective adaptation and institutional capacity
Pitman B. Potter

55 **China-Africa Development Relations**
Edited by Christopher M. Dent

56 **Neoliberalism and Culture in China and Hong Kong**
The countdown of time
Hai Ren

57 **China's Higher Education Reform and Internationalisation**
Edited by Janette Ryan

58 **Law, Wealth and Power in China**
Commercial law reforms in context
Edited by John Garrick

59 **Religion in Contemporary China**
Revitalization and innovation
Edited by Adam Yuet Chau

60 **Consumer-Citizens of China**
The role of foreign brands in the imagined future China
Kelly Tian and Lily Dong

61 **The Chinese Communist Party and China's Capitalist Revolution**
The political impact of the market
Lance L.P. Gore

62 **China's Homeless Generation**
Voices from the veterans of the Chinese civil war, 1940s–1990s
Joshua Fan

63 **In Search of China's Development Model**
Beyond the Beijing consensus
Edited by S. Philip Hsu, Suisheng Zhao and Yu-Shan Wu

64 **Xinjiang and China's Rise in Central Asia, 1949–2009**
A history
Michael E. Clarke

65 **Trade Unions in China**
The challenge of labour unrest
Tim Pringle

66 **China's Changing Workplace**
Dynamism, diversity and disparity
Edited by Peter Sheldon, Sunghoon Kim, Yiqiong Li and Malcolm Warner

67 **Leisure and Power in Urban China**
Everyday life in a medium-sized Chinese city
Unn Målfrid H. Rolandsen

68 **China, Oil and Global Politics**
Philip Andrews-Speed and Roland Dannreuther

69 **Education Reform in China**
Edited by Janette Ryan

70 **Social Policy and Migration in China**
Lida Fan

71 **China's One Child Policy and Multiple Caregiving**
Raising little Suns in Xiamen
Esther C.L. Goh

72 **Politics and Markets in Rural China**
Edited by Björn Alpermann

73 **China's New Underclass**
Paid domestic labour
Xinying Hu

74 **Poverty and Development in China**
Alternative approaches to poverty assessment
Lu Caizhen

75 **International Governance and Regimes**
A Chinese perspective
Peter Kien-Hong Yu

76 **HIV/AIDS in China – The Economic and Social Determinants**
Dylan Sutherland and Jennifer Y.J. Hsu

77 **Looking for Work in Post-Socialist China**
Governance, active job seekers and the new Chinese labor market
Feng Xu

78 **Sino-Latin American Relations**
Edited by K.C. Fung and Alicia Garcia-Herrero

79 **Mao's China and the Sino-Soviet Split**
Ideological dilemma
Mingjiang Li

80 **Law and Policy for China's Market Socialism**
Edited by John Garrick

81 **China-Taiwan Relations in a Global Context**
Taiwan's foreign policy and relations
Edited by C.X. George Wei

82 **The Chinese Transformation of Corporate Culture**
Colin S.C. Hawes

83 **Mapping Media in China**
Region, province, locality
Edited by Wanning Sun and Jenny Chio

84 **China, the West and the Myth of New Public Management**
Neoliberalism and its discontents
Paolo Urio

85 **The Lahu Minority in Southwest China**
A response to ethnic marginalization on the frontier
Jianxiong Ma

86 **Social Capital and Institutional Constraints**
A comparative analysis of China, Taiwan and the US
Joonmo Son

87 **Southern China**
Industry, development and industrial policy
Marco R. Di Tommaso, Lauretta Rubini and Elisa Barbieri

88 **State-Market Interactions in China's Reform Era**
Local state competition and global market building in the tobacco industry
Junmin Wang

89 **The Reception and Rendition of Freud in China**
China's Freudian slip
Edited by Tao Jiang and Philip J. Ivanhoe

90 **Sinologism**
An alternative to Orientalism and Postcolonialism
Ming Dong Gu

91 **The Middle Class in Neoliberal China**
Governing risk, life-building, and themed spaces
Hai Ren

92 **The Chinese Corporatist State**
Adaption, survival and resistance
Edited by Jennifer Y.J. Hsu and Reza Hasmath

93 **Law and Fair Work in China**
Sean Cooney, Sarah Biddulph and Ying Zhu

94 **Guangdong and Chinese Diaspora**
The changing landscape of Qiaoxiang
Yow Cheun Hoe

95 **The Shanghai Alleyway House**
A vanishing urban vernacular
Gregory Bracken

96 **Chinese Globalization**
A profile of people-based global connections in China
Jiaming Sun and Scott Lancaster

97 **Disruptive Innovation in Chinese and Indian Businesses**
The strategic implications for local entrepreneurs and global incumbents
Peter Ping Li

98 **Corporate Governance and Banking in China**
Michael Tan

99 **Gender, Modernity and Male Migrant Workers in China**
Becoming a 'modern' man
Xiaodong Lin

100 **Emissions, Pollutants and Environmental Policy in China**
Designing a national emissions trading system
Bo Miao

101 **Sustainable Development in China**
Edited by Curtis Andressen, Mubarak A.R. and Xiaoyi Wang

102 **Islam and China's Hong Kong**
Ethnic identity, Muslim networks and the new Silk Road
Wai-Yip Ho

103 **International Regimes in China**
Domestic implementation of the international fisheries agreements
Gianluca Ferraro

104 **Rural Migrants in Urban China**
Enclaves and transient urbanism
Fulong Wu, Fangzhu Zhang and Chris Webster

105 **State-Led Privatization in China**
The politics of economic reform
Jin Zeng

106 **China's Supreme Court**
Ronald C. Keith, Zhiqiu Lin and Shumei Hou

107 **Queer Sinophone Cultures**
Howard Chiang and Ari Larissa Heinrich

108 **New Confucianism in Twenty-First Century China**
The construction of a discourse
Jesús Solé-Farràs

109 **Christian Values in Communist China**
Gerda Wielander

110 **China and Global Trade Governance**
China's first decade in the World Trade Organization
Edited by Ka Zeng and Wei Liang

111 **The China Model and Global Political Economy**
Comparison, impact, and interaction
Ming Wan

112 **Chinese Middle Classes**
China, Taiwan, Macao and Hong Kong
Edited by Hsin-Huang Michael Hsiao

113 **Economy Hotels in China**
A glocalized innovative hospitality sector
Songshan Sam Huang and Xuhua Michael Sun

114 **The Uyghur Lobby**
Global networks, coalitions and strategies of the World Uyghur Congress
Yu-Wen Chen

115 **Housing Inequality in Chinese Cities**
Edited by Youqin Huang and Si-ming Li

116 **Transforming Chinese Cities**
Edited by Mark Y. Wang, Pookong Kee and Jia Gao

117 **Popular Media, Social Emotion and Public Discourse in Contemporary China**
Shuyu Kong

118 **Globalization and Public Sector Reform in China**
Kjeld Erik Brødsgaard

119 **Religion and Ecological Sustainability in China**
Edited by James Miller, Dan Smyer Yu and Peter van der Veer

120 **Comparatizing Taiwan**
Edited by Shu-mei Shih and Ping-hui Liao

121 **Entertaining the Nation**
Chinese television in the twenty-first century
Edited by Ruoyun Bai and Geng Song

122 **Local Governance Innovation in China**
Experimentation, diffusion, and defiance
Edited by Jessica C. Teets and William Hurst

123 **Footbinding and Women's Labor in Sichuan**
Hill Gates

124 **Incentives for Innovation in China**
Building an innovative economy
Xuedong Ding and Jun Li

125 **Conflict and Cooperation in Sino-US Relations**
Change and continuity, causes and cures
Edited by Jean-Marc F. Blanchard and Simon Shen

126 **Chinese Environmental Aesthetics**
Wangheng Chen, translated by Feng Su, edited by Gerald Cipriani

127 **China's Military Procurement in the Reform Era**
The setting of new directions
Yoram Evron

128 **Forecasting China's Future**
Dominance or collapse?
Roger Irvine

129 **Chinese Migration and Economic Relations with Europe**
Edited by Marco Sanfilippo and Agnieszka Weinar

130 **Party Hegemony and Entrepreneurial Power in China**
Institutional change in the film and music industries
Elena Meyer-Clement

131 **Explaining Railway Reform in China**
A train of property rights re-arrangements
Linda Tjia Yin-nor

132 **Irony, Cynicism and the Chinese State**
Edited by Hans Steinmüller and Susanne Brandtstädter

133 **Animation in China**
History, aesthetics, media
Sean Macdonald

134 **Parenting, Education and Social Mobility in Rural China**
Cultivating dragons and phoenixes
Peggy A. Kong

135 **Disability Policy in China**
Child and family experiences
Xiaoyuan Shang and Karen R. Fisher

136 **The Politics of Controlling Organized Crime in Greater China**
Sonny Shiu-Hing Lo

137 **Inside Xinjiang**
Space, place and power in China's Muslim far northwest
Edited by Anna Hayes and Michael Clarke

138 **China's Strategic Priorities**
Edited by Jonathan H. Ping and Brett McCormick

139 China's Unruly Journalists
How committed professionals are
changing the People's Republic
Jonathan Hassid

140 The Geopolitics of Red Oil
Constructing the China threat
through energy security
Andrew Stephen Campion

China's Unruly Journalists
How committed professionals are changing the People's Republic

Jonathan Hassid

LONDON AND NEW YORK

First published 2016
by Routledge

2 Park Square, Milton Park, Abingdon, Oxfordshire OX14 4RN
711 Third Avenue, New York, NY 10017

Routledge is an imprint of the Taylor & Francis Group, an informa business

First issued in paperback 2018

Copyright © 2016 Jonathan Hassid

The right of Jonathan Hassid to be identified as author of this work has been asserted by him in accordance with sections 77 and 78 of the Copyright, Designs and Patents Act 1988.

All rights reserved. No part of this book may be reprinted or reproduced or utilised in any form or by any electronic, mechanical, or other means, now known or hereafter invented, including photocopying and recording, or in any information storage or retrieval system, without permission in writing from the publishers.

Notice:
Product or corporate names may be trademarks or registered trademarks, and are used only for identification and explanation without intent to infringe.

British Library Cataloguing in Publication Data
A catalogue record for this book is available from the British Library

Library of Congress Cataloging-in-Publication Data
Hassid, Jonathan.
   China's unruly journalists : how committed professionals are changing the People's Republic / Jonathan Hassid.
      pages cm. — (Routledge contemporary China series ; 139)
   Includes bibliographical references and index.
   ISBN 978-1-138-95574-5 (hardback) — ISBN 978-1-315-66611-2 (ebook) 1. Journalism—Political aspects—China. 2. Journalism—China—History—21st century. 3. Press and politics—China—History—21st century. 4. Government and the press—China—History—21st century. I. Title.
   PN5367.P6H36 2015
   079'.51—dc23
   2015026669

ISBN: 978-1-138-95574-5 (hbk)
ISBN: 978-1-138-60895-5 (pbk)

Typeset in Times New Roman
by Apex CoVantage, LLC

For Amanda and Carlotta

Contents

List of tables xviii
Acknowledgements xix
List of abbreviations and acronyms xxi

1 Censorship and its discontents 1

Introducing the Chinese media 1
Liberalization: economic, not political 2
Beijing vs. the media 3
An uncertain control 5
Research questions 7
A preview of the argument 8
Limitations 12

2 Four models of the Fourth Estate: a typology of contemporary Chinese journalists 19

Introduction 19
Methodology 21
Making professional Chinese journalists 22
Conclusion 27

3 "Throat and tongue:" the communist professionals 30

Professional and *communist 33*
Who are the communist professionals? 35
Conclusion 36

4 "Guard against fire, theft, and journalists": the workaday reporters 40

The forms of Chinese media corruption 41

Causes of corruption 43
Corruption and the profession 45
Corruption and the state 46
Conclusion 47

5 Neutral, objective, and rare: the American-style journalists   50

American desires, Chinese reality 51
The rise of American-style journalism 52
The limits of objectivity 56
Conclusion 57

6 Representing "the people": the advocate professionals   60

Advocacy and nationalism 61
The limited power of markets 63
Factors pushing advocacy journalism 66
A long tradition 67
Advocacy, path dependence, and the news media 69
Conclusion 71

7 Pressing back   74

Introduction 74
What is pushback? 74
Pushback in context 77
Causes of pushback 78
Explaining pushback, take 1: the problem with economic determinism 78
Computer-assisted content analysis 81
Explaining pushback, take 2: political opportunity structures 93
Explaining pushback, take 3: China's professional journalists 95
Advocacy journalism and pushback 96
Pushback's effects 98
Conclusion 99

8 Beyond pushback   107

Introduction 107
Case one: the China Youth Daily *open letters 108*
Case two: the strike at the Beijing News *113*
Supplemental case: the Southern Weekend *strike that wasn't 116*
The theoretical payoff 118
Conclusion 123

9 Chinese journalism in the Internet age   128
The Internet should not be seen in isolation 133
The gatekeepers 134
Conclusion 135

10 Conclusion   139
Uncertainty: obstacle and opportunity 139
The utility of the pushback concept 141
Pushback and social movement theory 141
Why does the CCP allow pushback? 142
From pushback to resistance 144
The importance of the professions 146
Corruption's corrosion 147
Advocacy's short-term consequences 149
Advocacy's longer-term consequences 149
Future research 150
The Chinese future 152

Appendices   161
   Appendix A: list of Chinese newspapers analyzed, by province 161
   Appendix B: newspaper rank-order lists 162
   Appendix C: list of newspaper topics analyzed 165
   Appendix D: category means 166
Index   175

Tables

2.1	A typology of Chinese journalism	20
2.2	Fieldwork sites	21
2.3	Characteristics of the four types	26
7.1	Pushback in context	79
7.2	Dependent variables	86
7.3	Independent and control variables	89
7.4	Regression results	90
7.5	Standardized regression coefficients	91
7.6	Predicted percent change in results, from the lowest to highest observed values, holding other factors constant	92
9.1	Approximate number of article reprints in mainstream media Weibo feeds	134

Acknowledgements

I am profoundly grateful for the time I have spent at the University of California, Berkeley; the University of Technology, Sydney; and Iowa State University in the company of so many extraordinary scholars, colleagues and friends.

A special thanks goes to Kevin O'Brien for his time, mentorship, and insight on this and other projects over the years. His help has made this project significantly better. I owe a tremendous debt to other scholars, benefitting from Lowell Dittmer's wisdom and enthusiasm, Tom Gold's insights and impressive historical perspective, Wanning Sun's insights into the Chinese media, and Todd LaPorte's unfailing ability to see interesting similarities and differences between China and other parts of the world.

I am also grateful for help and comments from Margaret Boittin, Jennifer Brass, Anita Chan, Zongshi Chen, Jenny Chio, Josh Chin, Julia Chuang, Dai Lu, Mark Dallas, Gregory Distelhorst, Jennifer Dixon, Ashley Esarey, Eli Friedman, Steven Goldstein, Gong Wenxiang, Samuel Handlin, Amanda Hassid, Timothy Hidebrandt, Min Jiang, Allison Kaufman, Jody LaPorte, Liu Xiaobiao, Peter Lorentzen, Fen Lin, Will Lowe, Eva Mok, Dann Naseemullah, Sara Newland, Elisa Oreglia, Raymond I. Orr, Yancey Orr, Ran Jijun, Maria Repnikova, Rachel E. Stern, Daniela Stockmann, Christopher Sullivan, George Tsai, Carsten Vala, Leslie Wang, Bartholomew Watson, Susanne Wengle, Jason Wittenberg, Jakub Wrzesniewksi, Suowei Xiao, Xiao Qiang, Lu Ying, Zhan Jiang, and the many Chinese citizens who provided key information but must remain nameless. Special thanks goes out to my research assistants, Ming Tan and Li-Chia Lo. All errors are of course my own.

And finally, this project was funded in part by a Fulbright-Hays Doctoral Dissertation Abroad Fellowship, two Foreign Language and Area Studies (FLAS) fellowships, the China Times Cultural Foundation, support from Berkeley's Center for Chinese Studies, grants from the UC Berkeley Graduate Division, and grants from the Faculty of Arts and Social Sciences and the China Research Centre, University of Technology, Sydney.

Portions of Chapter 1 previously appeared as "Controlling the Chinese Media: An Uncertain Business," © 2008 by The Regents of the University of California. Reprinted from *Asian Survey*, Vol. 48, No. 3, pp. 414–30, by permission of the Regents. A greatly condensed and modified version of Chapter 2 appeared as

"Four Models of the Fourth Estate," © 2011 by *China Quarterly* and the School of Oriental and African Studies, Vol. 208, pp. 813–32, reprinted by permission. Portions of Chapter 8, heavily modified, appeared originally as "China's Contentious Journalists," in *Problems of Post-Communism*, Vol. 55, No. 4, July/August 2008, pp. 52–61, © 2008 by Jonathan Hassid.

Abbreviations and acronyms

ACJA	All-China Journalists' Association
CCTV	China Central Television
CASS	Chinese Academy of Social Sciences
CCP	Chinese Communist Party
CPD	Central Propaganda Department
CCA	computer assisted content analysis
DV	dependent variable
GAPP	General Administration of Press and Publication
HHI	Herfindahl-Hirschman Index
HLM	hierarchical linear model
IV	independent variable
IOJ	International Organization of Journalists
NPC	National People's Congress
NGO	nongovernmental organization
POS	political opportunity structure (concept in political process theory)
PPT	political process theory
PRC	People's Republic of China
RMB	Renminbi, the Chinese currency
SAPPRFT	State Administration of Press, Publication, Radio, Film, and Television (successor agency created by merger of GAPP and SARFT in 2013)
SARFT	State Administration of Radio, Film, and Television
SARS	Sudden Acute Respiratory Syndrome
SCIO	State Council Information Office
SOEs	state-owned enterprises

1 Censorship and its discontents

In the summer of 2008, I was having coffee with a prominent Chinese journalist for one of the country's top newspapers. As we were talking, she received a phone call from her boss. The news was bad; another prominent paper had scooped their story on the corrupt activities of a high-level Chinese Communist Party (CCP) official. Worse, because the other paper's story was gaining so much attention, the Central Propaganda Department (CPD), the Party organization in charge of media censorship, had decreed that further stories on the topic were forbidden. Weeks of hard work were suddenly useless. Far from being angry or even surprised, my friend was simply resigned. She knew further argument was useless – editors at her paper had been imprisoned in the recent past for defying the Party – and she knew there would be other opportunities to print similar stories. Ultimately, she shrugged her shoulders, and we continued drinking our coffee.

This incident exposes much about the lives of Chinese journalists and the complex relationship they have with the regime. It shows that reporters must act in the shadow of the state, always calculating the risks (often high) and rewards (mostly low) of stories that are unfavorable to power holders. But more than that, it also demonstrates that some Chinese reporters are willing to pursue stories on sensitive topics, despite the real risk that they are wasting their time or even that publication will result in fines, demotion, firing, or imprisonment. What this vignette does not tell us though, is *why*. Why do knowledgeable people used to working within the state censorship apparatus every day of their professional lives decide to begin challenging their official role as CCP mouthpieces? Answering this question is the motivating force behind this book. Although this opening vignette has a somewhat unhappy ending, and the Chinese media environment is even more restricted than it was at the time, I have a bit of optimism about the future. The fact that there are Chinese journalists as committed as my friend has huge consequences for China and beyond. What is more, I have found that such feisty professionals are thriving and perhaps even multiplying in China, a nation known for stringent censorship.

Introducing the Chinese media[1]

China's press control is hardly new. During the Mao era (1949–1976), the state tightly controlled all media outlets, restricting not only their numbers, but also their content, length, and format (He 2000). From 1949 until the mid-1990s, all news providers were funded either directly by the state, indirectly through a policy of forced subscriptions that kept circulation numbers artificially high, or through "back scratching" arrangements across organizations (i.e., "We'll subscribe to your publication if you subscribe to ours") (Ashley Esarey, personal communication). During the Cultural Revolution (1966–1976), the media were especially curtailed, and entertainment options were at times limited to a library of "eight plays, eight songs, and three film clips" (Lynch 1999: 24). All told, these mechanisms meant that "the vast majority of the Chinese did not even have the ability to be suspicious of the CCP's political system, because they didn't know that in the outside world a different, worthier life (*geng you jiazhi de shenghuo* 更有价值的生活) even existed" (He Qinglian 2004: 4).[2] Control of information was close to total.

Many aspects of the relationship between state and press began to change with Deng Xiaoping's reforms of the late 1970s. Commercialization, advertising, and market competition were allowed for the first time, and the number of news providers and range of acceptable content both dramatically increased. For example, between 1980 and 2009, the number of newspaper titles alone has risen from 188 to 1937, with the number of television stations, radio stations, and satellite broadcasters also proportionally increasing (Chinese Academy of Social Sciences News Research Institute [*Zhongguo Shehui Kexueyuan Xinwen Yanjiusuo* 中国社会科学院新闻研究所], various years). As the number of news providers has soared, so have their financial resources and day-to-day independence from the government. While Mao-era journalism relied entirely on state funding, today the Chinese news business is market-driven, with advertising revenue increasing from zero at the start of the reform era to 343.7 billion RMB (US$56.5 billion) in 2010 (Wood 2011), or around 0.9% of China's gross domestic product. The vast majority of publications in China now rely entirely on the market for funding; even semi-official papers like *Guangming Daily* (*Guangming Ribao* 光明日报) rely on commercial advertising and joint ventures to pay for their operations (Interview HH20–2). To sum up the results of a long, complicated market transition, the Chinese media are now – with an occasional notable exception – entirely commercialized.

Liberalization: economic, not political

Commercialized, however, hardly means free. All media in China are regulated by the CPD[3] and its lower-level equivalents (Brady 2008: 13) and by various state agencies like the State Administration of Press, Publication, Radio, Film, and Television (SAPPRFT); the State Council Information Office (SCIO); and the State Council Internet Office.[4] Since there are few detailed, academic studies of the CPD itself,[5] however, it is hard to know the extent to which power is shared among the CPD, provincial and local propaganda departments, and various state agencies. Responsibility and bargaining among different levels of the media control system remain unclear, and this book concentrates mainly on how news workers react to the control regime, not the control regime itself.

The Chinese press is very different from that of thirty years ago. Today, the media play a crucial role in the Chinese polity, affecting areas from elite politics and policy analysis ("the media ... have greatly affected CCP decision-making" (Yan Jiaqi 1995: 13) to studies of collective action among the peasantry ("even publication of a single letter or report detailing a case ... can instantly nationalize and legitimize a focus for popular action" (Li and O'Brien 1996: 48). But despite this importance, and the fact that nearly all Chinese papers rely on the market for readers and finance, economic liberalization has not translated into much political freedom. Beijing has made clear that it will continue to exercise very tight control over the news media for the foreseeable future by banning wayward publications, jailing dissident journalists, and attempting to consolidate control under huge government-run conglomerates (Zhao 2000). Meanwhile, China periodically undergoes media crackdowns where control is even tighter than usual. One blogger calls these the "thorny stretch of the path" (Qian Gang 2009), and they tend to recur every few years.

Beijing vs. the media

So how has Beijing managed to control the media so effectively in the face of the market juggernaut? After all, newspapers have noticed that exposé-style investigative reporting draws readers – and advertising money. Adventurous papers like *Southern Weekend* saw their circulation soar in the late 1990s and early 2000s on the strength of investigative reporting, and the two-thirds decline in circulation the paper took after the replacement of its boldest editorial staff in 2003–2004 (Interview FY22–0A) provides solid evidence that its readership was indeed responding to its muckraking style.

More generally, one prominent scholar has claimed that "The higher the level of marketization, the greater the degree of self-liberalization. Strong market forces [have] reduced the effectiveness of government censorship of the media by multiplying the channels of production and dissemination" (Pei 1994: 155). One academic goes even further, arguing that "those media which are most exposed to market competition will become free and pluralistic most rapidly" (Lawson 2002: 181). But in China, this argument seems premature. Why? How is it that "the party obviously feels safe enough to entrust commercialized papers with the task of getting the propaganda messages across" to the extent that it is actually encouraging further commercialization (Brendebach 2005: 42)?

Most answers to this question series fall into three broad categories: monetary, legal/structural, and coercive. Beyond arguing, as the former publisher of *Beijing Youth Daily* (*Beijing Qingnian Bao* 北京青年报) puts it, that "marketization and political orientation of the news are not incompatible" (Zhao 1998: 149), monetary control theorists go further in arguing that the state can actually use marketization to its own advantage. Media scholar Ashley Esarey writes that "the state developed market incentives to encourage media to produce news that was politically acceptable and popular with consumers" (Esarey 2005: 37). Critically, the top managers of most papers are appointed directly by the CPD and CCP or by the local propaganda department branch, and they are typically very well compensated for their efforts (Esarey 2005: 57). Further down the ladder, reporters' pay is often "tied to the number and length of stories that are broadcast or published," and so "journalists who fall out of favor with their superiors, or whose work is frequently censored, find themselves quickly out of the money" (Esarey 2005: 58).

This media control regime also uses legal and structural mechanisms. Among the most important of these constraints is the fact that all media units must be subordinated to a sponsoring government unit in their geographic area. Publications must also obtain a publication number (*kanhao* 刊号) from the General Administration on Press and Publication (GAPP) and its successor the SAPPRFT, which is often difficult to obtain legally.[6] Indeed, experimental regulations first trialed in 2010 are designed to eliminate small players from entering the industry, requiring extensive, additional state review for publications whose circulation fall below 3% of the local market, a review that may ultimately lead to forced closure (Cui Baoguo [崔保国] 2011: 42). This regulation system ensures that aside from a few illegal *samizdat*-style publications, there are no officially independent media outlets. Although oversight is usually hands-off, the fact that sponsoring units retain ultimate responsibility over the content published by their attached news units creates a strong incentive to set appropriate boundaries. After all, few players in Chinese politics want to invite greater scrutiny from central leaders, and many news outlets have internal censors seconded from the sponsoring agency and placed to ensure that things do not get out of hand.

Equally critical is the fact that top editors of most newspapers can be appointed and removed directly by the CPD and CCP Organization Department rather than by the sponsoring government unit or the newspaper itself. This creates a natural incentive for editors to feel themselves responsible not to their individual newspaper but to Beijing and the CPD. Although these papers are "commercially oriented media, they are still under the ideological leadership of the Party" (Zhao 1998: 161). Ultimately, this often leads to a policy of "being critical on small issues and being supportive on major issues" (*xiaoma da bangmang* 小骂大帮忙) (Zhao 1998: 163), a result encouraged by at least nine specific laws and regulations (He Qinglian 2004: 5).[7]

Finally, many scholars argue coercion is the last critical component of this control regime. Unlike the former Soviet Union, the Chinese press has never used pre-publication censorship as its primary media control. Instead, the CCP expects newspapers and magazines to toe the party line, and those occasional publications that go too far are subject to *post facto* suppression, sometimes involving punishment of the journalists who wrote the offending articles. Frank Smyth of the Committee to Protect Journalists, a Washington-based NGO, illustrates a typical view among Western journalists and academics:

> In decades past, Chinese authorities relied on censorship[8] and legal action as the main tools to silence the press, but in today's dynamic climate, the Communist Party has increasingly resorted to jailing journalists in order to silence some of the nation's most enterprising reporters.
> (U.S.-China Economic and Security Review Commission 2005: 92)

Zhou He writes that "coercion – in such forms as imprisonment, exile, purge and unemployment – has become the main means of safeguarding the supremacy of the Chinese version of Communist ideology. This is particularly true in the media" (He 2003: 208).

But this is only part of the story. It is true that Reporters sans Frontières, a French-based NGO, claims that China has more journalists imprisoned than any other country, and ranks 176th out of 180 rated countries on press freedom (Reporters sans Frontières 2015). But at the same time, the jailing of 29 journalists (Reporters sans Frontières 2013) out of over 173,000 registered[9] represents a tiny .017% of the total. Coercion like this has an outsized impact, and the climate of fear it creates is critical for keeping the press in line, but such punishment is clearly not the major way China controls its journalists (Stern and Hassid 2012). Likewise, although the Chinese control regime certainly does rely on both monetary and structural restraints on the press, none of these explanations – even in combination – tells the full story.

An uncertain control

Self-censorship, a powerful information control strategy, refers to "a set of editorial actions ranging from omission, dilution, distortion, and change of emphasis to choice of rhetorical devices by journalists, their organizations, and even the entire media community in anticipation of currying reward and avoiding punishments from the power structure" (Lee 1998: 57). Media scholars, contentious politics theorists, and others have long recognized the power of self-censorship in the Chinese press, but few have elucidated the mechanisms that make it so pervasive. Statements like "self-censorship is the major form of media control in China" (Chen Yali 2003) are common, but few reporters or academics have explored why the self-censorship regime is so effective.[10]

The CPD's power to determine what is and what is not acceptable news coverage lies at the heart of China's effective regime of self-censorship. The CPD and subsidiary agencies alone have the authority to demarcate the boundaries of acceptable coverage, and it does so in such a vague way that even professionals with decades of experience can be caught off guard by its decisions. It is this uncertainty about how far they can push coverage without facing a harsh and arbitrary punishment that keeps many reporters and editors from being too aggressive in their coverage. In other words, the uncertainty that surrounds the CPD's post hoc decisions on specific news topics is critical to controlling news workers.

Organization theorists have long recognized the power of uncertainty. Writing in 1964, French sociologist Michel Crozier analyzed the link between predictability of behavior and bargaining power. He argues that "the power of A over B depends on A's ability to predict B's behavior and on the uncertainty of B about A's behavior." He continues, "As long as the requirements of action create situations of uncertainty, the individuals who have to face them have power over those who are affected by the results of their choice" (Crozier 1964: 158). In other words, those with the ability to make unpredictable decisions ultimately have the power.

And the CPD has just this power. Without pre-publication censorship, it is often impossible for reporters to know ahead of time what will be a safe story. It is true that the CPD sends out specific briefings outlining which current topics are unacceptable,[11] and some topics are so clearly off-limits[12] that the media know better than to attempt them. But without clear guidelines on every single topic or story, and with subtly shifting political winds, even long-time journalists can often get in trouble for stories they and their editors thought were acceptable or that had gone unnoticed in the past. "It's something we are all aware of, we sense it, but we can't really express it," one veteran reporter says about which topics are allowable day-to-day (Pan 2000: 82), though this ad hoc approach naturally fails at times. Because the CPD uses its agenda-setting power to change its standards about acceptable topics so often, a story praised yesterday or last week might get a reporter into trouble the next time it is published.

One of the best-known examples of this phenomenon is the fallout that resulted from the Sun Zhigang case in 2003. Early that year, designer Sun Zhigang, originally from Hubei province, moved to the southern Chinese city of Guangzhou to begin working for a garment company. In April 2003, he was detained by Guangzhou police for not carrying his temporary residence permit. While in police custody in an internal migrant detention facility, he was beaten to death by the facility's staff members. After the aggressive *Southern Metropolis Daily* (*Nanfang Dushi Bao* 南方都市报) reported the circumstances of Sun's death on April 25, 2003, newspapers all over the country reprinted the article in the face of a national uproar. Ultimately, the pressure on the government to act was so great that the decades-old law authorizing the use of such internal detention facilities was repealed in what amounted to a major victory for a watchdog press (Hand 2006).

This victory was short-lived, however, as just a few months later police raided the *Southern Metropolis Daily* and "detained the top editor and six other officials in what many journalists regarded as retribution for aggressive reporting" (Kahn 2004) on this and their earlier story reporting the government's SARS cover-up.[13] Ultimately, the managing editor and one other official were sentenced to prison time on weak evidence of alleged corruption, an outcome "many journalists knew" was the result of "local officials' retaliation for the paper's coverage of Sun's case" (Beach 2005). And the chilling effect was immediate: "A former editor at another popular Guangzhou-based newspaper, who spoke on condition of anonymity for fear of reprisal, called the arrests 'the most serious blow to the Chinese media in the last decade'"(Beach 2005). The *Southern Metropolis Daily*'s top staffers were replaced by CCP appointees, and the paper has never quite regained its prominent pre-arrest reputation.[14]

The example of the *Southern Metropolis Daily* demonstrates how coercion and uncertainty and coercion work together to great effect. Ultimately, it is not the limited coercion itself, but the central government's vast and possibly deliberate amplification of its effect that makes this form of control so particularly powerful. For the Chinese media, uncertainty is so effective in amplifying the effects of coercion that the state is able to control newspapers even with the jailing of fewer than one in five thousand reporters (Stern and Hassid 2012). This amplification happens in part through the proliferation of control parables, a particular type of "didactic story that invent or recapitulate an understanding of why certain types of action are dangerous or even impossible" (Stern and Hassid 2012: 1240). Control parables represent journalists and other public professionals' attempts to make sense of a chaotic, dangerous work environment. Ultimately, "speculation surrounding a warning or punishment generates a set of imagined rules designed to prevent future clashes with authority. Without state involvement or necessarily even knowledge, then, control parables dissipate political possibilities from below" (Stern and Hassid 2012: 1241).

But uncertainty has a flip side, as well, allowing those few journalists brave enough to challenge the system space to work between its interstices. Many of these journalists are advocate professionals, a category discussed more fully in Chapter 6. Ultimately, although the CPD's uncertain control keeps most journalists in line, it does allow an intrepid handful the plausible deniability to work on specific issues like uncovering cases of local corruption or incompetence. As one journalist notes, "There are very few smart and courageous journalists who are willing to go to the edge of a cliff. I want to tell them that I am dancing ballet at the edge of the cliff, and the scenery is all right! But most journalists do not dare to join me" (Repnikova 2014: 115). Given that many topics are not banned outright, news workers with a careful feel for timing and a bit of political acumen can attempt to push the boundaries and "play edge ball" (*da cabianqiu* 打擦边求).

Research questions

And attempt they do. In August 2005, for example, several letters from top *China Youth Daily* (*Zhongguo Qingnian Bao* 中国青年报) editors excoriating their superiors and party management were "accidentally" leaked onto the Internet and generated a sensation across the media world (Marquand 2005). In late December of that year, a group of over a hundred journalists went on strike to protest the removal of Yang Bin, the *Beijing News* (*Xin Jing Bao* 新京报) editor-in-chief, by top CCP officials (Gill 2005). And in August 2008, months after having been forced to discipline a commentator for a controversial piece, the liberal *Southern Weekend* (*Nanfang Zhoumo* 南方周末) published a new editorial by the same author urging that "openness be the rule and secrecy the exception" in government life (Chang Ping [长平] 2008). All three of these incidents – and hundreds of similar, though less visible ones – have taken place in recent years despite one of the most sophisticated censorship systems in the world.

This book concentrates both on situations similar to the contentious *Southern Weekend* editorial, which is an example of what I term pushback,[15] and on cases of outright resistance like the aggressive open letters and media strike. I define pushback as contention that takes place when actors privileged by professional or traditional standing oppose power holders or their policies in ways that they perceive to be within the boundaries of the permissible. Pushback, although on the spectrum between quiescence and rebellion, is distinct from resistance because it

8 *Censorship and its discontents*

is neither intended nor seen as a direct challenge to power holders. Pushback happens in many contexts around the world, often creating an effective spur to change organizations from within. Although pushback does not directly cause rebellion, it does provide the preconditions that make it more likely. As such, the theory is situated within the literature on contentious politics that looks at movement emergence. Pushback, I argue, is part of the explanation for *why* actors move to directly challenge power holders, acting as a fertile ground to breed potential challengers. Even if pushback never develops into outright resistance, however, journalists who practice it can still play a major role in slowly, fitfully changing the Chinese status quo. I will examine pushback in theoretical context more fully in Chapter 7, and Chapter 8 examines cases that move from pushback to overt resistance.

Given China's harsh media environment then, why *do* Chinese journalists sometimes deliberately challenge the Party-state despite, not only the risks involved, but also after years or decades of passive acquiescence to the Chinese media control apparatus? Will these confrontations push China toward liberalizing its censorship regime or other aspects of state policy? This book explains why the concept of pushback helps answer these and other questions.

In answering these questions, I engage with literature on contentious politics and social movements, political communication, media theory, and the sociology of professions. Throughout the book, I rely on a mixed methodological approach that allows simultaneous examination of both large-scale structural factors and nuanced individual motivations. To examine the structural factors in Chinese society that are associated with contention, I have undertaken a large-scale, computer-assisted content analysis of Chinese newspaper articles, with a corpus of 15.4 million words among 18,897 articles gathered from 26 Chinese newspapers. To gauge the critical individual factors that lead Chinese journalists to resist a powerful authoritarian state, I have conducted seventy-one interviews with current and former reporters, editors, academics and others in four Chinese cities[16] and the United States over fifteen months of fieldwork (in 2005, 2006, 2007–2008, and 2013). Together, these data provide a comprehensive picture of contention, both obvious and subtle, in one of the most tightly controlled media systems in the world. Given this context, this research provides a highly conservative, "least likely" case on which to build theory; if journalists in China can be contentious, surely there are lessons here for scholars of other, more open political systems elsewhere in the world.

A preview of the argument

Moving into the structure of the book, Chapter 2 introduces the Chinese journalists themselves, illuminating their professional lives through interview data and starting to illustrate their backgrounds, thoughts, and motivations. The core of this chapter introduces a typology of Chinese journalists with four professional types: communist professionals, workaday journalists, American-style journalists, and advocate professionals. My work in so doing engages a recent strand of political communication research that has started to disentangle the fraught meaning of "professional" for journalists (Hallin and Mancini 2004). Media scholars like Hugo de Burgh or Chin-Chuan Lee have noticed Chinese ideas of professionalism that differ from Western models, but the literature in general has not advanced much beyond this recognition (Lee 2001; de Burgh 2003). My four-fold typology demonstrates that one type of journalistic professionals – the advocacy journalists – tend to disproportionately engage in resistive behavior, including pushback.

The following four, shorter chapters give an in-depth account of each of the four types and explain how the work together in the Chinese media ecosystem. Chapter 3 is an examination of China's communist professionals, a class sometimes seen as the archetypal type of Chinese journalist. Ideologically a holdover from the Maoist era, communist professionals believe in the supremacy of the CCP and in Marxist-Leninist theories that hold the press to be the "throat and tongue" of the Party. Although these journalists have sharply declined in numbers and importance since the start of the reform era in the late 1970s, they continue to have an outsized influence on outside observers of the Chinese media. A crucial argument in this chapter is that even though communist professionals may not meet Western newsroom standards, they are nonetheless true professionals who are committed to their jobs and to public service.

Next, I look at the workaday reporters, those who see their work as not a calling but merely a source of income. Although I estimate that workaday journalists comprise an outright majority of all Chinese news workers, they have been largely ignored by both Chinese and Western scholars of the Chinese press. Concerned primarily with making money, such reporters encourage a culture of corruption and complaisance in the press that arguably does more to keep the Chinese media supine than the enduring legacy of heavy press censorship. In Chapter 4, I examine the backgrounds and motivations for some of these reporters and examine both the causes and consequences of the pervasive culture of corruption that surrounds them.

Chapter 5 examines American-style journalists. While workaday journalists have been largely ignored in scholarly analysis, American-style journalists' outsized impact is far in excess of their rarity on the ground. Although Chinese journalists who think the press should follow Anglo-American–style neutrality and objectivity do indeed exist, there is a fundamental disconnect between this group's goals and practices and the realities of day-to-day Chinese journalism. This disconnect ensures that American-style journalists do not have nearly as much impact on the Chinese political system as some observers have argued. Instead, such journalists are often politically marginalized, making them more effective at getting the attention of the press than of changing its behavior.

Far more politically relevant are the advocate journalists, discussed in Chapter 6. These are reporters who wear their hearts on their sleeves, mix editorial and news content, and produce polemics aimed at solving specific social or political problems. Although this approach might be shunned in a Western newsroom,[17] in China it can be very effective in mobilizing public opinion to move a conservative and deeply entrenched bureaucracy. Part of advocate journalists' effectiveness lies in their congruence with Chinese traditions that give a privileged role to educated observers to comment on – and change – wrong-headed policies. Seizing this ancient literati role, advocate journalists aim to provide a kind of loyal opposition who speak for the voiceless and nudge the CCP toward making necessary reforms. While American-style journalists might wish to change the Chinese press wholesale, advocate journalists derive their effectiveness from pushing back and working inside the system to change some of its more objectionable features.

Chapter 7 elaborates on who pushes back and why. Turning from the mostly qualitative analysis used so far, this chapter introduces the methodology and results of a large-scale, computer-assisted content analysis of the Chinese press. These quantitative data, supplemented by qualitative interviews and case studies, allow me to investigate the macro- and micro-scale factors that drive aggressive or sensitive press coverage. In doing so, this chapter demonstrates why a purely economic approach cannot account for individual acts of pushback or resistance, despite both liberal and critical orthodoxy that holds competition and ownership structures to be crucial drivers of press content. Instead, I find that professional orientation – and especially that of the advocate journalists introduced in the previous chapter – is the main engine of challenge to power holders. This resistive behavior, in turn, may lead to long-term changes in the power dynamic of the Chinese polity, something I will draw out here and in the concluding chapters of this book.

This chapter also relies on the notion of openings in the political opportunity structure to help explain why pushback occurs when it does. Advocacy journalists, motivated to change particular policies or a general policy thrust of the Chinese government, are able to sense micro-opportunities to publish sensitive articles. They are keenly attuned to timing, for a false move might get them fired or sent to prison. And journalists who push back are not generally interested in an outright challenge to the Chinese state.

For those reporters who *are* interested in overt resistance, Chapter 8 offers an explanation of why and when they choose to challenge the powerful. I answer these questions in part by turning to the two cases of overt resistance mentioned early in this chapter: an open letter severely criticizing CCP management of *China Youth Daily* and the brief strike at the *Beijing News* (*Xin Jing Bao* 新京报), both of which took place in late 2005. Further evidence is given by the lead up and outcome of the widely publicized journalists' protests at *Southern Weekend* in early 2013. The published record of these cases is supplemented by my interviews with many of the major participants in both incidents, by other written sources, and by interviews with other media workers. The results demonstrate that reporters who push back are likely to turn to overt resistance when they have specific types of grievances against power holders. Specifically, the journalists in these cases moved from pushback to resistance when actions by the state (or its proxies) disrupted their everyday lives – what Snow et al. call the "disruption of the quotidian" (Snow et al. 1998) – when they had a clear target or targets, when they were able to draw on a language of moral outrage, and when they were already engaging in daily pushback. Moreover, although reporters closely followed changes in the political opportunity structure (POS) when pushing back, when moving toward overt resistance, their behavior was no longer governed by these changes. In other words, this chapter offers a potential way to reconcile those scholars who hold that opportunities govern protest and those who argue that grievances are equally or more important.

Although the news workers in Chapter 8 have moved beyond pushback into overt resistance, this progression demonstrates the theoretical utility of the pushback concept as a causal factor in later rebellious behavior. Although neither necessary nor sufficient to predict later resistance, pushback does seem to make outright resistance more likely. Together, Chapters 7 and 8 address the questions at the heart of the book and help show why some reporters challenge an authoritarian CCP – even when they might feel that the CCP is, on the whole, a good steward of the Chinese polity.

The previous chapters have mostly concentrated on the Chinese newspaper industry. Chapter 9 updates the story with an investigation of the Chinese Internet. As in the West, the Internet has produced profound social, cultural, and economic change in China. Indeed, because the Internet allows ordinary citizens to participate in political discussions for the first time in Chinese history, its impact is arguably more fundamental than in Western democracies. The newspaper business, too, has felt the impact of declining circulation and an ever-shorter news cycle. This chapter also explains why many Chinese news workers are more sanguine about the Internet's impact on their industry than those in the West. Finally, I argue here that the Internet should not be seen in isolation from other media. As with elsewhere in the world, the Chinese Internet is not *sui generis*, and Internet opinion and commentary often acts in concert with that expressed in the traditional media, creating a complex ecosystem that is sure to drive future changes in the Chinese polity.

Chapter 10 concentrates on the future of China and its media. Here, I extend the empirical and theoretical insights of earlier chapters toward areas outside of the Chinese media. For example, there is evidence that the "regime of uncertainty" discussed in this chapter has applicability in analyzing other areas of the Chinese political system as well (controlling lawyers and other public professionals as well) and perhaps even helping control public challenges in other authoritarian contexts. As this concept is ultimately built on the insights of organization theory, I will argue it has far-ranging implications for scholars of authoritarianism and state control. And finally, I point to future directions within the Chinese media itself. I do so, in part, by tracing long-term changes in the media environment created by reporters' pushback and by attempting to project these trends into the future.

For scholars of contentions politics, this book offers a potential way forward out of the "winding, snarling vine" of overly structural theories to explain the emergence of contentious action (Goodwin and Jasper 1999). Throughout, I refer both to structural and attitudinal factors that make contention more likely and introduce the concept of pushback as a way to think about resistive behavior that does not directly challenge authorities. Pushback and related activities happen around the world, whether in a Brazilian telecom (Rodrigues and Collinson 1995), inside the corporate sector (Meyerson and Scully 1995), or among stock market activists (den Hond and de Bakker 2007), and the attitudinal and professional factors I present here should have relevance for scholars of other areas. Finally, my arguments about why and when pushback moves to outright resistance have applications to studies of movement emergence and authoritarian longevity. The Arab Spring has once again brought home Mao's dictum that "a single spark can start a prairie fire,"[18] and I hope that my arguments about the preconditions necessary to spark such a fire have utility around the world.

Limitations

As with any research project, this book is subject to a number of limitations. Below, I lay out some potential qualifications to both the qualitative and quantitative research presented throughout. Although I believe the methods used have a solid foundation, I present these limitations to allow readers to judge for themselves and to make allowances where they might disagree with choices I have made.

Qualitative limitations

The qualitative side of project has a number of potential limitations, many of which are unavoidable in this kind of research. Most obviously, all the opinions and conclusions presented throughout the book are mine and are subject to any unconscious biases I carry with me. I have tried hard to let conclusions flow from the data and to allow Chinese news professionals to speak in their own words, but I have necessarily streamlined the results and drawn conclusions from a sometimes messy set of interview data. Like anyone else, I am subject to confirmation bias, the process by which people tend to ignore data that disconfirm their ideas (Nickerson 1998). I have tried to fight this tendency, but readers will have to make up their own minds about how successful I have been.

Issues surrounding Chinese politics can elicit intense debate within China and around the world, and there are necessarily scholars and writers who choose to advance polemical arguments rather than aiming for objectivity. It is possible, or even likely, that passionate advocates on either side of issues like China's potential for democratization will be displeased with what they read here. The arguments I make in this and other equally contentious areas are nuanced and contingent, a situation that might displease those who are looking for a clear answer or an unvarnished conclusion. The real world is messy, but this fact does not mean that messy conclusions are any more accurate than those in black and white. Again, readers will have to judge for themselves.

Other qualitative limitations are easier to evaluate. The interviews done throughout my fieldwork were based on snowball samples, where earlier interviewees recommended – and sometimes contacted – later ones. This method is far from perfect and brings with it the potential for a number of well-established problems. First, I cannot claim that I researched a representative sampling of the Chinese newspaper profession. The reporters and editors I spoke with were all generally in the same professional and epistemic community and tended to be much more elite than the average Chinese news worker. These are journalists at the apex of their profession, often working for top papers, and generally furnished with a prestigious education. Such reporters are more likely than average, I suspect, to be aggressive and to engage in the kinds of pushback I investigate in the book. This fact will necessarily color my conclusions, and might make me overstate the frequency and effectiveness of this kind of resistive behavior. And second, people often introduced me to their friends or acquaintances. (Indeed, it would be strange if they gave me entrée to their enemies!) The problem of homophily – like associating with like – rears its head here. Because friends tend to have convergent preferences and opinions (McPherson, Smith-Lovin, and Cook 2001), it is possible that I received a biased view of even elite Chinese journalism and that a proportion of even elite journalists have totally different views than the ones I talked to. I tried to maximize the number of entry points into arranging interviews and to conduct a sufficiently large number that these problems would be minimized, but I cannot entirely discount the danger from this issue.

Another potential bias along these lines is related to the limited number of cities in which I conducted interviews. Throughout the fieldwork process, I lived in Beijing, making trips of varying lengths to the other field site cities (Shanghai, Guangzhou, and Chongqing). Most of my interviews and experience, therefore, were with Beijing-based journalists. I tried to balance out this exposure with multiple visits and dozens of interviews in the other cities, but the end result is still a sample that is largely drawn from elite journalists in China's capital. On the other hand, although not all "pushy" journalists are investigative reporters, a substantial number are. Recent survey work shows that a majority (53.3%) of China's investigative journalists are based in Beijing, Shanghai, and Guangzhou, and this fact arguably makes my fieldwork results less biased and more in line with the realities of Chinese journalism (Shen and Zhang 2013: 382).

And finally, there are the problems associated with interview work in general, especially in a second language. It has been well established that people often tell interviewers what they think the interviewers want to hear (Fisher 1993). This "social desirability" bias is unavoidable with interview research, but throughout the project, I took steps to minimize its impact. I generally asked open-ended questions and followed up on what the news workers were telling me, taking pains to keep my expression and tone neutral. There is also no evidence that surveys done in China have higher levels of social desirability bias (Tang 2005: ch. 2), but it remains a danger in any human research.

With just a few exceptions, all seventy-plus interviews were conducted in Chinese. I am proficient in the language but cannot approach the fluency of a native speaker. This fact necessarily means that I sometimes missed the nuances of what interviewees were trying to tell me, or, perhaps, their entire argument. Although most reporters speak excellent Mandarin Chinese, I conducted a few interviews – especially in Guangzhou and Chongqing – where the reporters spoke to me with such a heavy local accent that it was sometimes difficult to follow what they were saying. For the safety and anonymity of my interviews and to satisfy human research ethics requirements, I did not record any interviews. I generally took notes, but without recordings, it can be difficult to judge tone or to go back over difficult passages. This is yet another area where I'm afraid readers must judge my success or failure for themselves.

For this kind of qualitative research, I suspect that use of a snowball sample is inevitable,[19] and I have tried hard to minimize biases. No research is perfect, but I have always aimed at quality.

Quantitative limitations

The quantitative work, too, suffers from number of potential biases and limitations related to data availability, sampling methods, analytical limitations, and others. For the computer-assisted content analysis (CCA), I rely on a three-year (2004–2006) sample of twenty-six Chinese newspapers. Although twenty-six newspapers is a relatively large number and the papers cover much of the country, they were not randomly selected. Creating a true random sample of Chinese newspapers from the mid-2000s is a nearly intractable problem. Most obviously, many of the smaller papers did not then have online content, meaning that I would have had to somehow obtain physical copies of the newspapers for the whole analytical time span. I would then have had to scan or otherwise input the content, correcting any mistakes introduced by imperfect optical character recognition (OCR). This would have been an extremely tedious and time-consuming process and would necessarily have limited me to a much smaller sample. I think the trade-offs involved in picking only papers available in the CNKI database and aiming to maximize geographic, ownership and circulation diversity were reasonable, but others may disagree.

The three-year sample is also a possible source of problems. Although I wanted to minimize the disruptions of day-to-day events and ephemera involved with a shorter time-span, a longer collection period would have been even more beneficial. Happily, this period includes both the very end of Jiang Zemin's incumbency as president of the PRC and chairman of the Central Military Commission and the beginnings of the rule of his successor, Hu Jintao. Nonetheless, leadership transitions are often a time of fraught politics in China, and new leaders sometimes take years to consolidate their power. It is therefore possible that even a three-year horizon did not capture enough of China's social and political events during more "normal" times. And finally, this corpus is already getting old and will not reflect the latest trends in the Chinese media. I have tried to update my conclusions based on interview work, but an updated sample might be necessary to be truly convincing.

Another issue with a CCA is keyword – "dictionary" – selection. CCA is essentially a giant word count, and if the dictionaries are not properly set up, the process risks over- or undercounting terms of interest. For this project I relied on a factor analysis approach to inductively build initial dictionaries from a subset of the data and then refined them based on input from native Chinese speakers (see Chapter 7 for more details). I also relied on research showing that a Chinese term list of approximately 500 words is enough to capture virtually all terms of interest and arranged my own dictionary accordingly (Jin and Wong 2002). I am happy to provide full dictionary lists to anyone who wishes to evaluate my methods here.

Finally, there are limitations to the statistical analysis based on the unreliability of Chinese statistics. To alleviate incommensurability, I used circulation and market data from a single source – the official *China Journalism Yearbooks*, published by the Chinese Academy of Social Sciences New Research Institute – but even this has limitations. Chinese newspapers are known to overestimate their circulation data to improve their standing with advertisers, and without an independent organization to audit circulation figures, there is little way to gauge the reliability of their supplied statistics. The best that can be said here is that, in choosing data from a single source, I have tried to ensure that any bias is at least consistent and so should not much affect papers' standings *relative to each other*. The potential unreliability of these circulation figures is unfortunate, but without a viable alternative, this remains the best data source available.

Notes

1 This section is adapted from Hassid (2008) with permission of *Asian Survey* and the University of California Press.
2 This translation from Chinese was done by the author. All other translations in the book are also done by the author unless otherwise noted.
3 The official Chinese name is the Chinese Communist Party Central Committee Propaganda Department (*Zhongguo Gongchandang Zhongyang Weiyuanhui Xuanchuanbu* 中国共产党中央委员会宣传部), but the official English name was changed in 1998 from the Central Propaganda Department to the Central Publicity Department.
4 The SAPPRFT (*Guojia Xinwen Chuban Guangbo Dianshi Dianying Zongju* 国家新闻出版广播电视电影总局) was created in 2013 with the merger of the General Administration of Press and Publication (GAPP *Xinwen Chuban Zongshu* 新闻出版总署) and the State Administration of Radio, Film, and Television (SARFT *Guojia Guangbo Dianshi Dianying Zongju* 国家广播电视电影总局). The State Council offices are the *Guowuyuan Xinxi Bangongshi* (国务院信息办公室) and the relatively new *Guowuyuan Hulianwang Bangongshi* (国务院互联网办公室).
5 Only Brady (2008) has attempted a book-length analysis of the CPD's workings, and Shambaugh (2007) has written an article on the subject.
6 Though they are apparently easy to get – illegally – via a secondary market run by publishers assigned extra numbers.
7 These include "Regulations Strictly Prohibiting Obscene Products" (1985), "Notice Regarding Striking Hard against Illegal Publications" (1987), "Rules for Managing Foreign Journalists and News Bureaus" (1990), "Regulations Governing Satellite Television Receiving Equipment" (1994), "Rules Governing Audio-Visual Products" (1994), "Regulations Governing Films" (1996), "Regulations Governing Publishing" (1997), "Regulations Governing Printing" (1997), and "Regulations Governing Broadcast Television" (1997).
8 Again, this is not strictly true, as even *overt* post-publication censorship was and remains relatively rare.
9 Data obtained from the official General Administration on Press and Publication (GAPP) website at http://press.gapp.gov.cn/tongji/type_sex.php, accessed June 20, 2009, but is no longer available online.

10 Link (2002) is a notable exception.
11 See http://chinadigitaltimes.net/china/ministry-of-truth/ for a partial list.
12 Topics like Taiwanese or Tibetan independence, the 1989 Tiananmen massacre, problems with Han-Uyghur relations in Xinjiang, and the like.
13 It is unclear, however, whether this crackdown was initiated by the CPD itself or by local or provincial authorities. One reporter at a sister paper claims in an interview (2007) that the crackdown was initiated at the highest levels of the provincial government, though this must surely have been with the knowledge and acquiescence of the CPD.
14 Several interviews with current and former print journalism reporters, including *Southern Metropolis* staff in 2005.
15 Note that for grammatical reasons when used as a noun, I term this phenomenon "pushback," but when used as a verb it becomes the two-word verbal phrase "pushing back."
16 Beijing, Shanghai, Guangzhou, and Chongqing, chosen to maximize variation in the Chinese media economic and political environment. See Chapter 2 for more details.
17 Or perhaps not, considering the growing partisanship in the Western press. Consider the rise of Fox News or its left-leaning competitors.
18 This is the title of a 1930 essay by Mao. The Arab Spring was apparently triggered by a literal fire – the self-immolation of a Tunisian fruit vendor Mohamed Bouazizi.
19 The SAPPRFT (formerly the GAPP) has a database of all legally registered journalists in China, and I suspect the All-China Journalists' Association does as well. Based on these lists, in theory, it would be possible to arrange a true random sample of Chinese news workers, but gaining access to the lists would likely prove extremely difficult. Others scholars have approximated a random sample in other ways. See, for example, Lin (2010) and Shen and Zhang (2013).

References

Beach, Sophie. 2005. "The Rise of Rights?" *Dangerous Assignments*, Spring/Summer, 31–33.
Brady, Anne-Marie. 2008. *Marketing Dictatorship: Propaganda and Thought Work in Contemporary China, Asia/Pacific/Perspectives*. Lanham, MD: Rowman & Littlefield.
Brendebach, Martin. 2005. "Public Opinion – A New Factor Influencing the PRC Press." *Asien, Deutsche Zeitschrift für Politik, Wirtschaft und Kultur* (96):29–45.
Chang Ping (长平). 2008. "The Public Should Be Public, the Private Should Be Private" (公开该公开的, 保密该保密的). *Southern Weekend* (南方周末), Aug. 27. Accessed November 24, 2008. http://cmp.hku.hk/2008/08/28/1208/.
Chen Yali. 2003. Statement by Chen Yali, Research Associate, Center for Defense Information, before the Congressional Executive Commission on China (CECC).
Chinese Academy of Social Sciences News Research Institute [Zhongguo Shehui Kexueyuan Xinwen Yanjiusuo]. Various years. *China Journalism Yearbook* [Zhongguo xin wen nian jian]. Beijing: China Journalism Yearbook Publishing [Zhongguo Xin Wen Nian Jian She].
Crozier, Michel. 1964. *The Bureaucratic Phenomenon*. Chicago: University of Chicago Press.
Cui Baoguo (崔保国), ed. 2011. *Report on the Development of China's Media Industry (2011)* (2011年: 中国传媒产业发展报告), *Blue Book of China's Media* (传媒蓝皮书). Beijing: Social Sciences Academic Press (社会科学文献出版社).
de Burgh, Hugo. 2003. *The Chinese Journalist: Mediating Information in the World's Most Populous Country*. London; New York, NY: Routledge.
den Hond, Frank, and Frank G.A. de Bakker. 2007. "Ideologically Motivated Activism: How Activist Groups Influence Corporate Social Change Activities." *Academy of Management Review* 32 (9):901–924.

Esarey, Ashley. 2005. "Cornering the Market: State Strategies for Controlling China's Commercial Media." *Asian Perspective* 29 (4):37–83.

Fisher, Robert J. 1993. "Social Desirability Bias and the Validity of Indirect Questioning." *Journal of Consumer Research* 20 (2):303–315.

Gill, Chris. 2005. "Beijing Paper's Staff Strike After Editor's Removal." *The Guardian*, Dec. 31. www.guardian.co.uk/international/story/0,3604,1675736,00.html.

Goodwin, Jeff, and James M. Jasper. 1999. "Caught in a Winding, Snarling Vine: The Structural Bias of Political Process Theory." *Sociological Forum* 14 (1):27–53.

Hallin, Daniel C., and Paolo Mancini. 2004. *Comparing Media Systems: Three Models of Media and Politics*. Cambridge; New York: Cambridge University Press.

Hand, Keith J. 2006. "Using Law for a Righteous Purpose: The Sun Zhigang Incident and Evolving Forms of Citizen Action in the People's Republic Of China." *Columbia Journal of Transnational Law* 45 (1):114–195.

Hassid, Jonathan. 2008. "Controlling the Chinese Media: An Uncertain Business." *Asian Survey* 48 (3):414–430. doi:10.1525/as.2008.48.3.414.

He Qinglian. 2004. *Media Control in China* [中国政府如何控制媒体]. New York: Human Rights in China.

He, Zhou. 2000. "Chinese Communist Party Press in a Tug of War: A Political-Economy Analysis of the Shenzhen Special Zone Daily." In *Power, Money, and Media: Communication Patterns and Bureaucratic Control in Cultural China*, edited by Chin-Chuan Lee, 112–151. Evanston, IL: Northwestern University Press.

He, Zhou. 2003. "How Do the Chinese Media Reduce Organizational Incongruence? Bureaucratic Capitalism in the Name of Communism." In *Chinese Media, Global Contexts*, edited by Chin-Chuan Lee, ch. 10. New York: Routledge.

Jin, Honglan, and Kam-Fai Wong. 2002. "A Chinese Dictionary Construction Algorithm for Information Retrieval." *ACM Transactions on Asian Language Information Processing* 1 (4):281–296.

Kahn, Joseph. 2004. "Police Raid Chinese Newspaper That Reported New SARS Case." *The New York Times*, Jan. 8. Accessed October 9, 2006. http://query.nytimes.com/gst/fullpage.html?sec=health&res=9D05E6DC1131F93BA35752C0A9629C8B63.

Lawson, Chappell H. 2002. *Building the Fourth Estate: Democratization and the Rise of a Free Press in Mexico*. Berkeley: University of California Press.

Lee, Chin-Chuan. 1998. "Press Self-Censorship and Political Transition in Hong Kong." *Harvard International Journal of Press/Politics* 3 (2):55–73.

Lee, Chin-Chuan. 2001. "Servants of the State or the Market?" In *Media Occupations and Professions: A Reader*, edited by Jeremy Tunstall, ch. 27. Oxford; New York: Oxford University Press.

Li, Lianjiang, and Kevin O'Brien. 1996. "Villagers and Popular Resistance in Contemporary China." *Modern China* 22 (1):28–61.

Lin, Fen J. 2010. "A Survey Report on Chinese Journalists in China." *China Quarterly* 202:421–34.

Link, Perry. 2002. "The Anaconda in the Chandelier: Chinese Censorship Today." *The New York Review of Books* 49 (6).

Lynch, Daniel C. 1999. *After the Propaganda State: Media, Politics, and "Thought Work" in Reformed China*. Stanford, CA: Stanford University Press.

Marquand, Robert. 2005. "Chinese Media Resisting Party Control." *Christian Science Monitor*, Aug. 26, Asia Pacific. Accessed September 1, 2006. www.csmonitor.com/2005/0826/p01s04-woap.html.

McPherson, Miller, Lynn Smith-Lovin, and James M. Cook. 2001. "Birds of a Feather: Homophily in Social Networks." *Annual Review of Sociology* 27:415–444.

Meyerson, Debra E., and Maureen A. Scully. 1995. "Tempered Radicalism and the Politics of Ambivalence and Change." *Organization Science* 6 (5):585–600.

Nickerson, Raymond S. 1998. "Confirmation Bias: A Ubiquitous Phenomenon in Many Guises." *Review of General Psychology* 2 (2):175–220.

Pan, Zhongdang. 2000. "Improvising Reform Activities: The Changing Reality of Journalistic Practice in China." In *Power, Money, and Media: Communication Patterns and Bureaucratic Control in Cultural China*, edited by Chin-Chuan Lee, 68–111. Evanston, IL: Northwestern University Press.

Pei, Minxin. 1994. *From Reform to Revolution: The Demise of Communism in China and the Soviet Union*. Cambridge, MA: Harvard University Press.

Qian Gang. 2009. "How Should We Face Hu Shuli's Departure from Caijing?" China Media Project, University of Hong Kong. Accessed November, 19, 2009. http://cmp.hku.hk/2009/11/13/3068/.

Repnikova, Maria. 2014. "Investigative Journalists' Coping Tactics in a Restrictive Media Environment." In *Chinese Investigative Journalists' Dreams: Autonomy, Agency and Voice*, edited by Marina Svensson, Elin Saether, and Zhi'an Zhang, 113–132. Lanham, MD: Lexington Books.

Reporters sans Frontières. 2013. "China." Accessed January 22, 2013. http://en.rsf.org/report-china,57.html.

Reporters sans Frontières. 2015. "2015 World Press Freedom Index." http://index.rsf.org.

Rodrigues, Suzana B., and David L. Collinson. 1995. "Having Fun? Humor as Resistance in Brazil." *Organization Studies* 16:739–768.

Shambaugh, David. 2007. "China's Propaganda System: Institutions, Processes and Efficacy." *The China Journal* (57):25–58.

Shen, Fei, and Zhi'an Zhang. 2013. "Who are the Investigative Journalists in China: Findings from a Survey in 2010." *Chinese Journal of Communication* 6 (3):374–384.

Snow, David A., Daniel M. Cress, Liam Downy, and Andew W. Jones. 1998. "Disrupting the 'Quotidian': Reconceptualizing the Relationship Between Breakdown and the Emergence of Collective Action." *Mobilization* 3 (1):1–22.

Stern, Rachel E., and Jonathan Hassid. 2012. "Amplifying Silence: Uncertainty and Control Parables in Contemporary China." *Comparative Political Studies* 45 (10):1230–1254. doi:10.1177/0010414011434295.

Tang, Wenfang. 2005. *Public Opinion and Political Change in China*. Stanford, CA: Stanford University Press.

U.S.-China Economic and Security Review Commission. 2005. Hearing on China's State Control Methods and Mechanisms. April 14. U.S. Government Printing Office.

Wood, Laura. 2011. "Research and Markets: China Advertising Industry Report, 2010–2011 – The Chinese Advertising Market Grows by 22.5% Totalling RMB343.7 billion in 2010." *Business Wire*, Jul. 29. www.businesswire.com/news/home/20110728006148/en/Research-Markets-China-Advertising-Industry-Report-2010–2011.

Yan Jiaqi. 1995. "The Nature of Chinese Authoritarianism." In *Decision-Making in Deng's China: Perspectives from Insiders*, edited by Carol Lee Hamrin and Suisheng Zhao, 1–14. Armonk, NY: M. E. Sharpe.

Zhao, Yuezhi. 1998. *Media, Market, and Democracy in China: Between the Party Line and the Bottom Line*. Urbana: University of Illinois Press.

Zhao, Yuezhi. 2000. "From Commercialization to Conglomeration: The Transformation of the Chinese Press Within the Orbit of the Party State." *Journal of Communication* 50 (2):3–26. doi:10.1093/joc/50.2.3.

2 Four models of the Fourth Estate

A typology of contemporary Chinese journalists

Introduction

Media oversight is thought to be so important to effective governance that the press is sometimes referred to as the Fourth Estate. Although the media in China cannot freely exercise this oversight role, an awareness is building among scholars and others that the practice of Chinese journalism has changed dramatically from the era where the *People's Daily* (*Renmin Ribao* 人民日报) was seen to be the profession's standard bearer. Recent work concentrating on the growth of a "professional" identity among Chinese journalists, although an excellent start, has sometimes elided the fact that media professionalism is not a monolithic construct, even in the West.[1] Professionalism, in all its forms, is clearly increasing in the Chinese media. But as media scholars Qian Gang and David Bandurski write,

> In Chinese academic circles and the media industry, the concept of professionalism . . . has taken on greater importance in recent years. While there is often little agreement about what professionalism entails, a number of trends point to the emergence of a professional journalism community.
>
> (Qian Gang and Bandurski 2011: 57)

Disentangling the fraught concept of "professionalism," I argue that Chinese news workers belong to at least four ideal-type professional orientations. Below, I examine each of these orientations and explain why a nuanced typology of professional Chinese journalists is important for understanding political and social developments in the People's Republic, drawing on sociologist Rodney Benson's urging that "political communication studies draw upon the sociology of the news media far more extensively than has been the case in the past" (Benson 2004: 276).

Although the Chinese press ranks among the world's least free (Reporters sans Frontières 2015), at times its journalists have shaped policy in impressive ways (Hassid 2008a). Perhaps because of these visible successes, some have argued that the growth of an "American-style"[2] professional ethos built on a commitment to neutral, independent reporting might represent the vanguard of an inevitable professionalization. Such journalists do exist, but their rarity, incongruence with the domestic media context, and disinterest in advocacy mean that they are unlikely to be transformational. While the foreign optimism attached to these few reporters is perhaps misplaced, it is equally erroneous to see all contemporary news workers as they were during the Maoist era, the "throat and tongue" (*houshe* 喉舌) of the Chinese Communist Party (CCP). Some Chinese reporters are indeed still "communist professionals" who take CCP marching orders, but scholarly focus on "the conventional dichotomy of 'Western professionalism vs. party journalism'" (Lin 2010a: 176) misses the importance of two additional – and more numerous – groups: "advocate journalists," independent-minded crusaders who wear their opinions on their sleeves and aim to push policy change, and "workaday journalists," who care for little but money or steady employment.

These four types differ principally on two dimensions: their level of commitment to journalistic *independence* and their level of commitment to *advocacy*. Journalistic independence refers to the idea that news workers themselves should determine standards of newsworthiness rather than writing stories with an eye toward pleasing higher-ups or the CCP. Advocacy refers to reporters and editors' willingness to stand up for causes they believe in, even when these causes might be politically sensitive. In other words, independence is about control, and advocacy about content. More concretely, if a reporter's support for independence is high but advocacy is low (as with the American-style professionals), she would be likely to support press freedom without pushing any specific political agenda. By contrast, a journalist with a commitment to advocacy but not independence (i.e., a communist professional) would tend to push his agenda in internal CCP memoranda while sincerely believing in the publicly expressed values of the Party/state.

Typologizing people is necessarily imprecise, and these categories are only meant to reflect ideal types.[3] Individual news workers may not neatly fall into categories and indeed may shift types over time or issue area. Advocacy can be an especially risky strategy in an environment where political boundaries can shift day-to-day and where news workers faced with ambiguous Party/state signals often must rely on their own shared understandings of the limits of acceptable discourse (Stern 2013; Stern and Hassid 2012). In other words, even journalists with a high commitment to advocacy might be unwilling to "play edge ball" (*da cabianqiu* 打擦边球) on certain issues or at certain times, and even communist professionals might suddenly find themselves on the wrong side of an issue. I discuss

Table 2.1 A typology of Chinese journalism

Commitment to advocacy		Commitment to journalistic independence	
		High	Low
	High	Advocate professionals	Some communist professionals (esp. when writing internal reports on social or political problems)
	Low	American-style professionals	Workaday journalists; some communist professionals

Reprinted with permission from "Four Models of the Fourth Estate," *China Quarterly* and the School of Oriental and African Studies, Vol. 208, 2011.

the strategies these news workers employ in Chapters 7 and 8. Here, and in the four short chapters following, I categorize Chinese news workers and discuss their often unique sense of professional mission. Although this typology cannot explain all aspects of Chinese media, it marks a start toward bringing the Chinese media into comparative perspective. As Benson notes, "Comparative research, at least initially, may be less able to resolve questions about causality than to punch holes in existing assumptions. But this alone would be an impressive step forward" (Benson 2004: 285).

Methodology

This chapter and those following are principally based on seventy-one in-depth interviews with Chinese professional news workers, academics, and others collected in China over fifteen months of fieldwork done between 2006 and 2013. These interviews lasted between forty-five minutes and two hours, with a median time of one hour, usually conducted over lunch or coffee. The vast majority were entirely in Chinese, though some were done in English or a mix of the two languages. On several occasions, I was fortunate to be invited to training sessions, conferences, or dinners not included in the interview total; these sessions were all highly informative, though necessarily informal. Note that, because of political sensitivity, the names of interview subjects are pseudonyms. To increase generalizability, I selected four fieldwork sites: Beijing, Shanghai, Guangzhou, and Chongqing. As the national capitol and headquarters of many of China's most prominent publications, Beijing is a natural choice. Moreover, Beijing's media market is highly commercialized, and the level of political control varies from high (during major political meetings or sessions of the National People's Congress) to *relatively* low (the rest of the time). Although the phenomenon of cyclical political opening and tightening is true across China (Baum 1994), the level of control seems to vary most in Beijing. Shanghai represents a curious example of a city with both a highly marketized media environment and a very high level of media control.[4] Guangzhou is a natural choice by virtue of its status as the most politically open journalistic environment in the country. Finally, Chongqing was selected as a more "typical" Chinese city, with relatively low levels of market competition and high

Table 2.2 Fieldwork sites

		Level of media commercialization	
Level of state media control		High	Low
	High	Shanghai Beijing (esp. sensitive times)	Chongqing
	Low	Beijing ("normal" times) Guangzhou	—

Reprinted with permission from "Four Models of the Fourth Estate," *China Quarterly* and the School of Oriental and African Studies, Vol. 208, 2011.

state media control. Chongqing also helped make the sample more indicative of China as a whole, rather than simply rich, coastal cities.

Within these cities, I relied on my network of journalistic contacts to provide a snowball sample of news workers, concentrating on elite journalists or those who worked at particularly influential papers. Obtaining a truly representative sample of China's 150,000 or so journalists is impossible without the cooperation of the Chinese government, and my 71 in-depth interviews can hardly represent the entire universe of Chinese journalists This snowball method does present a risk of a biased sample, as does the preponderance of elite journalists in the sample. My results are thus unlikely to be representative of all Chinese journalists but should be a fairly robust portrait of those at the top of the profession.

Making professional Chinese journalists

Before further detailing differences among the four ideal types, it is helpful to first discuss commonalities. Although their backgrounds differ, the vast majority (91% says Lin [2010b: 423]) of Chinese journalists have a college degree, compared with around 2.2% of the general population (Rong and Shi 2001: 113, measuring three years of attendance). All legally employed journalists in China must have a press card issued by the State Administration of Press, Publication, Radio, Film, and Television (SAPPRFT *Guojia Xinwen Chuban Guangbo Dianying Dianshi Zongju* 国家新闻出版广播电影电视总局),[5] under a system nationally unified in February 2009.[6] To obtain this press card, reporters are "required to take a training program in official ideology, media policies and regulations, journalism ethics, communication theory, and related topics" (Zhao 2008: 29). Indeed, the SAPPRFT does more than force journalists to attend these training sessions; to actually receive the card, they must also pass a test that includes Marxist-Leninist press theory (Interview ET02–3). In training reporters, the CCP emphasizes the importance of the "Party principle" (*dangxing yuanze* 党性原则), which is the idea that the Party/state should dominate the media (Zhao 1998: 19). Current training sessions continue to emphasize the priority of the CCP over the media and attempt to instill a Marxist-Leninist ideology of the press as transmission belt between rulers and ruled. This system is a holdover from Maoist times, when the CCP enjoyed absolute dominance over Chinese mass communication. Although the situation has clearly changed since that era (Hassid 2008a), Chinese journalist training curricula still officially demand that the press serve as the CCP's voice.

Chinese journalists are also formally guided by an ethos of public service put forward by their official professional association, the All-China Journalists' Association (ACJA) (*Zhonghua Quanguo Xinwen Gongzuozhe Xiehui* 中华全国新闻工作者协会). All Chinese journalists must belong to the ACJA, a theoretically autonomous social organization that is actually run by the Central Propaganda Department (CPD) as part of the Party/state's media control apparatus (Hassid 2008b; Brady 2008: 10). Although described by one interviewee – quite typically – as an organization that "doesn't train, doesn't help and doesn't protect journalists" (Interview GM14–2B), the ACJA does promulgate a code of professional conduct and, at least in theory, advocates for the profession. The code requires that journalists report the truth and not take bribes or blackmail sources, and the GAPP (and successor agency SAPPRFT) sometimes publicly posts a rotating list of news workers who have committed such professional misconduct.[7] The ACJA also posts moralizing stories and exhortations on its website, with a typical example arguing "fake news confuses public opinion and throws it into disorder (*raoluan yulun* 扰乱舆论), becoming a harmful and malignant cancer (*duliu* 毒瘤) on society."[8] Journalists, then, are required to be truthful and honest in their reporting. The ACJA has always been thoroughly co-opted by the CCP, but its existence as a formal, professional journalistic organization advancing a code of conduct and norms of public service strengthens the case that official Chinese journalists are all, structurally at least, professionals.

Journalists and scholars sometimes disparage old-line practitioners of communist journalism and propaganda. Prominent former editor Lu Yuegang (卢跃钢), for instance, writes that "the media playing the 'mouthpiece' role" can be summarized in eight characters, "when you are an accomplice to evil, you are hitting a man when he is down," (*zhuzhouweinüe, luojingxiashi* 助纣为虐,落井下石) a view that is often echoed in the foreign press (Lu Yuegang (卢跃刚) 1999: 3). This persistent attitude makes it important to draw out the argument that these news workers are indeed professional journalists. Clearly the standards of the Party press – including a reliance on Marxist/Leninist ideology and an uncritical acceptance of CCP decisions – are unlikely to appear on any Western journalism curriculum. It is a mistake, however, to translate a normative dislike of the training and practice of communist journalism into a claim that such reporters are not professionals. I argue that even those news workers who unabashedly take up their role as the "throat and tongue" of the CCP share the three core features of a profession laid out by political scientist Harold Wilensky (1964): 1) membership in a professional association, 2) widely acknowledged ethical norms, and 3) a commitment to public service.[9]

While all legally employed Chinese journalists have the *structural* aspects of professional membership, it is "The combination of the structural and the attitudinal aspects [that] serves as the basis for the professional model" (Hall 1968). Journalists' attitudes towards their role, and in particular their commitment to public service, are critical to their professional status. Many Westerners, and especially Americans, are enamored with the notion that professional journalism is synonymous with objectivity;[10] even in the contemporary United States, however, the daily partisan mudslinging of Fox News or MSNBC seriously challenges a reliance on objectivity as the sole criterion of "professional" journalism. The typology of Chinese news professionals I present here and in the following chapters therefore takes aim at those who argue that "Objectivity is the ethical precondition for determining whether a journalist is a professional or not" (Tong 2011: 100).

The first key to the professional ethos of many Chinese journalists is the highly networked nature of their work. Although the ACJA is useless as a formal advocate and coordinator for Chinese reporters, "Studies in the 1970s and 1980s found that, compared to lawyers and doctors, journalists tend to participate less in a shared professional culture that is promoted by professional bodies" around the world (Tumber and Prentoulis 2005: 66). In China, informal organizations and contacts replace many of the ACJA's socializing functions. At least three semi-formalized groups of reporters meet regularly in Beijing centered around environmental, law, and entertainment journalism, respectively, and a similar grouping of prominent news journalists meets regularly in Guangzhou.[11] Strictly speaking, these groups are illegal, and the CCP tends not to tolerate organized groups it cannot control. Indeed, Guangzhou authorities regularly shut down the group in that city, but the participants tend to ignore the ban, with one editor saying "they can't stop friends from meeting" (Interview HL8–4AZ).

The Beijing-based environmental and legal reporting groups are often well organized, with journalists, academics, and others making presentations, sharing new professional developments, and even organizing conferences. Even sensitive issues are discussed at times but always with a careful eye toward timing. One conference organized by law journalists was postponed for weeks, for example, because one of the invited speakers was outspoken – and recently disciplined – media advocate Lu Yuegang. When his talk was scheduled to take place during the politically sensitive annual meeting of the National People's Congress (NPC), authorities contacted the organizers, and they were forced to delay his presentation until after the NPC was over. These groups are hardly hiding in the shadows, however. The environmental journalism group, for example, has met once a month since 2000 and has offices in central Beijing, near the Yonghegong Lama Temple. The group is also so institutionalized that it has published a book, entitled *Green Journalist Salon*, popularizing the environmental cause (Wang Yongchen [汪永辰] and Xiong Zhihong [熊志红] 2005), and other members active in the group have written similar publications (e.g. Feng Yongfeng [冯永锋] 2007).

For those in other cities or other parts of the profession, "The Internet continues to serve as a protection and an important network for journalists in China, linking them to a global professional community" (Bandurski and Hala 2010: 72). Most Chinese journalists are highly networked, an unsurprising fact given the nature of their work, and often electronically trade stories and tips on the popular QQ, MSN, and WeChat networks. What may be more unexpected is the frequency of reporters' physical meetings; an astonishing 100% of respondents in a small, unscientific pilot survey (n=24) meet their colleagues outside of work at least a few times a month, with one quarter seeing their colleagues socially every day and an additional quarter doing so several times a week. And these professional networks are truly domestic, generally not including foreign journalists. Nearly 20% have never met a foreign reporter off the job, and an additional 60% do so only a few times a year.

Many Chinese journalists also meet Wilenksy's (1964) second professional criterion, sharing a commitment to widely acknowledged ethical norms. The norms of the profession vary, often paper by paper, but most newspaper journalists are aware that common acts like taking bribes to cover up or publicize stories are both illegal and unethical. Even if these norms are not always followed, it is enough that "unethical practices receive uniform condemnation at least in public statements" (Pan and Lu 2003: 225). I will discuss the unethical behavior of China's "workaday journalists" more fully in Chapter 4, but most journalists are aware that undesirable behavior violates ethical standards.

And finally, many Chinese news workers share a normative commitment to public service. Although some may disagree on who "the public" might be, professional journalists nonetheless believe that journalism is a higher calling. American-style professionals see their role as neutral, objective information provider and checking government and corporate excess, and advocate journalists often believe in helping protect vulnerable social groups. Even communist journalists, much derided in the West as Party hacks, propagandists, or worse, often believe that in serving the CCP they are guiding China's public interests. This is not to claim that Chinese journalists are happy with their work – my small experimental survey shows that 60% of them would "definitely" or "probably" change jobs if they could – but they often derive satisfaction out of serving the public interest. As media scholars Tumber and Prentoulis (2005: 63) write, "As an autonomous practice unwilling to compromise its ethic of 'public service' – in order to serve particular interests – journalism makes a strong claim to being a profession." In the chapters following, I discuss the four Chinese professional ideal types in greater detail.

Admittedly, this commitment to public service comes for some journalists after they enter the profession, not before. Many of my interviewees entered journalism because they were involuntarily thrust onto the journalism track in their university studies or because they could not easily find another job after graduation. Young *Beijing News* reporter Lei Hua (Interview HB24–2), for example, entered the field because she needed work. For her, it was just a job, not a profession or calling, but as she became more exposed to the professional model, she started to see that it was important to have balance in stories, quote people properly, and strive for objectivity. Although for many the work remains just a job, she argues, there is increasing professionalization in the career path directing more and more journalists toward a sense of mission.

Even after time on the job, though, not all journalists professionalize. Another reporter at the state-run *Guangming Daily* argues that unprofessional or corrupt reporters are not a reflection on journalism *per se* but on Chinese society everywhere. China, he argues, has very few people who do really bad things but also very few doing good. Like most Chinese citizens, he says, most Chinese journalists are just a mass of people muddling along and not putting much thought into their work one way or another (Interview HH20–2). Many of these reporters are unlikely to adopt the sense of public service necessary to define their professional mission, but on the whole, the number of reporters just interested in a quick buck seems to be slowly diminishing. Chinese reporters, in other words, are professionalizing.

Table 2.3 Characteristics of the four types

Reporter ideal type	Role conception	Other characteristics	Effect on stories and behavior	Normative self-assessment
Advocacy professionals	High independence, high advocacy. Representing "the people," "vulnerable social groups" (ruoshi qunti 弱势群体) or others against the predations of society or the state. May also support other causes.	Tendency to think of themselves as educators and problem-solvers driven by nationalism, coupled with a strong literati tradition.	Contentious political behavior tends to come from this group. They often write with emotionally charged language and use much self-reference in stories.	American-style professionals.
American-style professionals	High independence, low advocacy. Aim to be a neutral, objective information provider. Some see themselves as a check on state power, though this view is limited by the needs of objectivity.	Tendency to write in unemotional terms. Emphasis on separation of editorial and journalistic content. Tend to be explicitly influenced by, and admiring of, the U.S. media system.	Can use objectivity as a shield from controversy, meaning little (though not zero) confrontation with power holders.	American-style professionals.
Communist professionals	Low independence, varying degrees of advocacy (usually in internal reports). Mouthpiece, or "throat and tongue," of the CCP.	Usually (though not exclusively) work for the old-line CCP papers, like the People's Daily.	Very unlikely to engage in combative political behavior.	Muddled, but often communist professionals.
Workaday journalists	Low independence and advocacy. No professional ethos. Reporters are out to make money or have a steady job.	This is a diverse group without clear characteristics or tendencies.	This diverse group tends to avoid political controversy, preferring to stay under the radar.	Muddled. Either American-style or advocacy professionals.

Reprinted with permission from "Four Models of the Fourth Estate," *China Quarterly* and the School of Oriental and African Studies, Vol. 208, 2011.

Conclusion

Some speak of the increasing American-style professionalism of Chinese journalists with a barely concealed normative approval that often glosses over important empirical and theoretical differences among a heterogeneous group of journalists. At the same time, however, few Chinese journalists maintain their role as the "throat and tongue" of the Party. Indeed, both orientations are rare and have neither the normative appeal nor practical effects to warrant their near monopoly on scholarly attention. In the past, communist professionals dominated the Chinese press, and one day American-style journalists will perhaps dominate, but both periods are a long way off.

In addition to problematizing the very notion of a "professional" Chinese journalist, I hope to focus attention away from the common, but often inaccurate, notion that only a true American-style journalist is capable of independent political action. Indeed, the biggest drivers of day-to-day political change in the Chinese news environment are not these "American-style" journalists, or even market pressure, but the advocate professionals. Although media professionalization is clearly advancing in China, it is not a monolithic construct, and we cannot directly point from "professional journalism" to state challenges. It is the *kind* of professionalism that matters. It is time to step back from the Procrustean bed of a Western media theory that refuses to see advocates as anything other than "unbalanced" polemicists and engage with the empirical realities faced by actual – not idealized – Chinese reporters. Ultimately, it is the advocate professionals, discussed further in Chapter 6, who have the most congruity with Chinese intellectual and media tradition. We should therefore not be surprised to find them at the vanguard of sensitive coverage and of policy and media change in China, as I will show in the chapters to come.

Notes

1 Though among recent exceptions are Lin (2010a), Zhao (2008), and Lee (2005).
2 The term is adapted from Hallin and Mancini (2004) who refer to such journalists as belonging to the "North Atlantic" or "Liberal" model of journalism.
3 Note that the four categories are derived primarily from interviews and research on Chinese periodicals, and their application to radio, TV, or Internet journalists is somewhat speculative. Without a sample from a representative survey, I cannot provide reliable frequency estimates.
4 Chin-Chuan Lee, Zhou He, and Yu Huang (2007) discuss this phenomenon and contend that Shanghai, Beijing, and Guangzhou represent the three types of party-market media relations extant in China.
5 Hassid (2008b: 427). Note that the SAPPRFT is a new agency, created in 2013 and inheriting the previous mandate of the General Administration of Press and Publication (GAPP *Xinwen Chuban Zongshu* 新闻出版总署).
6 From the GAPP website at http://press.gapp.gov.cn/cms/html/285/index.html, accessed May 27, 2011.
7 For example http://press.gapp.gov.cn/cms/html/285/2259/List-1.html, accessed May 27, 2011, but since removed from the web. Interestingly, the large majority of these disgraced reporters were accused of accepting bribes and not of other misconduct.

8 http://news.xinhuanet.com/zgjx//2009–03/18/content_11028741.htm, accessed June 5, 2009.
9 In this case, the belief that they serve society by serving the CCP.
10 Many European journalists, for instance, would disagree. For the fault lines between American and European "professional" journalists, see Hallin and Mancini (2004).
11 I was fortunate enough to attend several meetings and conferences of the environmental and legal journalists' groups in 2007–2008.

References

Bandurski, David, and Martin Hala. 2010. "The Kingdom of Lies: Unmasking the Demons of Charity." In *Investigative Journalism in China: Eight Cases in Chinese Watchdog Journalism*, edited by David Bandurski and Martin Hala, 61–72. Hong Kong: Hong Kong University Press.

Baum, Richard. 1994. *Burying Mao: Chinese Politics in the Age of Deng Xiaoping*. Princeton, NJ: Princeton University Press.

Benson, Rodney Dean. 2004. "Bringing the Sociology of Media Back In." *Political Communication* 21:275–292. doi:10.1080/10584600490481299.

Brady, Anne-Marie. 2008. *Marketing Dictatorship: Propaganda and Thought Work in Contemporary China*, Asia/Pacific/Perspectives. Lanham: Rowman & Littlefield.

Feng Yongfeng (冯永锋). 2007. *Don't Criticize the Head of the Environmental Protection Bureau: Beijing's Perspective on the Way Forward for Chinese Cities' Environmental Protection* (不要指责环保局长: 从北京看中国城市环保局出路). Beijing: World Knowledge Press (世界知识出版社).

Hall, Richard H. 1968. "Professionalization and Bureaucratization." *American Sociological Review* 33 (1):92–104.

Hallin, Daniel C., and Paolo Mancini. 2004. *Comparing Media Systems: Three Models of Media and Politics, Communication, Society, and Politics*. Cambridge; New York: Cambridge University Press.

Hassid, Jonathan. 2008a. "China's Contentious Journalists: Reconceptualizing the Media." *Problems of Post-Communism* 55 (4):52–61.

Hassid, Jonathan. 2008b. "Controlling the Chinese Media: An Uncertain Business." *Asian Survey* 48 (3):414–430. doi:10.1525/as.2008.48.3.414.

Lee, Chin-Chuan. 2005. "The Conception of Chinese Journalists: Ideological Convergence and Contestation." In *Making Journalists: Diverse Models, Global Issues*, edited by Hugo de Burgh, 107–126. London; New York: Routledge.

Lee, Chin-Chuan, Zhou He, and Yu Huang. 2007. "Party-Market Corporatism, Clientalism and Media in Shanghai." *Harvard International Journal of Press/Politics* 12 (3):21–42.

Lin, Fen J. 2010a. "Organizational Construction or Individual's Deed? The Literati Tradition in the Journalistic Professionalization in China." *International Journal of Communication* 4:175–197.

Lin, Fen J. 2010b. "A Survey Report on Chinese Journalists in China." *China Quarterly* 202:421–34.

Lu Yuegang (卢跃刚). 1999. "Our Basic Position (我们的基本立场)." In *The Fourth Right: From Watchdog Journalism to Rule of Law in the Media* (第四种全力: 从舆论监督到新闻法治), edited by Zan Aizong (昝爱宗), 1–4. Beijing: Minzu Chubanshe (民族出版社).

Pan, Zhongdang, and Ye Lu. 2003. "Localizing Professionalism: Discursive Practices in China's Media Reforms." In *Chinese Media, Global Contexts*, edited by Chin-Chuan Lee, 215–236. New York: Routledge.

Qian Gang and David Bandurski. 2011. "China's Emerging Public Sphere: The Impact of Media Commercialization, Professionalism, and the Internet in an Era of Transition." In *Changing Media, Changing China*, edited by Susan L. Shirk, 38–76. New York: Oxford University Press.

Reporters sans Frontières. 2015. "2015 World Press Freedom Index." http://index.rsf.org.

Rong, Xue Lan, and Tianjian Shi. 2001. "Inequality in Chinese Education." *Journal of Contemporary China* 10 (26):107–124.

Stern, Rachel E. 2013. *Environmental Litigation in China: A Study in Political Ambivalence, Cambridge Studies in Law and Society*. Cambridge: Cambridge University Press.

Stern, Rachel E., and Jonathan Hassid. 2012. "Amplifying Silence: Uncertainty and Control Parables in Contemporary China." *Comparative Political Studies* 45 (10):1230–1254. doi:10.1177/0010414011434295.

Tong, Jingrong. 2011. *Investigative Journalism in China: Journalism, Power, and Society*. London; New York: Continuum.

Tumber, Howard, and Marina Prentoulis. 2005. "Journalism and the Making of a Profession." In *Making Journalists: Diverse Models, Global Issues*, edited by Hugo de Burgh, 58–74. London; New York: Routledge.

Wang Yongchen (汪永辰) and Xiong Zhihong (熊志红), eds. 2005. *Green Journalists' Salon (绿色记者沙龙)*. Beijing: China Environmental Science Publishers (中国环境科学出版社).

Wilensky, Harold L. 1964. "The Professionalization of Everyone?" *American Journal of Sociology* 70 (2):137–158.

Zhao, Yuezhi. 1998. *Media, Market, and Democracy in China: Between the Party Line and the Bottom Line*. Urbana: University of Illinois Press.

Zhao, Yuezhi. 2008. *Communication in China: Political Economy, Power, and Conflict, State and Society in East Asia*. Lanham, MD: Rowman & Littlefield.

3 "Throat and tongue"
The communist professionals

Although such reporters like are often seen as an anachronistic relic of Maoist times, communist professionals still make up a substantial, though shrinking, proportion of Chinese journalists. While many younger reporters have grown disillusioned with communist-style news or even quit the profession entirely because, in the words of one former reporter, they "told lies" (*sa huang* 撒谎) (Interview HY14–2), others continue the tradition of communist professionalism.

Despite their shrinking numbers and stature in the PRC, communist professionals are very commonly discussed in Western academic and media circles. When stories refer to "China's official media" as "ignoring or twisting" the words of Western leaders (York 2008) or when scholars call the CCP mouthpiece *People's Daily* the paper that "sets the tone for all other media in China" (Yin 2007: 35), they reinforce the sense that most Chinese journalists are still communist professionals. Often seen as an anachronistic relic of Maoist times when all journalists were state employees distributing rigidly standardized propaganda, communist professionals have been declining in importance since the reform era began in 1978. Although many such journalists still ply their trade, they hardly merit their occasional position as *the* stereotypical representatives of the contemporary Chinese news media.

Party membership remains disproportionate among journalists – in 2008 about 40% of reporters were party members (Lin 2010b: 423) compared to about 5% of the general public[1] – but this number that has been declining in recent years. In the late 1990s, for example, about 54% of reporters held CCP membership, a drop of nearly one-third in only a decade and despite virtually no change in the total number or composition of China's newspapers.[2] These declining numbers are a manifestation of the decreasing appeal of communist ideology to many journalists, with one former *Southern Weekend* journalist claiming (with some exaggeration) that "half of reporters want to criticize the government, while the other half want to make money" (Interview EL30–0). The power of Chinese communist ideology among news workers has been declining since at least the late 1970s, with prominent journalists like Liu Binyan writing famous reportage that implicitly critiqued the CCP (Liu Binyan [刘宾雁] 1979). By the time of the 1989 Tiananmen Square uprising, journalists were "the first organized group of intellectuals on the streets," often voicing demands for more autonomy (Jernow and Thurston

1993: 51–52). Even journalists at the party mouthpiece *People's Daily* and the state broadcaster CCTV "shouted slogans like, 'We Must Speak the Truth,' 'Don't Force Us to Lie,' and carried banners that proclaimed, 'Don't Force Us to Spread Rumors,' . . . 'I Love Free Press,' and 'Free Minds, Free Press'" (Jernow and Thurston 1993: 56).

Related to the decline of journalists' Party membership is the decreasing proportion of journalists who work for Party "mouthpiece" papers. While all newspapers in China must retain a Party/state "sponsor" (*zhuguan bumen* 主管部门), very few continue to rely on public money to fund their operations. Even papers like *Worker's Daily* and *China Environment News* (*Zhongguo Huanjing Bao* 中国环境报), the official paper of the Ministry of Environmental Protection, are now entirely marketized, and the requirement to sell subscriptions and advertising at times interferes with their expected propaganda role. Indeed, *China Environment News* struggles even in comparison with other small papers, receiving in 2007 more than half of its 20 million RMB ($3.2 million) advertising revenue in the form of technically illegal "paid news" – often company press releases (Interview HH12–2). This cozy reliance on paid business funding means that if even executives at *China Environment News* and similar papers wanted to maintain their mouthpiece function, they would be hard pressed to do so. Among China's nearly 2,000 newspapers, only a handful continue to receive any state funding at all; this decline has directly contributed to China's shrinking number of communist professionals.

Party membership, however, is neither necessary nor sufficient to make a communist professional; instead, these are news workers who aim to serve as the CCP's mouthpiece regardless of official affiliation. As CCTV journalists joke:

> I am a dog of the Party, sitting in front of the Party's house. I attack whomever the Party wants me to, and I attack as many times as the Party wants me to. I am a dog of the Party, sitting in front of the Party's house. I kiss whomever the Party wants me to, and I kiss as many times as the Party wants me to.
> (Zhao 2004: 43)

Marxist-Leninist press theory supports this view, holding that the news media should serve as a transmission belt that helps inform both officials above and people below of decisions and on-the-ground conditions (Dittmer 1994). Journalists are expected to report and explain official decisions to the people and in turn describe popular reaction to their superiors. As one CCP media official puts it, even today "Firmly grasping the propaganda role (*yulun daoxiang* 舆论导向) is a prerequisite for improving the competitiveness of the entire newspaper industry," and "The newspaper industry must preserve the leadership of the Party from start to finish, preserve the leading role of Marxism in publishing newspapers, and promote advanced socialist culture" (Shi Feng [石峰] 2007).

Even as Party officials and communist professionals acknowledge that technology and media commercialization have irreversibly changed the role of official media outlets, they still work diligently to preserve these outlets' leading role in delivering official propaganda and "guiding" public opinion. Politics scholar and

Xinhua journalist Shen Rufa (沈汝发), writing in the magazine of the official state journalists' organization, acknowledges that China's transformation has created "social contradictions" that have led to the growth of what she terms "radical public opinion" (*guoji yulun* 过激舆论). Unlike responsible media, which rely on the Party/state to pass "laws and regulations that solve social problems," and "safeguard social order," these non-Party journalists and netizens "lack any sense of responsibility, leading to the publication of excessive speech, even to the point that lawless people publish false information and concoct fake news" that challenges social stability. This situation takes place in large part, Shen argues, because the "vast majority of netizens" – unlike communist-approved journalists – "have not received professional training" (Shen Rufa [沈汝发] 2010: 79).

The view that the communist press most properly serves as a transmission belt helping guide and improve the nation from on high initially achieved such traction because of its complementarily with earlier precommunist views of the media's role. Historian Joan Judge writes of

> [a] Chinese student in American who contributed an editorial to the newspaper [*The Times*, or *Shibao* 时报] in 1906 defined the general objective of education – to be led, in part by journalists – "as 'cultivating civic qualities and developing the nation's ability to defend itself against foreign aggression.'"
> (Judge 1996: 105)

Today, communist professionals see the CCP as playing this very role.

Although many noncommunist journalists dismiss such talk as official boilerplate or worse, many contemporary Chinese journalists clearly continue to believe in the Party's leading role in public life. For example, Hu Zhibin, a former journalist at *The First* (*Jing Bao* 竞报), notes that his role is determined in relationship to the CCP:

> As to whether I will be able to practice my journalistic ideals, I really can't decide by myself. This is because, firstly, I am a Communist Party member, and, secondly, journalism still is the mouthpiece of the Party and government and must fulfill propagandistic requirements. I don't think doing propaganda is necessarily bad; you are serving your country.
> (Polumbaum and Xiong 2008: 99)

The result of this tension between practicing "journalistic ideals" and serving the CCP, as media scholar Chin-Chuan Lee notes, is that communist

> [j]ournalists serve two masters: party leaders and the masses. Potential conflicts inherent in the unequal power between these two masters may be harmonized at the level of abstract theorization (by making an *a priori* claim, for example, that the vanguard party represents the masses), but not in practice.
> (Lee 2005: 116)

In practice, of course, journalists' superiors in the Party historically were listened to far more often than "the masses," especially given top leader Liu Shaoqi's insistence that "journalists use Marxist class conflict and dialectical materialism to analyze concrete phenomena" (Lee 2005: 115). As the theory has remained the same for six decades, even the language often remains unchanged, employing the same stuffy clichés of Maoist yesteryear. A typical exhortation in an official publication urges reporters to "diligently improve the ability to guide public opinion" (*yulun daoxiang nengli* 舆论导向能力), to "persist in correct guidance" of the people and to "reform managerial control" (Wang Chen [王晨] 2007: 243), phrases that would not have been out of place in the 1950s.

Within this system, the *People's Daily* has always had a special role to play, a role that it continues to stress. Wang Chen (王晨), then head of the *People's Daily* news agency, in 2007 proclaimed that the "*People's Daily's* greatest political responsibility" was to "persist in the correct political line, and persist in correctly guiding public opinion . . . unflinchingly and unwaveringly" (Wang Chen [王晨] 2007: 243). The *People's Daily* certainly maintains this role for communist professionals and official provincial papers throughout China, though its circulation – and relevance for most journalists and the general public – continues to decline precipitously. Official figures for the *People's Daily Overseas Edition*, for example, suggest that its circulation dropped by over 80% between 2006 and 2009.[3]

Professional *and* communist

Although Western scholars might see communist professionals working for the *People's Daily* and other papers as more "communist" than "professional," this view is a mistake. Communist professionals remain professionals, having experience with what political scientist Jane Curry calls the four elements "involved in transforming an individual into a professional" (Curry 1990: 16). These are

> (1) the recruitment and training process; (2) work experiences and the resulting interaction with fellow professionals; (3) the structures and rules for controlling professionals' behavior that are . . . codified and reinforced by formal and informal professional associations; and (4) the impact of external images of the profession held by the society.

Many Chinese journalists, even those who work at hardline mouthpiece papers and remain deeply committed to the goals of the party, have clearly been shaped by this four-element professionalizing process. And to these four, I would add a fifth element: the impact and influence of international norms.

Even if communist professionals are not often active in China's several semi-formalized journalism training groups, "Informal organization, characterized as it is by colleague network, is the vital link in professional life. Formal professional organizations are really structural concessions to represent a profession to nonprofessionals" (Curry 1990: 16). In other words, the tight core of professionalized, public-minded journalists at the heart of the profession helps make up for the structural failings of China's official reporters' association.

These organizations aside, communist professionals have their own view on what journalistic professionalism means in practice. As one media scholar puts it, "the Marxist view of the press is the crux, and together with a professional spirit and professional ethical foundation are united and inseparable" (Xin Yan [辛言]2010: 22). Exposure to Western journalism theory and practice might at first seem incongruous with this "Marxist view of the press," but communist journalists might disagree. Many apply Western training to their style and interview technique, rather than in reshaping their views of the media's proper relationship with the state. Wang Yunbo (Interview GX16–2), a former reporter and editor at the *Farmer's Daily* (*Nongmin Ribao* 农民日报) had formal journalism training in school and continuing education at work, with his instructors placing special emphasis on emulating *The New York Times*. Rather than adopting the (idealized) view of *Times* staff that reporters should supervise and critique the government, however, Wang and his colleagues continued to think of themselves as the CCP's "throat and tongue," an attitude that did not change in the newsroom over the course of his employment at the paper despite the end of government subsidies. Nonetheless, Wang's long training as an undergraduate and in the newsroom, his commitment to public service, and even his exposure to Western press ideals mark him as a communist professional.

In addition to their desire to serve the CCP, communist professionals also share demographic features, typically being older, male, and working at government-run or noncommercial papers. Although their desire for media independence from the CCP is low, many communist professionals have a high commitment to advocacy, especially those who view intrabureaucracy internal reference reports[4] as "an alternative that could help solve problems, given the current state-media regime" (Lin 2010a: 179). Editor Li Lei is interested in more than just "supervising" the government, but instead is interested in being "a builder" (*jianshezhe* 建设者) who "participates in building the country." Criticism is easy, she claims, but helping solve problems is much harder. Rather than simply criticize, she argues, helping the CCP is like "helping an old friend." If the old friend has problems, it is best to point them out gently and constructively, with an aim toward improving the situation (Interview HB20–2). In this respect, Li Lei echoes those journalists of a century earlier who accepted state power as a given and believed that "civil society must maintain an intimate and harmonious, rather than a hostile and antagonistic, relationship with the state" (Judge 1996: 202). Other media scholars have noted the unique position this harmonious relationship gives many communist professionals. David Bandurski and Martin Hala note that "It can sometimes be difficult to differentiate the work of reporters from that of public investigators or government regulators, while, at the same time, the press has in many ways come to be viewed as a cost-effective complement to them" (Bandurski and Hala 2010: 91).

Who are the communist professionals?

Communist professionals tend to dominate outlets like the *People's Daily, Farmer's Daily,* the various papers of the provincial party committees (e.g., the *Sichuan Daily* [*Sichuan Ribao* 四川日报]), China Central Television (CCTV), and others, though all of these media groups also employ journalists of the other three types. These news workers are hardly the bottom of the barrel either, as *People's Daily* staff in particular are "Drawn from the ranks of the best trained and most talented, with a strong sense of professionalism" but they "also must have finely honed political sensitivities" (Polumbaum and Xiong 2008: 43). The official news agency Xinhua, meanwhile, is reputed to have many staff members unhappy with their mouthpiece role but unable (or unwilling) to openly push for change. One former senior journalist, for example, left the agency to expand his domestic influence and better solve national problems but still believes in the primacy of the Party (Interview KM1–2). In short, many – if not most – employees of these "mouthpiece" organizations remain committed to CCP leadership and communist-style journalistic professionalism.

This commitment to CCP leadership tends to be less self-reflective among older journalists. For example, Chen Hu (Interview HY20–5B), a 50-ish editor at the *Workers' Daily* (*Gongren Ribao* 工人日报) clearly thought of himself as representing the Party spirit and seemed pleased with the status quo. Although Chen vaguely claimed to "represent the people," when pressed he equated their interests with those of the CCP. As is common among communist professionals working for the few remaining state "mouthpiece" newspapers, he slowly rose through the ranks, beginning his journalism career as a writer for a coal company's newsletter during the late 1970s. It was very common for large employers to have their own newspapers during this era, and many of the older communist professionals became reporters through this kind of on-the-job training, rather than obtaining a university degree in journalism.

This commitment to the CCP is not limited to older workers, however. One young reporter told me that he supports the Party because it brings stability, and "preserving stability" (*weiwen* 维稳) is the most important role of the press. Too much media freedom is a terrible thing, he claims, and indeed he claims that even in the US reporters cannot criticize the government willy-nilly (Interview KM1–2). Younger communist professionals like Li Lei (Interview GM05–2), a twenty-something female journalist for a paper sponsored by the official Xinhua News Agency, tend to think more critically about their role within Chinese society. Li is avowedly quite "conservative" (*baoshou* 保守) and thinks that it is not for individual journalists to decide their own role. Rather, she believes, the state should decide such questions, especially since both she and the state share the goal of developing Chinese society. Although at times unhappy with what she sees as the CCP's overly heavy-handed control of the press, she is nonetheless comfortable with its overall role in the media. Li Fang (Interview ET09–2B), a young radio reporter, explicitly considers himself the "throat" (*houlong* 喉咙) of the government but not its "tool" (*gongju* 工具). Unlike a "tool," a "throat" has two facets: When the government wants to speak, it uses the throat, but the rest of the time the throat can and should speak on its own. Such a statement does not undermine the characterization of Li as a communist professional and is consistent with early survey work suggesting that, regardless of their orientation, "Chinese journalists' job satisfaction has less to do with material rewards . . . than with their perceptions of job autonomy" (Chen, Zhu, and Wu 1998: 25).

Conclusion

Communist professionals, then, are neither a distant relic of the Maoist past nor the most numerous and powerful representatives of the Chinese media. On the whole, they are a contented group who have little wish to rock the boat. For example, here is an excerpt from a front-page story on October 21, 2009, in the *People's Daily,* a paper that by all accounts is heavily staffed by communist professionals:

> The Dalai Lama has always shielded himself with the "democracy" sign to cater to westerners. . . . However on September 9, Jamyang Norbu, a radical Tibetan separatist, published a long article on a "pro-Tibet independence" website . . . which pitilessly exposed the Dalai Lama's "democracy myth" and again helped people see through the true autocratic features of the Dalai Lama clique.
>
> *(People's Daily* Staff 2009)

Stories like this are entirely noncontroversial (within China) and highly unlikely to cause trouble for anyone. Any irony about a CCP functionary criticizing the Dalai Lama as "autocratic" is unremarked – and unintended. Similarly, stories on diplomatic visits to China often use recycled boilerplate like "'building stronger bilateral ties' to describe, with never a variation, the purpose of meetings between national VIPs" (David 1992: 19). These reporters, in other words, aim to express *only* the CCP viewpoint and strive to toe the official Party line, at least when reporting for direct public consumption.

Although such reporting is a hallmark of China's contemporary communist professionals, the CCP has made sporadic attempts in the past to distance communist journalism from this wooden formulism. Mao Zedong himself railed against "stereotyped Party writing" that "fills endless pages with empty verbiage" (Mao Tse-Tung 1965: 56), arguing that authors who employ such language "fear refutation, are very cowardly, and therefore rely on pretentiousness to overawe others, believing that they can thereby silence people and 'win the day'" (Mao Tse-Tung 1965: 57). Mao's advice to Chinese authors to "consider their audience and bear in mind those who will read their articles" (Mao Tse-Tung 1965: 59) has always been more honored in the breach than in the observance but nonetheless provides a fitting reminder that writing in a stereotypical "communist" style is associated with, but does not define, China's communist professionals.

More recently, many CCP scholars have recognized that Mao was right. To survive, they have argued, China's official papers and communist professionals need to become more relevant and economically competitive while still remaining under the tight control of propaganda officials. To achieve this balancing act, officials are turning away from "controlling" and toward "guiding" public opinion in what media scholar David Bandurski terms "Control 2.0" (Bandurski 2009). In this model, communist professionals are encouraged to write stories that are more interesting and relevant than their previous insipid offerings. Hong Kong University's China Media Project writes that

> In January 2003, [propaganda boss] Li Changchun announced top leadership would take a "Three Closenesses" [*san tiejin* 三贴近] approach to the control of mass media: "Closeness to reality, closeness to the masses and closeness to real life" (贴近实际, 贴近群众, 贴近生活). Li said the emphasis of propaganda work should be uniting the "spirit" of the Party with public opinion. This was an elaboration of Jiang Zemin's notion of "guidance of public opinion," the idea being that people should be both guided and given media they found more attractive, interesting and relevant (in other words, could actually *consume*).
>
> (China Media Project Staff 2008)

The end result has been to encourage communist professionals to become less communist and more committed to generalized norms of public service. While still communist, these journalists have also become increasingly professional. In short, while communist professionals have clearly lost ground over time to the other types of Chinese news worker, it is far too soon to count such reporters out. As long as reporters like Hu Zhibin retain their strong faith in the CCP, they will continue to play a crucial role in contemporary Chinese society.

Notes

1 According to *The Economist* at www.economist.com/countries/China/profile.cfm?folder=Profile-Political%20Forces, accessed August 5, 2009.
2 Journalist party membership data is from Chen, Zhu, and Wu (1998), newspaper data from Chinese Academy of Social Sciences News Research Institute (中国社会科学院新闻与传播研究所, various years).
3 Dropping from a daily average of 165,000 to 30,500 according to the Chinese Academy of Social Sciences News Research Institute (中国社会科学院新闻与传播研究所, various years). Circulation data in China – especially for official papers – are unreliable, and during the same period, the domestic *People's Daily* has claimed a small circulation increase. This supposed increase is unlikely to be legitimate, however (Interview KX24–2Z), and the data for the *Overseas Edition* might be seen as less politically sensitive and less prone to manipulation.
4 That is, articles written for the Party/state bureaucracy only and not for the general public.

References

Bandurski, David. 2009. How Control 2.0 Found Its Poster Boy in Yunnan. *China Media Project*. Accessed Jan. 16, 2012. http://cmp.hku.hk/2009/02/24/1483.

Bandurski, David, and Martin Hala. 2010. "Undercover Reporting: Ah Wen's Nightmare." In *Investigative Journalism in China: Eight Cases in Chinese Watchdog Journalism*, edited by David Bandurski and Martin Hala, 73–93. Hong Kong: Hong Kong University Press.

Chen, Chongshan, Jian-Hua Zhu, and Wei Wu. 1998. "The Chinese Journalist." In *The Global Journalist: News People around the World*, edited by David H. Weaver and Wei Wu, 9–30. Cresskill, NJ: Hampton Press.

China Media Project Staff. 2008. The Three Closenesses. *China Media Project*. Accessed January 16, 2011. http://cmp.hku.hk/2007/03/20/212/.

Chinese Academy of Social Sciences News Research Institute (中国社会科学院新闻与传播研究所). Various Years. *China Journalism Yearbook* (中国新闻年鉴). Beijing: China Journalism Yearbook Publishers (中国新闻年鉴社).

Curry, Jane Leftwich. 1990. *Poland's Journalists: Professionalism and Politics*. Cambridge; New York: Cambridge University Press.

David, John. 1992. "Pioneering Xinhua's International Journalism Training Centre." In *Reporting the News from China*, edited by Robin Porter, 16–39. London: Royal Institute of International Affairs.

Dittmer, Lowell. 1994. "The Politics of Publicity in Reform China." In *China's Media, Media's China*, edited by Chin-Chuan Lee, 89–112. Boulder, CO: Westview Press.

Jernow, Allison Liu, and Anne F. Thurston. 1993. *"Don't Force Us to Lie": The Struggle of Chinese Journalists in the Reform Era*. [New York]: Committee to Protect Journalists.

Judge, Joan. 1996. *Print and Politics: 'Shibao' and the Culture of Reform in Late Qing China, Studies of the East Asian Institute*. Stanford, CA: Stanford University Press.

Lee, Chin-Chuan. 2005. "The Conception of Chinese Journalists: Ideological Convergence and Contestation." In *Making Journalists: Diverse Models, Global Issues*, edited by Hugo de Burgh, 107–126. London; New York: Routledge.

Lin, Fen J. 2010a. "Organizational Construction or Individual's Deed? The Literati Tradition in the Journalistic Professionalization in China." *International Journal of Communication* 4:175–197.

Lin, Fen J. 2010b. "A Survey Report on Chinese Journalists in China." *China Quarterly* 202: 421–34.

Liu Binyan (刘宾雁). 1979. "People or Monsters? (人妖之间)." *People's Literature (人民文学)*.

Mao Tse-Tung. 1965. *Selected Works of Mao Tse-Tung*. Vol. 3. Peking: Foreign Languages Press.

People's Daily Staff. 2009. "Tibetan Separatist Exposes Dalai Lama's 'Democracy Myth.'" *People's Daily English Edition*, Oct. 21. http://chinatibet.people.com.cn/6789022.html.

Polumbaum, Judy, and Lei Xiong. 2008. *China Ink: The Changing Face of Chinese Journalism*. Lanham, MD: Rowman & Littlefield.

Shen Rufa (沈汝发). 2010. "Contributing Factors and Responses to Online 'Radical Public Opinion' (网络'过激舆论'的社会成因及应对)." *Chinese Journalist (中国记者)* 11:79–80.

Shi Feng (石峰). 2007. "Improve the Competitiveness of China's Entire Newspaper Industry, Initiate a New Phase in China's Newspaper Development (提升中国报业整体竞争力,开创中国报业发展新局面)." In *The Development Report of China's Newspaper Industry* (中国报业发展报告), edited by Lin Jiang (林江) and Feng Yuming (冯玉明), 1–6. Beijing: Social Sciences Academic Press (社会科学文献出版社).

Wang Chen (王晨). 2007. "Resolutely Improve the Ability to Guide Public Opinion (努力提高舆论导向能力)." In *China Journalism Yearbook* (中国新闻年鉴), edited by the Chinese Academy of Social Sciences News Research Institute (中国社会科学院新闻与传播研究所), 243–244. Beijing: China Journalism Yearbook Publishers (中国新闻年鉴社).

Xin Yan (辛言). 2010. "A Book Helpful for Studying and Understanding the Marxist View of the Press (一本有助于深入学习、理解马克思主义新闻观的书)." *Chinese Journalist* (*中国记者*) 12: 22.

Yin, Jing. 2007. "The Narrative Function of News: A Comparative Study of Media Representation and Audience Interpretation of China-U.S. Trade Relationship." *China Media Research* 3 (3):33–42.

York, Geoffrey. 2008. "China Twisting Harper's Message; State-Controlled Media Have Either Ignored Pm's Advice on Human Rights or Reported His Opposition to a Boycott." *The Globe and Mail*, Apr. 10, A14.

Zhao, Yuezhi. 2004. "Underdogs, Lapdogs and Watchdogs: Journalists and the Public Sphere Problematic in China." In *Chinese Intellectuals between State and Market*, edited by Edward Gu and Merle Goldman, 43–74. New York: RoutledgeCurzon.

4 "Guard against fire, theft, and journalists"
The workaday reporters

On July 14, 2008, just weeks before the Beijing Olympics, explosives improperly stored in the illegal Lijiawa coal mine in Yuxian County, Hebei, blew up, trapping dozens of coal miners and killing thirty-five. Such disasters are sadly common in China's poor coal mining regions, and the only notable feature of the Lijiawa disaster is that it was eventually reported in the media. While 2.6 million RMB (~US$400,000) in bribes to reporters – a huge amount of money in rural China – had managed to keep the story out of the papers for nearly three months, eventually a disgruntled county employee posted about the disaster online. The pioneering *China Youth Daily* (*Zhongguo Qingnian Bao* 中国青年报) picked up the story, and the resulting investigation led to the jailing of dozens of county officials and, remarkably, ten unnamed reporters (Tian Guolei [田国垒] 2010). This incident captures both the promise and pitfalls of the contemporary Chinese news media. While capable of sparking substantial political change, the Chinese press is also awash in corruption, often beholden to the interests and pocketbooks of power holders and usually politically supine.

Conventional wisdom – and numerous academic studies (e.g., Stapenhurst 2000; Brunetti and Weder 2003; Rose-Ackerman 1978) – argue that sunshine is the best disinfectant. A free media, in other words, by helping to uncover and prevent corruption, is claimed to improve the quality of governance (Hassid and Brass 2015). But what happens when there is widespread corruption in the media itself? Although research on the Chinese media has emphasized state censorship as the major institutional block to a free press (Esarey 2005, 2006; Brady 2008; Hassid 2008; He Qinglian 2004), rampant media corruption is a serious obstacle toward the evolution of an effective news media that can monitor and even check overweening state power. The corruption in the press mirrors, and ultimately masks, the corruption endemic in Chinese society. Media corruption, officially tolerated or even encouraged, retards professionalization and prevents or delays political change in the People's Republic.

Definitions of corruption vary, of course, based on cultural contexts and institutional norms. For this paper, I will sidestep the issue of providing a general definition by restricting my analysis to behaviors normatively (but often nominally) condemned by Chinese journalists and official guidelines. Below, I will detail the types and causes of corruption in the Chinese media and examine the factors that make such behavior an "institutional and occupational phenomenon involving the majority of journalists and the majority of media organizations" (Zhao 1998: 72). Finally, I will demonstrate how and why corruption impedes the consolidation of a professional ethos among Chinese journalists, a professional ethos that can encourage news workers to push for political and social change.

The forms of Chinese media corruption

Corruption among Chinese news workers runs the gamut from the small and commonplace to the spectacular and epic. Perhaps the most common form is "car fare" (*chemafei*), envelopes stuffed with between 200 and 500 RMB (~ US$30–80) provided by companies and even government bureaus to encourage journalists' attendance at news events. Most reporters readily and openly admit to taking car fare, and one even told me that press conferences "must" offer such envelopes (*chemafei shi yinggaide* 车马费是应该的) (Interview GM10–2B). Even otherwise professional news workers take such fees, for at news conferences all reporters take the envelopes "without exception" (Interview ET04–3). Indeed, "the payoffs have become so accepted that a reporter who showed up" for one company's news conference "complained loudly and walked out when he discovered he would be given only a bottle of mineral water, according to other reporters present" (Cody 2007). Although such petty corruption is nearly ubiquitous, most Chinese news organizations ban their reporters from taking car fare, a rule actively enforced only at a handful of top publications. Most reporters, too, agree that the practice is detrimental to their objectivity, although a vocal minority insists that such payment is fair reimbursement for travel expenses in a country where distances are often large and reporters' salaries small.

More serious is the phenomenon of "paid news" (*youchang xinwen* 有偿新闻), when reporters or papers are directly paid to produce articles favorable to corporations or powerful individuals. This phenomenon originated in the 1980s, when press commercialization and a gradual waning of state subsidies forced journalists and papers to look for new sources of revenue. By late 1993 this form of corruption it had "become so widespread and even socially accepted that some lower-level television stations began openly publishing prices" ranging from 500 to 5,000 RMB for favorable publicity (Lynch 1999: 62). This trend continues today, though less openly than in the 1990s.

Paid news is hardly the worst offense in the pantheon of Chinese media corruption. Journalists routinely demand "shut-up fees" (*fengkou fei* 封口费) to not report on negative news about companies or individuals. This type of blackmail is especially common after industrial or mining accidents, when real and fake reporters – often hundreds at a time – gather to be paid off. After a mine collapse in 2005, for instance, "reporters and their friends in Henan province dispatched a flurry of cell phone messages as soon as they heard the news – not because they were eager to report on it, but because they knew local officials would be eager to hush it up." So many people showed up that local officials ran out of cash and ended up paying out over 200,000 RMB (~US$32,000) to nearly five hundred journalistic extortionists. And such scenes are "very, very frequent," said Ma Yunlong, an editor at the newspaper that exposed this case (Cody 2007). For some industrialists, even paying hundreds of reporters hundreds of dollars apiece is cheaper than making basic safety upgrades or improving worker training. In one lurid case widely reported in 2003, journalists who had visited the scene of a gold mine collapse were later found to have gold bars stashed all over their houses as "hush money" payments (Interview HL9–4). Business reporters routinely play the stock market while writing stories to promote the stocks they own and make a quick profit, to the point of collectively organizing across papers to increase the positive "bump" on a stock from news stories (Interview GX30–2). Others try to blackmail companies with negative information, asking for as much as 300,000 RMB (~US$50,000) at a time (Interview GM05–2). Sometimes news workers even attempt to blackmail companies with fake information; one journalist told me of a colleague who broke into a Häagen-Dazs ice cream factory to plant evidence of dirty manufacturing practices in a failed effort to extort the company (Interview HL9–4).

More systemically, journalists and editors often hire their friends or relatives to be reporters without any training or aptitude, further encouraging cronyist behavior (Interview HL9–4). An equally common problem is the fact that media employers often do not provide their employees with an adequate travel budget, meaning that local officials and companies can step into the gap and provide reporters with all-expenses-paid junkets that can easily influence coverage. One veteran environmental reporter, for example, can exhaust his entire yearly travel allotment in just one trip to faraway Yunnan province, meaning he often has to rely on local power holders to finance his trips. Ultimately, he often finds it difficult to write critically about the very officials who paid for his travel (Interview HH12–2). Corruption even extends into the censorship apparatus, with some companies or powerful individuals having officials from the local publicity department call a paper to kill a story rather than pay the journalists off. For this reason, "mine owners often get chummy with propaganda department officials, and then when a problem happens, tap this resource to unilaterally shut things down, regardless of official policy" (Interview GM08–2).

Interestingly, with growing competition in the Chinese economy, some reporters think that corruption is increasing. In part this is because there is simply more money to go around, but more importantly, as new companies are started, they often pay reporters to promote positive stories about them in an effort to get noticed (Interview ET08–2). This blurring of the lines between news media and public relations is very common. But although news workers know that such behavior is problematic and that taking bribes is wrong, "the vast majority do it anyway while aspiring for a system in which it isn't necessary" (Interview HL6–4). The extent of corruption can be gauged by the rarity of newspaper reports about mining disasters in a country where 2,631 miners per year, or 7.2 per day, die on the job – by official figures (Associated Press 2010). The CCP's provincial paper in Shanxi province, for instance, has stories about natural and industrial accidents less frequently than does the party provincial papers in Anhui province, and only slightly more than the one in Chongqing, despite having a coal output between eight and ten times higher than the latter two areas.[1] In other words, though hundreds (or thousands) of miners die each year in Shanxi, corruption and media restrictions keep news about mining accidents to a trickle.

Causes of corruption

What causes such epic corruption? Many analysts concentrate on the incentives that monopolies (over purchasing, governing, information, etc.) create for rent seeking by officials and others. Susan Rose-Ackerman's early work, for instance, analyzes a hypothetical agency that is "very decentralized and fragmented, with numerous low-level officials" where "each individual official was granted exclusive authority" over a specific function (Rose-Ackerman 1978: 137). Such a system, with bureaucrats who have little oversight and accountability monopolizing specific policy areas, is a recipe for widespread corruption. In addition to accurately characterizing China's sprawling governmental machinery, this description also applies to many of China's media outlets, where reporters often work with little supervision over specific geographic areas or topics, rarely even entering their own offices.

Yuezhi Zhao writes that

> [j]ournalists, with their monopolistic access to state-controlled media resources, their overall cynicism toward the Party's propaganda operations and their job-mandated connections with the business sector . . . became one of the most readily co-opted intellectual groups. Their rental seeking activities encompass a wide range of unethical and illegal practices.
>
> (Zhao 2004: 51)

This monopolistic rent seeking is especially likely in areas served by only a single local paper, and this is undoubtedly part of the reason that smaller, regional papers are routinely seen as more corrupt than their central-level counterparts. Interestingly, this means that the effective salaries of reporters out in the countryside are often higher than those based in major media markets, because fewer rent-seeking opportunities in competitive media markets translates into lower reporter salaries (Interview GX31–2). Especially as the state has moved to end the system of forcing government offices or Party-affiliated mass organizations to subscribe to a number of newspapers, smaller papers or those in smaller advertising markets have scrambled to make up the lost revenue. Often this involves taking advantage of their lack of local competitors to get local businesses to purchase paid news and, increasingly, "paid no-news" (*youchang bu xinwen* 有偿不新闻) – that is, payments to avoid negative publicity (Interview HL2–2). The opposite can happen as well, with commercial pressure pushing journalists toward ever more sensational stories (whether true or not). *People's Daily* reporter Gong Wen complains that

> the status of journalists in China is declining. When I entered the career in 1992 journalists for organizations like *People's Daily* and Xinhua got

tremendous respect. These brand names still carry weight, but it's not like it was a decade or two ago when people would turn to media to reflect problems or convey grievances. The change is understandable; with more outlets and increased competition, some media hunt for novelty, grab scoops, and resort to hype.

(Polumbaum and Xiong 2008: 50)

While in theory competition and commercialization should help eradicate the monopoly that some media outlets have over information and therefore decrease corruption, most Chinese journalists agree that competition is only making things more complicated. A former editor at the *Farmers' Daily* (*Nongmin Ribao* 农民日报), for instance, argues that competition has had the paradoxical effect of making paid news, in particular, both more common and cheaper (Interview GX16–2). The proliferation of media outlets has made it harder for companies to get product recognition, making paid news an increasingly common tactic to stand out from the crowd. Interestingly, though, as paid news has proliferated it has become a less serious problem for companies because news outlets and journalists no longer have monopoly pricing power on publicity. In other words, as paid news has proliferated, its cost has declined.

The structure of local government in China and the incentives the CCP uses to control local officials also contribute to media corruption. County governments often rely heavily on local industrial concerns for tax revenue, and county officials are often personal shareholders in these (frequently illegal) companies. Moreover, when evaluating these officials for promotion, the CCP often prioritizes having a clean safety record and few "adverse events." The end result is a culture that ensures that information about local industrial accidents is kept secret at all costs. Media expert Zhan Jiang agrees, arguing that "local authorities in mining areas have come to rely on concealing work safety accidents through cutting information off from the public and using public funds for bribes," a system that creates a class of "professional blackmail journalists" (Liu Zhijie 2010).

Low salaries also play a critical role in encouraging corruption in the Chinese media. For example, Zhang Nan, an editor for a legal paper, says, "If you don't take red envelopes [bribes], you end up in poverty" (Interview GM14–2B). Another reporter argues that journalists simply are not paid enough money, and if a reporter can get 100 RMB for a short article but 200 RMB in "car fare" simply for showing up to a press conference, then the incentives are clear (Interview HB24–2). Reporters' salaries are so low, in part, because of how they are paid. In general, news workers are paid a minimal base salary, and the bulk of their income comes from "bonuses" based on how many of their stories appear in print. In addition to encouraging corruption, this system also provides heavy incentives for shoddy fact checking, plagiarism, and hasty writing to maximize income. It certainly does not help that many journalism students end up "studying journalism as a coincidence rather than of personal interests," revealing a lack of initial enthusiasm that no doubt contributes to unprofessional behavior later on (Dombernowsky 2014: 71).

Corruption and the profession

Although Chinese journalists are formally professionals, the field's rampant corruption keeps many of them from acting professionally – that is, by abiding the rules and procedures of their office. In particular, corrupt practices make a mockery of professional guidelines that require a commitment to public service. Instead of serving the public, corrupt media workers are interested in nothing more than lining their own pockets. As described above, such behavior badly distorts the accuracy and objectivity of the media, working to the advantage of the rich and powerful at the expense of the general public.

Although the media are a critical social and political actor in every modern society, the importance of the press cannot be overstated in China. Because the government routinely deems even the most anodyne information a state secret, the press is often the only source of information about basic political, social, and economic developments. And the public is hardly happy. A December 2005 telephone survey of Beijing residents conducted by the Chinese Academy of Social Sciences (CASS) and published in the official 2007 *China Journalism Yearbook*, for instance, found that a whopping 64.2% of survey respondents (n=554) agreed that news outlets "report only the good and hold back the bad" (*baoxi bu baoyou* 报喜不报忧), 59.4% think that "news reports far too rarely reflect the views of vulnerable social groups" (*ruoshi qunti* 弱势群体), 58.6% agree that news reports are far too often full of "empty or boastful rhetoric" (*konghua taohua dahua* 空话套话大话), 56.8% find that some news reports "conceal the truth" (*yangai shishi zhenxiang* 掩盖事实真相), 54.5% think news reports are too "one-sided" (*pianmianxing* 片面性), and 53.7% find that the foreign media cover stories the domestic media will not (Chinese Academy of Social Sciences News Research Institute [中国社会科学院新闻与传播研究所)] 2008: 477). And the results would likely be even worse outside the relatively strict oversight of the capital. Given this dissatisfaction, it is hardly surprising that one popular saying urges listeners to "guard against fire, theft, and journalists."

Writing about the United States, Susan Rose-Ackerman argues, "extortion can only be effectively checked by the professional ethical codes of journalists" (Rose-Ackerman 1978: 205). When these ethical codes are subverted by rampant corruption, the end result is a vicious circle that corrodes the power of journalistic professionalism and leads to more corruption. Many reporters agree that because the state and general public hold the media in low esteem, they are likely to have a lower self-worth and a negative sense of their own profession. One Chinese survey, for instance, found that nearly 80% of Chinese journalists would change careers if they could, in part because of a lack of social respect (Wang Zhuoqiong 2005). This lack of pride, in turn, encourages an "anything goes" attitude that ends up making corruption even worse. Corruption, in other words, is *both* a cause and an effect of the Chinese news media's general culture of unprofessionalism.

The fact that any professional Chinese journalists exist at all is due in part to a cohort of dedicated, highly networked exemplars at the core of the profession. Because news workers often look to their colleagues for ethical guidance, these groups can potentially serve as a nexus for reform. Reporter Zhu Hongxu agrees that corruption is really "about the ideology of the papers and reporters who work there" (Interview GM08–2). As a current employee of a major publication that bars its journalists from taking bribes, Zhu claims he would never do so, but in the past, when he worked for the *China Commercial Times* (*Zhongguo Shangbao* 中国商报), he used to do so all the time because it was part of the office custom. Professional context, in other words, matters a great deal. Reporters are embedded in professional networks and take their cues on acceptable behavior from the people around them. If corruption becomes increasingly unacceptable in the network – that is, if the professional ethos changes – then reporters seem to become less likely to take bribes. But if everyone in a reporter's professional network is corrupt, it makes being honest a good deal harder. As one veteran reporter put it, "to resist makes you stand out" (Interview HL6–4). And standing out in China can be a dangerous proposition.

Corruption and the state

When acting professionally and with an eye toward public service, Chinese journalists can be quite effective at pushing political change. Although the Sun Zhigang case (discussed briefly in Chapter 1) is the most well-documented case of the power a professionalized press can have in contemporary China, it is hardly unique. Among other recent cases, the press have exposed the following: the Chinese government's cover-up about the spread of Sudden Acute Respiratory Syndrome (SARS) in southern China and Beijing (Kahn 2004), revealed spectacular instances of corruption by local authorities (Interview GM08–2), rescued hundreds of adults and children from industrial slavery in Shaanxi brick factories (Zhu Zhe 2007), exposed the illegal commitment of government petitioners to psychiatric hospitals (Canaves 2008), investigated why so many schools collapsed in the 2008 Sichuan earthquake (Yang Binbin et al. 2008), broken the official silence about the existence of avian influenza (Interview HH31–2CZ), and encouraged the retrial of a suspected organized crime boss when it was rumored that bribes had gotten him a reduced sentence (Zheng 2008: 124). In short, it is clear that, when not beholden to power holders, the media can effect substantial changes in the Chinese polity.

Local officials, in particular, often wish to avoid these political changes and preserve the lucrative status quo, in part by simultaneously encouraging and taking advantage of rampant media corruption to withhold negative information from their superiors. From the perspective of corrupt local officials, then, having accurate, autonomous media is best avoided. The central state, though, seems to be of two minds about media corruption. On the one hand, central state organs like the General Administration on Press and Publication (GAPP) and co-opted ones like the All China Journalists Association (中华全国新闻工作者协会 Zhonghua Quanguo Xinwengongzuozhe Xiehui, ACJA) exhort against corrupt activities and shame journalists publicly caught breaking the rules. On the other hand, however, central and local authorities seem to encourage further corruption in an effort to more easily control journalists. When news workers cross a political line, charging them with corruption is an easy and believable way to ensure their silence.[2] This policy works even better if the accused journalists are actually guilty of corrupt behavior; the media's systemic problems means that such charges are often true.

When the Central Propaganda Department (CPD) forces an unwilling professor to offer "car fare" to journalists attending his press conference (Interview HH23–2), at a minimum, controlling corrupt journalistic behavior is not at the top of its agenda. Moreover, some of its directives strongly imply that the CPD itself is corrupt or at least in collusion with those who are. The fact that papers are not allowed to report on corruption in their local areas too frequently (He Qinglian 2004: 17) is evidence of this conclusion, as is the fact that one interviewee provided me with a CPD directive banning coverage of poor mobile phone service. A sudden increase in dropped calls hardly seems like a political issue, and it is reasonable to conclude that the (state-controlled) mobile phone companies bribed or otherwise pressured CPD officials to ban coverage for purely economic reasons. Data recently shared by UC Berkeley scholar Xiao Qiang also indicate that problems with real estate companies and private enterprises make up a substantial proportion of Chinese censorship directives, indicating the extent of systemic corruption.[3]

In the end, the systemic corruption of Chinese media workers makes professionalization less likely and keeps the media pliant. Writing about authoritarian, 1980s era Mexico, Susan Eckstein argues that "The regime, in particular, thrives on corruption. For decades such everyday defiance of the law enhanced the regime's stability; all groups had some stake in noncompliance with rational-bureaucratic rules" (Eckstein 1989: 42–43). Activists who stick to their principles and rock the boat are a threat to everyone; those at the top of the pile fear for their position and those at the bottom resent and mistrust colleagues who will not "play by the rules." A similar dynamic exists in China.

Writing about Chinese corruption specifically, Robert Harris argues that, "the political structure vests power in a small oligarchy of effectively unaccountable politicians, military leaders and officials. Secrecy is maintained through media control, fear, and punishment" (Harris 2003: 91). The media, in other words, are critical to exposing problems and pushing change in Chinese society. This situation puts central government officials in something of a bind; they need the media to expose problems in the localities at the same time as they do not want a press so free it endangers their own power. Given that local officials are often on the side of a corrupt, pliant media and central officials have – at best – a jaundiced view of press freedom, it is little wonder that the state does not take effective action to ensure an accurate, effective Chinese press.

Conclusion

In a country where incompetent, corrupt, or parasitic officials can simply bribe or blackmail their way into positive press coverage, journalists are unlikely to function freely or effectively even in the absence of political or legal restrictions. Even if China's Central Propaganda Department were eliminated tomorrow, rampant corruption would still prevent Chinese news workers from exercising the oversight functions so critical to effective governance. The core of professional, dedicated journalists who are responsible for many of the most dramatic and visible political and social changes of recent years demonstrates that an aggressive Chinese news media is hardly unthinkable. As long as the attention of scholars and activists is focused exclusively on political restrictions, however, the equally sinister problem of corruption will remain unaddressed.

The fact that Chinese journalists are highly networked and attuned to the behavior and attitudes of their colleagues presents reformers a double-edged sword. On the one hand, because many reporters see that their colleagues are willing to take bribes or blackmail power holders, these behaviors are seen as acceptable or even desirable throughout the field. On the other hand, however, the continued existence of genuinely effective, professional Chinese news workers serves as an example that encourages the growth of an ethos of public service. Exposing more current and potential news workers to these exemplars might be a successful way to improve the quality of the Chinese media – and of Chinese governance. Rather than directly challenging China's press censorship system, foreign and Chinese activists and NGOs might instead put more energy into training programs that aim to reduce media corruption – an approach both less confrontational and potentially more effective.

Notes

1 Disaster vocabulary represents about 0.24% of total word use in the *Anhui Daily* 安徽日报 (Anhui Ribao), 0.23% in the *Shanxi Daily* 山西日报 (Shanxi Ribao), and 0.22% of the *Chongqing Daily* 重庆日报 (Chongqing Ribao), differences that are not statistically significant. Coal output from China Data Online at http://chinadataonline.org/member/macroyr/macroyrtshow.asp.
2 By all accounts, this is how the CCP controlled papers in the Southern Group when they were becoming a political liability. See Kahn (2004); Esarey (2005).
3 Data analyzed by Ashley Esarey at a Berkeley workshop in mid-2013.

References

Associated Press. 2010. "China Coal Mines Safer, but More Changes Needed." *The New York Times*, Feb. 13. www.nytimes.com/aponline/2010/02/13/world/AP-AS-China-Mine-Deaths.html?_r=1&scp=3&sq=china coal&st=cse.
Brady, Anne-Marie. 2008. *Marketing Dictatorship: Propaganda and Thought Work in Contemporary China, Asia/Pacific/Perspectives*. Lanham, MD: Rowman & Littlefield.
Brunetti, Aymo, and Beatrice Weder. 2003. "A Free Press Is Bad News for Corruption." *Journal of Public Economics* 87 (7–8):1801–1824.
Canaves, Sky. 2008. "A Bold Media Move on the Psychiatric Detention of Complaining Citizens." *The Wall Street Journal: China Journal [Online]*, Dec. 9, China Journal. Accessed February 18, 2009. http://blogs.wsj.com/chinajournal/2008/12/09/a-bold-media-move-on-the-psychiatric-detention-of-complaining-citizens/?mod=rss_WSJBlog.
Chinese Academy of Social Sciences News Research Institute (中国社会科学院新闻与传播研究所). 2008. *China Journalism Yearbook* (中国新闻年鉴). Beijing: China Journalism Yearbook Publishers (中国新闻年鉴社).
Cody, Edward. 2007. "Blackmailing by Journalists in China Seen as 'Frequent.'" *The Washington Post*, Jan. 25, A1.

Dombernowsky, Laura. 2014. "Chinese Journalism Students: Balancing Competing Views." In *Chinese Investigative Journalists' Dreams: Autonomy, Agency and Voice*, edited by Marina Svensson, Elin Saether and Zhi'an Zhang, 53–74. Lanham, MD: Lexington Books.

Eckstein, Susan. 1989. "Power and Popular Protest in Latin America." In *Power and Popular Protest: Latin American Social Movements*, edited by Susan Eckstein and Manuel A. Garretón Merino, 1–60. Berkeley: University of California Press.

Esarey, Ashley. 2005. "Cornering the Market: State Strategies for Controlling China's Commercial Media." *Asian Perspective* 29 (4):37–83.

Esarey, Ashley. 2006. "Speak No Evil: Mass Media Control in Contemporary China." In *A Freedom House Special Report*. Freedom House. https://freedomhouse.org/sites/default/files/inline_images/Speak%20No%20Evil-%20Mass%20Media%20Control%20in%20Contemporary%20China.pdf

Harris, Robert. 2003. *Political Corruption: In and Beyond the Nation State*. London; New York: Routledge.

Hassid, Jonathan. 2008. "Controlling the Chinese Media: An Uncertain Business." *Asian Survey* 48 (3):414–430. doi:10.1525/as.2008.48.3.414.

Hassid, Jonathan, and Jennifer N. Brass. 2015. "Scandals, Media and Good Governance in China and Kenya." *Journal of Asian and African Studies* 50 (3):325–342.

He Qinglian. 2004. *Media Control in China [Zhongguo Zhengfu Ruhe Kongzhi Meiti]*. New York: Human Rights in China.

Kahn, Joseph. 2004. "Police Raid Chinese Newspaper That Reported New SARS Case." *The New York Times*, Jan. 8. Accessed October 9, 2006. http://query.nytimes.com/gst/fullpage.html?sec=health&res=9D05E6DC1131F93BA35752C0A9629C8B63.

Liu Zhijie. 2010. "Hush Money Journalism." *Caixin Magazine*, Feb. 4. http://english.caing.com/2010–02–04/100113698.html.

Lynch, Daniel C. 1999. *After the Propaganda State: Media, Politics, and "Thought Work" in Reformed China*. Stanford, CA: Stanford University Press.

Polumbaum, Judy, and Lei Xiong. 2008. *China Ink: The Changing Face of Chinese Journalism*. Lanham, MD: Rowman & Littlefield.

Rose-Ackerman, Susan. 1978. *Corruption: A Study in Political Economy*. New York: Academic Press.

Stapenhurst, Rick. 2000. The Media's Role in Curbing Corruption. World Bank Institute.

Tian Guolei (田国垒). 2010. "Investigation into Hebei's Yuxian County Mine Disaster: Over 2.6 Million Rmb Have Sealed the Lips of Which Reporters? (河北蔚县矿难调查:260多万元封住了哪些记者嘴?)." *China Youth Daily* [中国青年报], Feb. 1. http://shehui.daqi.com/article/2809510_1.html.

Wang Zhuoqiong. 2005. "Four in Five Reporters Want to Change Jobs." *China Daily*, Nov. 8. www.chinadaily.com.cn/english/doc/2005–11/08/content_492251.htm.

Yang Binbin, Zhao Hejuan, Li Zhigang, Chang Hongxiao, Zhang Yingguang, Chenzhong, and Xiaolu. 2008. "Why Did So Many Sichuan Schools Collapse?" *Caijing English Edition*, Jun. 17. http://english.caijing.com.cn/2008–06–17/100070077.html.

Zhao, Yuezhi. 1998. *Media, Market, and Democracy in China: Between the Party Line and the Bottom Line*. Urbana: University of Illinois Press.

Zhao, Yuezhi. 2004. "Underdogs, Lapdogs and Watchdogs: Journalists and the Public Sphere Problematic in China." In *Chinese Intellectuals between State and Market*, edited by Edward Gu and Merle Goldman, 43–74. New York: RoutledgeCurzon.

Zheng, Yongnian. 2008. *Technological Empowerment: The Internet, State, and Society in China*. Stanford, CA: Stanford University Press.

Zhu Zhe. 2007. "More Than 460 Rescued from Brick Kiln Slavery." *China Daily*, Jun. 15. Accessed Feb. 1, 2011. www.chinadaily.com.cn/china/2007–06/15/content_894802.htm.

5 Neutral, objective, and rare
The American-style journalists

Not all academics hew to the idea, discussed further below, that professional journalism in China is analogous to that of the United States. Chin-Chuan Lee, for example, differentiates among three models of Chinese journalism, but he does not further develop his model or discuss the many workaday journalists (Lee 2005). Lee's models are Confucian liberalism, Maoism, and communist capitalism, mainly divided by time period. Although the Maoist model (1949–present) and the communist capitalist model (after the 1980s, and especially after 1992) have some temporal overlap, the thrust of Lee's argument is that the Chinese press has moved in stages between these three models, which have both differences and commonalities. His analysis is insightful and intuitive, but it does not fully capture the present complexities of Chinese journalists' role.

More recently, sociologist Fen J. Lin has conducted survey work among Chinese news workers in which she sees a mixture of "three types of ideal elements – Western professionalism, literati tradition, and party journalism" that "coexist in the current Chinese journalism landscape" (Lin 2010: 176). While a useful counterpoint to more dogmatic assertions of the primacy of "professionalism" in the media, this view glosses over the existence of the nonideologically minded workaday journalists and does not fully acknowledge that advocacy can come, not only from what she terms "party journalism," but from more independently minded reporters as well. These exceptions aside, scholars have long been interested in American-style professional journalists dedicated to independent, objective reporting.

Media scholar Yuezhi Zhao, for example, speaks of "China's nascent culture of independent professional journalism" (Zhao 2008: 268) and refers to "journalists' growing sense of the liberal watchdog model" (Zhao 2008: 253). In one of the few large-scale surveys of Chinese journalists, Chen et al. conclude that "Chinese journalists are in the midst of professionalization," without further disaggregating the concept (Chen, Zhu, and Wu 1998: 29). But this characterization is not confined to recent work; as early as 1993, Allison Liu Jernow was able to see "a new generation of journalists at work," who "emphasized professionalism, not propaganda" (Jernow and Thurston 1993: 27). Even scholars like Li Liangrong, who has examined the historical waxing and waning of Western-style objectivity in China, occasionally made sweeping statements that "the principles of objectivity and fairness have become an irreversible trend after over a decade of profound reforms" (Li 1994: 234).

Academics and reporters in China, too, sometimes make the assumption that only one model of professional journalism exists and "use exemplars from the West to define 'professional standards'" (Pan and Lu 2003: 227). In *Watchdog Journalism and Global Democracy,* liberal scholar Zhan Jiang (展江) writes about the relationship between professional journalists and ethical codes, explicitly saying that "in the U.S. such [a model] is often called 'news professionalism'" (Zhan Jiang [展江] 2007: 37). And in interviews, journalists often conflate "professionalism" with "American-style professionalism." One reporter, for example, thinks that younger reporters are more professional than older ones because they have more formal training in college and journalism school and are "more influenced by America" (Interview HH05–2A). Another claims that the journalists at the *Beijing News* are professional because they cover stories with objectivity (Interview HE24–2). Admiration for an idealized American Fourth Estate is common. Many more reporters admire the ethical codes at American papers and link professionalism with ethics. Such journalists often specifically draw the comparison with Chinese journalists, whom they denounce as corrupt. In short, many journalists and scholars in China and abroad think that "professionalism" means emulating the U.S., and state that it is desirable to do so.

American desires, Chinese reality

This is not to say that American-style professionals, driven to present objective facts and include balanced opinions, are entirely absent. There certainly is a small core of journalists who "really look up to" an idealized American model of the press, which many have studied in school (Interview GX31–2). These professionals tend to work at the better known or more respected periodicals in China, publications like *Southern Weekend,* the *Beijing News, Finance (Caijing* 财经), and *Caixin – China Economics and Finance* (财新网).

The reality, however, is that most Chinese journalists are not American-style media professionals. One editor even stated that "if the media are too professionalized, it is a problem," because he finds such journalists to be overly objective and boring (Interview HL9–4). This quote is telling, as it came near the end of an interview in which the editor first claimed that reporters should be neutral information providers. Over the course of the interview, he revealed a common pattern: Many Chinese journalists initially claim to be objective, independent professionals but, when pressed, espouse values incompatible with the normative standards of American journalism. Note that my argument does not claim that journalists who do not practice the American model are unprofessional, nor do I hold American-style professionalism to be the normative model of good journalism. Indeed, I argue that such journalists remain professionals, but not *American-style* professionals.

At the beginning of an interview, for example, reporter Zhu Hongxu (Interview GM08–2) argued that the press should serve as a neutral Fourth Estate and "supervisor of the Party/state" (*dangzheng jiandu* 党政监督) and that his paper specifically looked to *The New York Times* for inspiration. When pressed further, however, he espoused a belief that the press should influence government policy directly, agreeing with prominent former editor Li Datong (李大同) that "news should influence today."[1] Another reporter at one of China's most influential papers claimed that a professional reporter is one who objectively reports the facts while also serving as a mediator between the people and the government (Interview GX31–2). A different interviewee argued that a professional journalist, while serving as the objective writer of the "manuscript of history" (*lishi de digao* 历史的底稿) should also be a *jiduzhe* (济度者), a Buddhist term meaning "one who provides salvation to the masses" (Interview HH5–2A). It is hard to simultaneously reconcile both roles under a single strand of professionalism, but this remains a typical attitude among elite Chinese news workers.

The rise of American-style journalism

The normative appeal of the American-style strand comes from abroad, where the (often unrealized) ideal of neutrality and objectivity has often displaced rival journalistic standards. As Hallin and Mancini put it, "A model of journalistic professionalism based on principles of 'objectivity' and political neutrality is increasingly dominant" (Hallin and Mancini 2004: 252), a model which has been exported from the United States. This "Americanization" of the media has been noted – and decried – for a long time, preoccupying scholars and media experts for the past several decades (Tunstall 1977). "Not only have European media and communication processes come to resemble American patterns in important ways," Hallin and Mancini write, but "there is clear evidence of direct American influence, starting at least from the late nineteenth century" (Hallin and Mancini 2004: 255).

Providing a full explanation of the power of American media norms around the world is outside the scope of this chapter, but it is helpful to briefly illustrate some of the trends pushing these norms' popularity. The post-World War II success of the United States and a triumphalist march toward international cultural Americanization clearly expanded the appeal of the American press model abroad, especially in an era where media providers in Europe and elsewhere struggled (Grainge 2004). But the uptake of American-style press norms abroad was hardly spontaneous; Margaret Blanchard describes in *Exporting the First Amendment* how the U.S. government and press often worked hand in glove to promote "honest and objective reporting" rather than the model of "European agencies [that] 'saw news as something that might be bent or twisted as necessary to serve diplomatic or imperial interests'" (Blanchard 1986: 7, quoting a 1949 book called *Freedom of Information*). Postwar reconstruction aid, for example, was often legally tied to freedom of the press. In 1946, for example, "both houses of Congress agreed to require all countries receiving aid to allow a 'reasonable number of properly accredited representatives of the American press to enter, observe and report on the distribution, and utilization of relief and rehabilitation supplies and services' without censorship" (Blanchard 1986: 72). As it happens, the American government simultaneously (and hypocritically) refused to let in many reporters from the Communist bloc, but the principle of nonstate interference in news reports took firm hold all over Europe.

Throughout much of the immediate postwar period and into the 1950s, the U.S. government and powerful U.S.-based agencies staunchly and explicitly encouraged the spread of the American press model abroad. In Germany and Japan, "Visiting journalists from the United States encouraged native reporters to employ American techniques in dealing with public officials," and "Japanese and German journalists established professional organizations modeled after" those in the U.S. (Blanchard 1986: 168). The success of this effort can be gauged by the Code of Newspaper Practices proposed by the World Association of Newspapers in 1981, a document that "clearly reflects the influence of the Liberal [or American] conception of press freedom and professionalism" with Point 2 advocating "the need for impartiality" and Point 3, "the separation of news from commentary" (Hallin and Mancini 2004: 256).

Some of these ideas seem to have had some success in precommunist China. P. H. Chang, the (Nationalist, noncommunist) Chinese delegate to the 1948 United Nations Conference on Freedom of Information, for example, argued that "A foreign correspondent should be 'a well-balanced, fair individual with a sense of fair play, and man of responsibility" (Blanchard 1986: 158). Admittedly, the quite authoritarian Nationalist Chinese government felt that freedom and objectivity could go too far. While noting that "China favored freedom of the press," Chang also argued that the Chinese government should retain the ability to "supervise whether it is news, gossip or lies that are printed, and check on the right of the press to make this decision" (Blanchard 1986: 159). Even such a small opening from the notoriously managerial Nationalist government was quickly quashed; the Communist Party's victory in the civil war just one year later ended even the possibility of a nascent trend towards news "objectivity." It was not until the reform era began in the late 1970s that American-style journalism again was held as a model for the Chinese press.

Today, the U.S. government and American and international NGOs continue to play a role in disseminating Western, and especially American, press norms and practices. The "soft support" (Stern 2009) offered by NGOs like Internews, a journalist advocacy and training group whose Chinese activities are primarily funded by the U.S. State Department (Interview EU30–3), continues to have potential influence on generations of Chinese reporters.

Internews, which was originally founded with an eye toward reforming the Soviet press, trains reporters all over the country in conjunction with local Chinese universities. Internews does not teach journalism *per se*, a topic deemed too sensitive even with the "protective umbrella" of a local university partner.[2] Instead, they concentrate on issues like scientific training, whereby they have expert speakers come talk to program participants about issues like HIV/AIDS or environmental reporting. A conference held in March 2011 in Shanghai, for example, billed as "A wide-ranging discussion of environmental science, corporate social responsibility, and journalism," brought together dozens of reporters and NGO staff from *Southern Metropolis Daily, 21st Century Business Herald, Oriental Morning Post, Jie Fang Daily, National Business Daily, Shanghai Times, Modern Express, Time Weekly, Wen Wei Po* and *Guiyang Daily*. The aim seems to have been to teach reporters techniques for accurate, balanced reporting of environmental issues, though no doubt Internews was happy with reporters like *Time Weekly*'s Chen Meng gushing that "It is quite inspiring as to how an environmental reporter can expose covert facts and be responsible to the public."[3]

While not *explicitly* promoting American-style news practices, the Internews staff ensure that training sessions conform to an internal office code emphasizing objectivity, truthfulness, and balance with an eye toward indirectly imparting these values. Ultimately, the program's goal, according to one staff member, is to "Americanize" the Chinese media (Interview GM09–2A). It is unclear what, if any, effect such training might have on graduates of the program,[4] but this and similar programs, like journalism training done by the U.S. government funded East-West Center,[5] clearly expose more Chinese news workers to American-style journalistic norms.

A second avenue of influence for the American press is the spate of journalist exchange and visiting scholar programs run across the United States. The University of California, Berkeley, for example, in the past has hosted several visiting scholars each year attached to the Graduate School of Journalism. These journalists, many from top papers like *Southern Weekend, China Youth Daily, Caijing, Caixin*, and others, attend journalism classes with their American counterparts and have special workshops where they share their experiences. Many distinguished American schools of journalism, including those at the University of Missouri, Columbia, the University of Iowa,[6] and elsewhere, have been making a greater push to engage with and train Chinese journalists. Quantifying the effect of such efforts is difficult, but it is reasonable to assume that this is a powerful avenue for American news ideology to permeate the Chinese news media. Note, however, that this is an idealized ideology and does certainly not reflect the recent re-emergence of muscular opinionated journalism in the U.S. (*à la* Fox News or MSNBC). This opinionated journalism is never emphasized in training, and in any case, elite Chinese journalists are often more interested in emulating more respected Western media outlets rather than those seen as controversial.

Finally, the informal professional organizations in China dedicated to journalistic training and discussion, previously mentioned in Chapter 2, disseminate norms of news practice throughout the profession. The highly networked and publicly visible nature of journalism ensures that colleagues who are widely respected can be a force for reform. Among elite journalists, at least, many seem well aware of the efforts of prominent colleagues to professionalize news practice. Even those who may not agree with this agenda are quickly made aware of it and must reckon with its effects. One American journalist I chatted with, for example, described a trip to a polluted village near Beijing that he participated in the late 2000s. The trip was organized by the environmental journalism group and, except for him, consisted entirely of Chinese colleagues. When one reporter concluded without evidence that a local chemical company was responsible for the pools of toxic sludge found all over the village, the other journalists vehemently condemned her conclusion as ill-founded and contrary to the group's professional evidentiary norms. In the end, according to the American reporter, she was pressured not to write the story.

Chinese journalists' awareness of international standards of reporting, in other words, is high and growing. Prominent former editor Li Datong writes about this process of internationalization:

> Starting in the 1980s, books of Western news media theories, principles, and techniques started to be translated. . . . And the result was that we started to see ourselves as members of the world news community, in the same profession as people in other countries. . . . And we started to realize that we were all in complete agreement: news is not the lackey of authority, but is instead the critic and arbiter of that authority.
>
> (Li Datong [李大同] 2006: 1)

In other words, Li and like-minded journalists started to look specifically toward the West – and the United States, in particular – for models of professional journalism.

This trend did not stop in the 1980s but continues today, especially in China's journalism schools. Chinese journalism students often explicitly learn American models of the press during their professional education, with nearly half of respondents in my small-scale, nonrandom sample pilot survey (n=24) indicating that they either learned "a lot" or a "relatively large amount" about the practice of American journalism. As one author notes in her overview of journalism education in China, exposure to the American model is dominant, with other areas like Japan and Europe far behind (Dombernowsky 2014: 59). A majority of pilot survey respondents, for example, reported learning "nothing" about Japanese journalism, despite the initial huge influence of Japan on Chinese journalism pioneers at the turn of the twentieth century and Japan's geographic proximity.

At the scholarly level, too, the push to learn from the West continues. Prominent academic Yu Guoming (喻国明), current deputy director of one of China's most prestigious journalism programs at People's University, has written and translated extensively from Western scholarship. He wrote and published the *Collection of Translated Essays on Mass Media Management* (传媒管理译丛), for example, because in the mid-2000s he saw an "urgent need" to "introduce accomplished scholarship from the developed countries of the West" (Yu Guoming [喻国明] 2005: 62). Of the book's nine sections, though, the only one explicitly concentrating on media practice abroad is called "The American Newspaper Industry," signaling the primacy of the U.S. model in China's view of "Western" journalism. Ultimately, he writes, this book was so badly needed that he received the publishing house's "warmest agreement and great thanks" for his work (Yu Guoming [喻国明] 2005: 62), which has gone through several printings. In short, China's journalists are quite familiar with at least an idealized American model, and this awareness inspires many to action.

The limits of objectivity

But rather than serving as a spur to bold reporting, a true American-style orientation can actually result in a more deferential Chinese media environment. Jingrong Tong writes that because journalists' overt opinions can lead to "political catastrophes, it is therefore necessary that journalists can stick to being objective if they want to be politically safe" (Tong 2011: 72). For example, Zhang Nan (Interview GM14–2B), an editor for a government-circulation[7] legal paper, feels so strongly that reporters should have enough technical knowledge to report news accurately that she helped found an informal organization for training legal reporters. This group avoids sensitive topics and concentrates on imparting basic skills to legal journalists so that they do not, for example, misreport laws or "incorrectly write the name of the Supreme People's Court."[8] Although this and similar informal organizations serve as a nexus of journalistic independence and an important way for norms and practices to spread through the profession, she herself feels that professional journalists should not push their own views in articles. Similarly, Lei Hua thinks that good journalism is mainly a technical exercise. She does not have a grand worldview and is not much interested in helping the country. Instead, she tries to report things properly according to strict technical professional standards and to stay out of trouble. Her commitment to "objectivity," then, can serve as a justification to avoid broaching dangerous topics (Interview HB24–2).

Even in the West, objectivity has long been seen as a "strategic ritual" and a way for reporters to avoid writing confrontational or controversial articles. In a highly influential 1972 article, Gaye Tuchman notes that even in the U.S. "every story entails dangers for news personnel and for the news organization. Each story potentially affects the newsmen's ability to accomplish their daily tasks, affects their standing in the eyes of their superiors, and affects that ability of news organizations to make a profit" (Tuchman 1972: 663–664). American reporters "cope with these dangers," Tuchman writes, "by emphasizing 'objectivity'" (Tuchman 1972: 664). Such news workers "assume that, if every reporter gathers and structures 'facts' in a detached, unbiased, impersonal manner, deadlines will be met and libel suits avoided" (Tuchman 1972: 664). So much more do these and other hazards menace Chinese journalists, who worry about more than just unhappy editors and libel suits. In short, not expressing an opinion, shying away from examining controversial issues and conforming to a strict technical definition of "objectivity" can help reporters safely navigate the calm waters of the American media.

This strategy is hardly limited to the United States. A 2007 study of the Hong Kong media has found that sometimes a culture of objectivity actually encourages self-censorship among news workers (Lee 2007), a phenomenon that is even more pressing in Mainland China. Such journalists can hide behind procedure and high-mindedness, while avoiding pushing an aggressive agenda. For example, a story on the planning of transport capacity during the Chinese New Year discusses the issue of rural labor mobility, a mildly sensitive issue in China,[9] but does so without commentary:

> This paper has learned from the provincial Labor and Society Protection Office that in order to ensure the orderly flow and transport of peasant labor (*mingong* 民工) during the busy Spring Festival period, the province [Jiangsu] has implemented an employment and labor mobility information forecasting system. The first areas selected will be Suzhou, Wuxi, Xuzhou, and Huai'anchu prefectures.
>
> (Huang Hongfang [黄红芳] and Yang Yong [杨涌] 2004)

Although it is impossible to know whether this story's reporters are in fact American-style professionals without interviewing them, such writing is a hallmark of the work that American-style journalists tend to produce. Unlike many Chinese language stories, for example, this piece avoids either emotional language or commentary on an issue that is ripe for both. Such attributes are common among the stories that American-style professionals aspire to write.

Conclusion

Ultimately, China presents a very different news environment than the United States. Those journalists who wish to work toward an idealized, independent, objective press find many institutional roadblocks and little encouragement. The practice of a true American-style reporter involves little more than producing neutral-sounding reports and avoiding corruption, something Chinese reporters can manage without challenging the powers that be. Confrontation is ultimately riskier than producing neutral stories on approved – or even mildly sensitive – topics and therefore requires a larger sense of commitment than simply behaving by "professional" norms. As one reporter told me, in the long run, China should move toward the American model, but the current Chinese news environment is better suited to more aggressive journalism (Interview HL6–4). In short, many Chinese reporters claim to be American-style professionals, many fewer actually are, and even those few tend toward political passivity. For aggressive boundary pushing in the Chinese media, we must look elsewhere.

Notes

1 The Li Datong quote is from the title of Li Datong (李大同) (2006).
2 For more on how universities can act to protect potentially sensitive issues in China, see Stern and Hassid (2012).
3 All from Internews' website. See www.internews.org/our-stories/program-news/chinese-language-earth-journalism-toolkit-released, accessed February 9, 2012.
4 See Stern (2009) for a discussion of the effectiveness for similar programs aimed at the Chinese legal profession.
5 The East-West Center receives around $23 million per year in U.S. State Department funding, some of which goes toward journalism training. Indeed, "The Center has expanded its journalist programs substantially, including recent additions of a program

involving U.S. journalists . . . and a North Pacific program (journalists from U.S., Japan, China, and Korea)." See the Congressional Budget Justification Fiscal Year 2012, p. 749, at www.state.gov/documents/organization/156215.pdf, accessed February 10, 2012.
6 Iowa has an explicit push to recruit Chinese journalism students, producing an outreach video in Chinese. See http://clas.uiowa.edu/sjmc/resources/featured-topics/china-outreach, accessed February 1, 2012.
7 Namely, their content is mostly, though not entirely, for internal government reference (*neibu* 内部) only and not for general circulation.
8 Something that happens surprisingly often, apparently.
9 Strictly speaking, one must have a residence permit to reside in Chinese cities, and the vast majority of rural laborers lack this permit, called a *hukou* (户口). For more on the *hukou* system, see Mallee (2003).

References

Blanchard, Margaret A. 1986. *Exporting the First Amendment: The Press-Government Crusade of 1945–1952, Longman Series in Public Communication*. New York: Longman.
Chen, Chongshan, Jian-Hua Zhu, and Wei Wu. 1998. "The Chinese Journalist." In *The Global Journalist: News People around the World*, edited by David H. Weaver and Wei Wu, 9–30. Cresskill, NJ: Hampton Press.
Dombernowsky, Laura. 2014. "Chinese Journalism Students: Balancing Competing Views." In *Chinese Investigative Journalists' Dreams: Autonomy, Agency and Voice*, edited by Marina Svensson, Elin Saether, and Zhi'an Zhang, 53–74. Lanham, MD: Lexington Books.
Grainge, Paul. 2004. "Global Media and Resonant Americanisation." In *Issues in Americanisation and Culture*, edited by Neil Campbell, Jude Davies, and George McKay, 213–225. Edinburgh: Edinburgh University Press.
Hallin, Daniel C., and Paolo Mancini. 2004. *Comparing Media Systems: Three Models of Media and Politics, Communication, Society, and Politics*. Cambridge; New York: Cambridge University Press.
Huang Hongfang (黄红芳) and Yang Yong (杨涌). 2004. "Information on the Provincial Labor Mobility Forecast (我省预报流动就业信息)." *New China Daily* (新华日报). Jan. 13.
Jernow, Allison Liu, and Anne F. Thurston. 1993. *"Don't Force Us to Lie": The Struggle of Chinese Journalists in the Reform Era*. [New York, N.Y.]: Committee to Protect Journalists.
Lee, Chin-Chuan. 2005. "The Conception of Chinese Journalists: Ideological Convergence and Contestation." In *Making Journalists: Diverse Models, Global Issues*, edited by Hugo de Burgh, 107–126. London; New York: Routledge.
Lee, Francis L.F. 2007. "Hong Kong Citizens' Belief in Media Neutrality and Perceptions of Press Freedom: Objectivity as Self-Censorship?" *Asian Survey* 47 (3):434–454.
Li Datong (李大同). 2006. *Using News to Influence Today – The Freezing Point Chronicle [用新闻影响今天 ——《冰点》周刊纪事]*: Hong Kong Peaceful and Virtuous Age Publishing Company [香港泰德时代出版有限公司].
Li, Liangrong. 1994. "The Historical Fate of 'Objective Reporting' in China." In *China's Media, Media's China*, edited by Chin-Chuan Lee, 225–237. Boulder, CO: Westview Press.
Lin, Fen J. 2010. "Organizational Construction or Individual's Deed? The Literati Tradition in the Journalistic Professionalization in China." *International Journal of Communication* 4:175–197.

Mallee, Hein. 2003. "Migration, *Hukou*, and Resistance in Reform China." In *Chinese Society, 2nd Edition: Change, Conflict and Resistance*, edited by Elizabeth J. Perry and Mark Selden, 136–157. London; New York: RoutledgeCurzon.

Pan, Zhongdang, and Ye Lu. 2003. "Localizing Professionalism: Discursive Practices in China's Media Reforms." In *Chinese Media, Global Contexts*, edited by Chin-Chuan Lee, 215–236. New York: Routledge.

Stern, Rachel E. 2009. "In Safety's Shadow: Suing Polluters in China." PhD dissertation, Political Science, University of California, Berkeley.

Stern, Rachel E., and Jonathan Hassid. 2012. "Amplifying Silence: Uncertainty and Control Parables in Contemporary China." *Comparative Political Studies* 45 (10):1230–1254. doi:10.1177/0010414011434295.

Tong, Jingrong. 2011. *Investigative Journalism in China: Journalism, Power, and Society*. London; New York: Continuum.

Tuchman, Gaye. 1972. "Objectivity as Strategic Ritual: An Examination of Newsmen's Notions of Objectivity." *The American Journal of Sociology* 77 (4):660–679.

Tunstall, Jeremy. 1977. *The Media Are American: Anglo-American Media in the World*. London: Constable.

Yu Guoming (喻国明). 2005. *The Changing Mass Media: Analyzing Problems in the Transformation of China's Communication Media (变革传媒: 解析中国传媒转型问题)*. Beijing: China Publishing House (华夏出版社).

Zhan Jiang (展江). 2007. "General Introduction: Watchdog Journalism and Civilized Governance (总论: 新闻舆论监督与政治文明)." In *Watchdog Journalism and Global Democracy (新闻舆论监督与全球政治文明)*, edited by Zhan Jiang (展江) and Zhang Jinxi (张金玺). Beijing: Social Science Document Publishers (社会科学文献出版社).

Zhao, Yuezhi. 2008. *Communication in China: Political Economy, Power, and Conflict, State and Society in East Asia*. Lanham, MD: Rowman & Littlefield.

6 Representing "the people"
The advocate professionals

Rather than writing for money, the CCP, or even objectivity, advocate journalists aim to push a specific, social, ideological, or economic viewpoint in their stories. They thus score high on commitment to both media independence and advocacy. As *China Youth Daily*'s Jin Yongquan says, "If someone asks [sensitive] questions, [propagandists] will try our best to minimize them down to zero. This is propaganda. Journalism, on the contrary, tries to maximize that zero" (Polumbaum and Xiong 2008: 67).

If occasionally stepping on official toes is the price that advocate journalists must pay for their independence, many remain unfazed by the challenges: "Despite insurmountable odds, a deeply held belief in justice spurs the investigative reporter into action" (Bandurski and Hala 2010c: 105). Such reporters often see themselves as serving a higher good than simply currying favor with higher-ups. Lu Yuegang, a prominent former editor who has been called "The journalist who won't give up" (Bandurski and Hala 2010b: 30), writes that he and other such reporters "stand for the public. Our legitimacy comes from the common good. We are, in other words, what has been called 'the Fourth Estate'" (Bandurski and Hala 2010b: 25). Often, news workers like Lu claim to represent "vulnerable social groups" (*ruoshi qunti* 弱势群体) in an attempt to better their plight. A special issue of *Southern Weekend*, for example, argues that the "function of the media was to 'show care for the weak, to give strength to the powerless,' and that journalists should express their 'social conscience' by revealing the truth to people" (Qian Gang and Bandurski 2011: 57).

An article published in Shanghai's *Unity Times* (*Lianhe Shibao* 联合时报) called "Who Is Concerned about Freelance Professionals?" for example, plaintively asks "who will protect the life and livelihood" of freelancers, those "between the boundary between employment and unemployment? Who will provide the necessary services for them?" (Feng Jinsheng [冯金生] 2004). Such freelancers, the author argues, are well educated, have good skills, and are allowed to "give free rein to their potential." But without a stable employer, these workers have no proper retirement, medical, and unemployment insurance, a lack that creates a source of constant anxiety. By providing such services, the author argues, Shanghai can become a "new heaven and earth" (*xin tiandi* 新天地),[1] helping the freelancers themselves and the rest of the city in turn.

But in standing for "the public," advocate journalists can agitate for a range of causes beyond the poor and vulnerable. For example, a 2005 story in *Southern*

Weekend with the poetic title "Venus: The Price inside the Wall for the Floating Fragrance outside the Wall,"[2] pushes for more support and sympathy for China's artistic community:

REPORTER: In 2000, after leaving the Beijing Modern Dance Troupe, Venus moved to Shanghai to make a fresh start and open the wholly owned Venus Modern Dance Troupe, China's only private modern dance group. . . .
VENUS: In China, the significance of opening a modern dance company is enormous. It far exceeds just opening another one in Europe, because my theatrical company represents the very existence of modern dance in China.
REPORTER: Is it easy to set up a dance company domestically?
VENUS: It is not easy. Actually, many students especially want to come dance with me, because with me they are able to find truth and freedom.
(Zhang Ying [张英] and Wu Yi [吴怿] 2005)

The writers' sympathy toward the notion that the arts, and modern dance in particular, should receive more social support is apparent in this section and throughout the article. These reporters, as advocate professionals do, wear their hearts on their sleeves.[3] Reporting the "truth" is still important, but as Jin Yongquan of the *China Youth Daily* writes, "As for other principles, truth is fundamental," but "discerning truth is not simple" in part because "Our current communications network and media exclude poor people. Simply following so-called impartiality actually will be unfair to some groups" (Polumbaum and Xiong 2008: 67).

Of course some advocate journalists, often those who report on the financial community, push for the relatively well off. The reporters at the business minded *Caijing*, for example, and now at its competitor *Caixin Media*, have carefully pushed for reforms that would increase China's political and economic transparency. Such measures would, at least initially, help mainly the investor class. Similarly, reporter Li Qinghua of the *China Economic Times* (*Zhongguo Jingji Shibao* 中国经济时报) notes that some of the problems contributing to a tenfold rise in uncollectable debt owed by foreign-invested companies between the late 1980s and 2004 include "local protectionism" (*difang baohuzhuyi* 地方保护主义); "misuse of government power" (*zhengfu lanyong quanli* 政府滥用权利); and "problems with the trustworthiness of the legal system itself, including judicial corruption" (*sifa fubai* 司法腐败) (Li Qinghua [李庆华] 2004). To be sure, Li levels most of his criticism against untrustworthy foreign-invested enterprises for which "breaking promises is a ubiquitous day-to-day management activity." But as with other carefully worded pieces in China's economic press, the clear implication is that many problems come from the Chinese government itself, and China needs to improve its act.

Advocacy and nationalism

This attitude towards improving China is not unusual; a striking number of such advocate journalists see their role as essentially nationalistic. As sociologist Fen J. Lin puts it, they see the "crucial function of news media is to serve the long-term goal of national development" (Lin 2010: 178). For them, being a reporter means solving social problems and engaging in the national project of pushing forward China's development. Sometimes this advocacy means publicizing weighty concerns like justice for pollution victims or the prevalence of local corruption, and other times, it might mean pushing less sensitive topics like greater arts funding. The common thread in all three of these examples, though, involves journalists trying to mobilize public opinion with an eye toward building a better China and pushing CCP policy in a way that it might not otherwise go.

Li Lei (Interview HB20–2), an editor at the *China Youth Daily*, is one such journalist. She likes the job because she can serve the country and see the direct results of her endeavors every day. She has relatives who are businesspeople, and although their jobs help improve the country's GDP, her gratification is much more direct. As a journalist, she can do more than just "supervise" the state; she can also impact policy in an effort to make China great. She believes in the importance of the CCP and respects its authority, but sometimes, she says, the Party bosses need a nudge in the right direction – and journalists can provide that nudge.

Many reporters say they consider their role as representing "the people," rather than the Party/state. One former reporter for *Southern Weekend* went further, claiming that "about half of reporters want to criticize and change the government" (Interview EL30–0). One reporter even told me that "being a reporter is impossible in China," in part because press restrictions make it difficult for reporters to push policy changes (Interview ET02–3).[4] These advocacy journalists have "an increasing tendency to distinguish between state and citizenry and to see themselves on the side of the latter" (de Burgh 2003: 93). For example, Zhang Yongchun (Interview GX20–2), a journalist of eleven years in his mid-thirties, works for a national opinion magazine and is avowedly "leftist," believing that the media should help the people and Chinese society rather than the state. Although Zhang is a bit more outspoken than most, his claim that journalists should explicitly side with the forces of "labor" and critique the forces of "capitalism" would not be out of place among other advocate journalists. Quoting – in English – the idea that "journalists shift our perceptions of the world," he thinks that the role of journalists is more educational and nuanced than offering straightforward political commentary. In other words, journalists should represent the people by "representing the world to the people."

Another *Southern Weekend* reporter, Fu Xiaohua (Interview HU5–2), told me of her aim to help solve national problems. She was inspired by the fact that the Chinese "nation" (*minzu* 民族) is the sole survivor of the great ancient civilizations, a fact that, to her, clearly demonstrates China's fundamental greatness. Even if there are many contemporary problems, she argued, China's unique and powerful cultural heritage makes her proud to help solve them. This desire to help was especially manifest in the aftermath of the devastating 2008 Sichuan earthquake, which killed thousands and left millions without power or food for days or weeks. Sent in as part of the first wave of reporters to the quake zone, Fu saw the devastation firsthand and wanted to make a difference. Five to six days after the quake, she was talking to a group of people with relatives in remote mountain villages that were entirely cut off from supplies. The relatives were worried that those in the villages were without food or water and that the situation might be growing increasingly desperate. To help, she immediately contacted her editor, who quickly posted a story online. Going beyond what many might do, she next informed the headquarters of the Chengdu Military Region of the situation. As a result of her efforts, the military airdropped supplies for the village the very next day, evacuating all the residents by airplane just a few days later. For Fu, her advocacy directly helped the situation of ordinary people.

Despite their claims to represent "the people," however, many advocate journalists do not clearly define who "the people" are. Many see "the people" as those left most vulnerable by the rapid changes in Chinese society. By speaking for the voiceless, many advocate journalists believe they are able to represent a huge proportion of the Chinese population who otherwise have no one to look after them. This attitude in turn allows them to challenge Western professional objectivity. Ultimately, though, "the people" are whoever the journalists say they are, and priorities and outlooks can change over time.

The limited power of markets

Although the structural changes that commercialization forced on the once closed media industry clearly sustain and encourage advocacy journalism, it is striking that many individual reporters do no pursue stories out of a desire for readership or with an eye toward marketability. "For some journalists, resolving problems and obtaining redress for aggrieved individuals is itself a goal, independent of the potential news value of the underlying grievance" legal scholar Benjamin Liebman writes (2011: 162). Many of the journalists I interviewed directly or indirectly echoed this sentiment, arguing they wrote not for market concerns but to solve problems. Sometimes they argue overcommercialization is a problem. One editor in Guangzhou takes the example of nearby Hong Kong as a fate to be avoided.

Historically, the Hong Kong media had a lot of influence in Guangdong province, but today he thinks that their media are viewed as good just for "entertainment and horoscopes" (*yule bagua* 娱乐八卦) among mainland journalists. "If we were given the same sort of media freedom they have, we could surpass them in two or three years," he says, echoing the danger that media marketization might trivialize, rather than strengthen, newsgathering (Interview HL9–4). In the next chapter, I present evidence from the quantitative content analysis that reinforces just how ineffective marketization is at producing, in the short run, an aggressive media.

On an individual level, advocates are often more committed to their story and solving the problems they uncover than in reaping the commercial benefits of a juicy scoop. After *Southern Weekend* reporter Zhai Minglei uncovered massive corruption at the government-sponsored charity Project Hope in 2001, the newspaper ran an initial story directing the blame towards poor management. Despite the fact that the published article was heavily redacted from the original story, "Zhai Minglei received hundreds of letters praising the newspaper's coverage" (Bandurski and Hala 2010d: 69). A follow-up story in the paper that pinned the blame on specific officials ended at the pulp mill after the Central Propaganda Department (CPD) "ordered the destruction of *Southern Weekend's* entire print run of roughly 300,000 copies." Zhai was undaunted, however, and both leaked the story to other newspapers and posted the entire text of the now-destroyed article on the Internet. This relinquishment of "a major, hard-earned scoop to another media organization – an idea that might seem abhorrent to journalists working in freer environments" was driven by personal conviction and a sense of mission, not by market forces (Bandurski and Hala 2010d: 70).

Indeed, sometimes advocates can come from within nonmarketized, strictly controlled government organizations. An officially commissioned article analyzing the lessons from China's 2003 Severe Acute Respiratory Syndrome (SARS) outbreak in the official 2007 *China Journalism Yearbook*, for example, squarely lays the blame at the Chinese government, and especially the Ministry of Health, for contributing to the media "muteness" (*shiyu* 失语) that made the epidemic much worse. The "root" of the problem, the author argues, was "the government's control of information and stifling of reporting," a bold claim in an officially authorized publication (Yin Yungong [尹韵公] 2007: 289).

Even reporters at the *People's Daily*, the official CCP mouthpiece, sometimes chafe at press restrictions and pine for a greater role in solving China's problems, according to former employees. One senior editor, for example, used to work for a marketized paper and was gratified that while there he was able to help call attention to social and political issues. After the paper was shuttered, he moved to the *People's Daily* for its salary, perks, and official access. While acknowledging the advantages of his current job, he is rueful that "whatever we do, it isn't news" (Interview KX24–2Z). What distinguishes such reporters from mainline communist professionals is their greater desire for media autonomy, within even the most tightly controlled media organizations in China.

Many of these gutsy boundary pushers are willing to challenge the system again and again, despite potentially serious consequences. Jin Yongquan, a *China Youth Daily* reporter and tireless advocate for people displaced by the construction of the huge Three Gorges Dam, was chastised for a story pointing out problems in the forced migration. Despite being disciplined, though, he went back later for follow-up reports:

> I'm a journalist, not a propagandist. That's why I got criticized. Knowing the leadership of the paper was under pressure from above, I requested time off for the next trip. . . . By the time I returned . . . I filed another major report on the big migration. I discovered that, having criticized you once, officials will find it awkward to criticize you again. They can't keep scolding you all the time.
>
> (Polumbaum and Xiong 2008: 64)

Similarly, a prominent journalist at a top paper who has gotten into trouble many times for his aggressive writing argues that reporters are increasingly tired of being the voice and tool of the Party/state and instead are now becoming the voice of the people. When asked if it is just the braver reporters who think this way, he responded that reporters all over the country are developing this attitude, brave and ordinary alike. Bold reportage, one scholar argues, "expresses the willingness and ability of investigative journalists and news organizations to provide . . . an institution that stands for justice in an authoritarian society" (Tong 2011: 99).

In 2000, for example, *China Newsweek* (*Zhongguo Xinwen Zhoukan* 中国新闻周刊) reporters Zhang Jinping and Zhang Jie learned that villages in the heartland province of Henan were wracked by an extraordinarily virulent AIDS epidemic. The epidemic was spread by a 1990s-era, Henan government-sponsored program that encouraged villagers to sell their blood to augment their meager incomes. The problem with this approach was that to save money and allow patients to give more blood, "donors of the same blood type [were] combined after isolation and re-transfused into donors," creating an AIDS transmission route of unprecedented efficiency (Bandurski and Hala 2010a: 40). Belatedly realizing the severity of the crisis in the late 1990s, provincial officials "moved preemptively against journalists likely to file news reports on HIV/AIDS," bribed the largest local newspaper with 80,000 RMB (US$11,500) in cash, and had several reporters "removed for trumped-up offences" (Bandurski and Hala 2010a: 42). When the two Zhangs learned about this crisis, in other words, they quickly became aware of its political sensitivity surrounding the issue. Despite the risks, *China Newsweek* "unflinchingly criticized government leaders, whom it said had buried information about the epidemic out of fear for their own political hides," and in so doing had "run a huge political risk" (Bandurski and Hala 2010a: 47). Zhang Jinping and Zhang Jie, in other words, had defied political control to publicize an issue and help solve a burgeoning problem. This kind of optimism – often in the face of strong counter-evidence – is what drives the advocates forward.

Some advocates, of course, question these tactics while supporting the overall goals of national problem solving. When prominent advocate journalist Li Datong (李大同) wrote a book challenging journalists to "influence today," one interviewee told me that this call sparked serious debate with the *Beijing News* newsroom about the role of the press, with many agreeing but others concerned about the propriety of this direct approach (Interview GM08–2). Fu Xiaohua, the reporter who helped stranded villagers in the aftermath of the Sichuan earthquake, disapproves of the more direct challenges to the CCP. For instance, she disapproves of the efforts of Li's efforts to aggressively push the state too far. Li, who was ultimately fired from his job as an editor of *China Youth Daily* for his aggressive reporting, believes that reporters should explicitly aim to be confrontational in pushing the boundaries of acceptable coverage. By challenging the state, he argues, journalists can best help the people (Li Datong [李大同]2006). Many subscribe to this view, but Fu does not, seeing his approach as too confrontational and best suited to a previous generation of Chinese news workers. Where Li would like to push China towards democratizing, Fu argues that "China is not ready for democracy."

Or as a prominent journalist argues, "Journalists should represent the people, but not directly. They represent the people by presenting truth, and this ultimately moves everything along and helps the system progress. But the representation is not direct. Multifaceted (*duoyuan*多元) journalism is best" (Interview GM14–2A). In other words, while advocates tend to argue for specific fixes to China's problems and have little reluctance to ditch Western norms of objectivity, not all see their job as being confrontational. The goal of helping people might be constant, but the tactics are constantly up for dispute.

Factors pushing advocacy journalism

Maoism temporarily destroyed the ideal of journalists and other intellectuals as a semi-independent power source. So how, then, did this idea (re)emerge in the reform era and gain currency among journalists? Interestingly, demographic features like sex, education level, or location in China seem to have little impact on this orientation, with older journalists being marginally more inclined toward advocacy.[5] Beyond demographic factors, two phenomena are key to the expansion of advocacy journalism orientation in contemporary China: first, the transnational spread of journalistic norms, mainly from the West, and second, the power of informal networks among the journalists themselves. It is beyond the scope of this chapter to describe the international spread of Western, especially liberal American, journalistic norms. Suffice it to say the idea of liberal journalism is powerfully normative, as the example of advocate journalists claiming to be neutral news observers illustrates. Hallin and Mancini write that "The Liberal Model has clearly become increasingly dominant across Europe . . . – as it has, no doubt, across much of the world – its structures, practices and values displacing, to a substantial degree, those of . . . other media systems" (Hallin and Mancini 2004: 251).

But the second factor – the power of informal networks within China – is both empirically interesting and theoretically fruitful. Journalists in China, as in most countries, are connected by a dense network of personal and institutional ties. For example, in an online pilot survey I conducted in late 2008, all journalists met with other Chinese journalists outside of work at least a few times a month, with the outright majority (54%) meeting at least a few times a week. These informal, domestic networks are likely to a much more efficient spread of norms than transnational ones; indeed, 80% of surveyed journalists met with foreign colleagues a few times a year or less. Such infrequent visits and the inability of even most highly educated reporters to speak English limit journalists' exposure to international norms, at least in the shorter term. Much more important are the "relationship web" (*guanxi wang* 关系网) that reporters develop in person and on the Internet.

In particular, blogging is gaining currency among news workers as a way to spread information and to network. Chapter 9 discusses the Internet's impact more fully, but now it is important to mention that most interviewees have had a blog at one time or another, as have nearly three-quarters of the respondents of an informal, online survey. Reporters often post on their blogs stories that were too sensitive for formal publication, and this is a way for many of them to get around the CCP's restrictions on information. Because most journalists are avid blog readers, even stories too sensitive for publication ultimately become common knowledge – at least among news workers. Because journalists often tend to write for other journalists, this system ultimately seems to encourage bolder reporting and, ultimately, more advocacy-style journalism. Blogs and microblogs are also now driving stories that journalists would otherwise miss; they thus serve as an excellent way for journalists to trade information (often sensitive), and are an important component of reporters' informal networking behavior.

The informal journalists' networking groups in Beijing help spread such norms. Guangzhou, too, has a more general professional group, though at times it has been deemed "illegal" (*feifa* 非法) according to one editor. Having personally attended meetings of both the Beijing-based legal and environmental groups, I can attest that they are very much attuned to encouraging advocacy journalism in their respective topic areas. For example, during a meal after a meeting of environmental journalists, I witnessed a discussion between news workers over how best to push environmental awareness. A discussion of the Nu (Salween) River dam project, for example, was ruled out because the CPD has already restricted coverage. Ultimately, these reporters decided to produce a report labeled as a diary of a local farmer affected by environmental issues. By doing so, these journalists and editors hoped to increase environmental awareness among readers and ultimately change policy. This group also discussed issues related explicitly to the profession, like the need for separation between editorial and business sides of newspapers and even a long-stalled potential national press law. In short, these groups act as "think tanks" that set agendas and professional norms across the journalistic field.

A long tradition

Though it has had a resurgence in recent years, Chinese advocacy journalism is hardly new. Such a role orientation has a long tradition, beginning with late nineteenth-century reformer Liang Qichao's efforts to establish newspapers that were "factional organs (*dangbao*)" and even "protopolitical opposition parties" (Judge 1996: 25). These early journalists still have relevance today, and several interviewees spoke explicitly of late Qing dynasty or early Republican-era media history. The view that journalists are essentially educators or intellectuals with a specific viewpoint and a desire to help "the people" and shape public opinion (*yulun* 舆论) goes back even further. "*Yulun*, the character compound [that early twentieth-century journalists] used for public opinion, dated back at least to the third century and had been used throughout Chinese history to describe elite opinion within the bureaucracy," historian Joan Judge writes (Judge 1996: 68). And far from dampening this desire, China's upheavals in the early twentieth century "reinforced the elite's consciousness of themselves as autonomous critics of political authority," a consciousness that continues today (Goldman and Cheek 1987: 2).

During the run-up to the Communist revolution in 1949, intellectuals again demonstrated their commitment to social and political advocacy based on imperial norms, with many of the leading writers of the day – including Lü Xun, Hu Shih, Chen Duxiu, and others – urging the government to attack China's growing problems (Bianco 1971: 44–48). Like contemporary advocate journalists, these writers and intellectuals "regarded social ills as but one element in 'the Chinese crisis,' which they saw in nationalist terms" (Bianco 1971: 86). *Da Gong Bao*, a winner in 1941 of the University of Missouri School of Journalism's foreign press award, set the standard for this era by advancing "a liberal vision of journalism akin, in spirit if not in practice, to the Western concept of professionalism." Despite its similarities to the Western press, the paper's underlying "normative standards were embedded in the moral responsibility of Confucian intellectuals, whereas Western media professionalism rose historically from the growth of the market economy" (Lee 2005: 111).

Soon after the 1949 revolution, however, "party leaders created a party-state with more control over the intellectuals than that of any dynastic ruler, including China's most despotic First Emperor of the Qin dynasty (221–209 BC), who supposedly burned the books and buried Confucian scholars alive," Merle Goldman writes (2002: 500). Except for brief periods, the CCP kept intellectuals on a very tight leash throughout the Mao era, at times launching campaigns designed to cow potential (and imagined) opponents of the regime. Although the traditional model of the Confucian scholar at liberty – and indeed, duty bound – to point out and correct national problems never went away entirely, it was severely curtailed during the harshest years of CCP rule.

Except during these years of high-Maoism, intellectuals, including journalists, have long had a privileged place in Chinese society to simultaneously critique the government by representing "the people" and, in turn, to educate the people as to how – the intellectuals believe – the people should think and act.[6] Judge argues that during the late nineteenth and early twentieth centuries,

> The press was, first of all, a metonym for "the people" – voicing its opinions, representing its desires, and supervising the government in its name. It was also the arena within which the reform publicists imagined and constructed "the people" as a unified collective distinct from, and often in conflict with, the imperial authorities.
>
> (Judge 1996: 79)

But as with many Chinese journalists today, these early news pioneers, "in spite of these heightened rhetoric about uplifting the broader citizenry . . . never clearly defined who constituted 'the people' or who was being addressed as the new citizenry" (Judge 1996: 81).

Chinese journalists, who still consider themselves intellectuals, have long been "committed not only to represent and inform but also mobilize their compatriots" (Judge 1996: 10). As early journalism pioneer Liang Qichao wrote in a famous 1896 essay, "without eyes and ears, without a tongue, nothing can be said," and the press serves that vital role (Liang Qichao [梁启超] 1896). This tradition, carried forward by journalists like Liu Binyan and Qin Benli, was nearly stamped out in the Maoist era, when the CCP often looked on intellectuals with deep suspicion. Since the early 1980s, however, China's intellectuals have begun to reclaim the traditional privilege of the Confucian literati to criticize government authority and help solve national problems. This historical role has deep relevance for contemporary advocate journalists, and in interviews, many mentioned explicitly being inspired by Liu, Qin, Liang, and others to be advocates and educators, in addition to learning from the West. As Ying Chan writes, "Chinese investigative journalism has strived to incorporate the best from Western journalism while adapting their practices to the realities of China" (Chan 2010: 17). Or as another scholar argues, "As social teachers, the literati pride themselves on proffering expert opinions, while Western media professionals separate news from opinions to attract the widest mass audience" (Lee 2005: 112). Just like the literati in imperial times, China's intellectuals during the reform era have seen themselves "the conduit through which political leaders learned of the defects of their policies and heard the demands of the people" (Goldman 2002: 503). In other words, the rebirth of investigative and advocacy journalism since 1978 was inspired by Western norms and successes, but is fundamentally based on the revival of a different, historically grounded relationship between intellectuals and the state.

The role of "educating the people" is one of these key traditional ideas that survives today. The role of journalist as educator is sometimes overt; one journalist told me his role is to provide his readership with salient facts and point out when "one plus one equals two," for example (Interview HE24–2). Or it can be subtle, as when Xiao Guangxu (Interview HL06–4), an editor for *Southern Weekend*, discussed a Chinese husband and wife team who live in the U.S. and report on their experiences abroad. Readers can then "make the comparison themselves" and see China's problems indirectly through the column. For Xiao, this sort of careful triangulation lets people know the situation in other countries without a direct, politically aggressive comparison. Sometimes the idea that journalists should educate the people blurs into contempt. Bai Xinguo (Interview GX30–2), for example, told me his magazine does not particularly care if readers are interested in a story, because he and his colleagues do not write for the readers' pleasure but for their benefit. He thinks that media outlets that too closely stick to readers' interests put out a low-quality product that does not sufficiently educate and guide readers, a desire that resonates with the heart of advocacy journalism.

Advocacy, path dependence, and the news media

In addition to the structural reasons that advocacy resonates in the Chinese media, individual papers' traditions and structural arrangements can also help spur advocacy (Polumbaum and Xiong 2008: 83). Not coincidentally, many of China's boldest papers are based in Guangzhou, a city renowned for the latitude allowed its political and economic entrepreneurs. In 1984, Guangzhou was among the first cities in China to be granted status as a Special Economic Zone. Coupled with its proximity to Hong Kong, this influence allowed rapid competition and commercialization opportunities in the local media. The relative media freedom in turn attracted some of China's boldest journalists, and soon path dependence ensured that the city developed a reputation as the most aggressive and freewheeling media environment in the People's Republic.

As political scientist Paul Pierson describes it, "path dependence refers to dynamic processes involving positive feedback, which generate multiple possible outcomes depending on the particular sequence in which events unfold" (Pierson 2004: 20). Pierson has argued that "the crucial feature of a historical process that generates path dependence is *positive feedback* (or self-reinforcement). Given this feature, each step in a particular direction makes it more difficult to reverse course" (Pierson 2004: 21, emphasis in original). Even though propaganda authorities have tried for years to rein in many of the Guangzhou papers, path dependence has made it very difficult for conservative censorship officials to do so, even with constant Party-mandated editorial changes.

In other words, economic freedom and proximity to the freer Hong Kong media made Guangzhou an initial media hotspot in the 1980s and 1990s, attracting sympathetic editors and writers and indelibly shaping the aggressive newspapers that continue today, despite high personnel turnover. As media scholar Jingrong Tong writes, "In the 1990s, a large group of journalists who shared similar views about the role of their work gathered" in papers that concentrated on investigative journalism, papers that were "led by certain 'spirit leaders' within these media organizations" who fostered a culture of advocacy (Tong 2011: 47). Guangzhou-based *Southern Weekend* journalist Liu Jianqiang gives a telling example from when he was considering a job at the paper. In the wake of the CCP's 2003 removal of top staff for overzealous reporting, Liu was worried that the new editor would reverse course and control the paper too tightly. The deputy editor, though, told him "the paper won't change that easily – rather, we hope we can change the new editor" (Polumbaum and Xiong 2008: 83).

But path dependence can work the other way as well, entrenching deep conservatism even within news outlets that are not closely scrutinized. Because papers like those in the Southern Group have a reputation for being "bad boys," as one long-time journalist told me, censors give them more leeway in approaching sensitive topics. Papers like the *Beijing Daily* (*Beijing Ribao* 北京日报), by contrast, hold tightly to the official line despite the fact that they are not actually scrutinized very closely by propaganda authorities. This reluctance to rock the boat is entrenched by the self-reinforcing path dependency of earlier generations of conservative journalists.

But if editors at these "good boy" papers go against tradition and decide act up, censorship authorities are often harsher in their punishments because the transgression was so unexpected (Interview KX24–2Z). Li Yang, a former

Xinhua journalist, writes of a story she did about a protest against illegal housing demolitions in Beijing's Chongwen district. After she "described the beating, the protest, the bloodstains, people writing grievance letters in blood, and so on," her internal circulation article prompted an aggressive response from powerful district officials (Polumbaum and Xiong 2008: 75–76). The officials issued an "Emergency circular regarding the Xinhua reporter deceiving the central authorities and blustering the district leadership" accusing Li of lying despite her extensive evidence. She also "received threatening phone calls at home. The callers said they had all [her] personal information. They wouldn't identify themselves; nor did caller I.D. show the source" (Polumbaum and Xiong 2008: 76). These events "terrified" her, and "when the propaganda chief of Chongwen District visited our branch and offered cigarettes to the bureau head," she quit Xinhua. Because more aggressive news outlets are often familiar with this kind of harassment, their reporters and editors have a personal and professional support network to help them cope. At Xinhua, by contrast, Li was unprotected and ultimately left for the greener pastures of *China Newsweek*, where "nothing similar has happened" since (Polumbaum and Xiong 2008: 77). Like Li, other reporters who might have a taste for sensitive stories quickly learn that a place like Xinhua is not the place for such work – to the benefit of their more aggressive competitors.

Conclusion

In sum, for historical, geographic, and cultural reasons, many of China's top papers, including *Southern Weekend*, the *Beijing News*, and *China Youth Daily*, are full of advocate journalists pushing their views with firmness but subtlety. This determination echoes that of the advocate journalists of one hundred years earlier who saw in mobilizing public opinion "the means of abolishing autocracy and moving toward constitutionalism" (Judge 1996: 69). As the modern analogs of these Confucian scholar-officials, contemporary advocate journalists carry on this tradition and are ultimately – and perhaps unexpectedly – among of the key drivers of policy change in China.

Notes

1 This is a phrase that has special relevance for a Shanghai audience, as it also refers to a former colonial part of town that has now become arguably the country's premier shopping district and a model for Shanghai's success.
2 This type of flowery language is very common in advocate journalists' writing. In this case, the title refers to the price that must be paid inside the artistic community, and the psychic wounds on the artists themselves, for the refinements they demonstrate to the world.
3 Such a role orientation is hardly exclusive to China. Hallin and Mancini (2004) speak of European reporters who "retain more of the 'publicist' role that once prevailed in political journalism – that is, an orientation toward influencing public opinion." They see this attitude prevalent in what they call the "Polarized Pluralist" model of the news, a model similar to that practice by China's advocate journalists. Such reporters aim to push a

specific agenda in their writing and influence public opinion through overt persuasion. See Hallin and Mancini (2004: 28).
4 For him, it was indeed impossible – he was later fired for his outspokenness.
5 See Shen and Zhang (2013: 380). Note that in this study, journalists associated with features of advocacy journalism like a desire to "promote social reform" are termed "populist mobilizers."
6 See Kluver (1999) for a discussion of the traditional role of intellectuals in Chinese society.

References

Bandurski, David, and Martin Hala. 2010a. "Breaking through the Silence: The Untold Story of the Henan Aids Epidemic." In *Investigative Journalism in China: Eight Cases in Chinese Watchdog Journalism*, edited by David Bandurski and Martin Hala, 35–60. Hong Kong: Hong Kong University Press.
Bandurski, David, and Martin Hala. 2010b. "The Danger of Libel: Wu Fang's Search for Justice." In *Investigative Journalism in China: Eight Cases in Chinese Watchdog Journalism*, edited by David Bandurski and Martin Hala, 19–33. Hong Kong: Hong Kong University Press.
Bandurski, David, and Martin Hala. 2010c. "The Journalist as Crusader: The Beijing Taxi Corruption Case." In *Investigative Journalism in China: Eight Cases in Chinese Watchdog Journalism*, edited by David Bandurski and Martin Hala, 95–108. Hong Kong: Hong Kong University Press.
Bandurski, David, and Martin Hala. 2010d. "The Kingdom of Lies: Unmasking the Demons of Charity." In *Investigative Journalism in China: Eight Cases in Chinese Watchdog Journalism*, edited by David Bandurski and Martin Hala, 61–72. Hong Kong: Hong Kong University Press.
Bianco, Lucien. 1971. *Origins of the Chinese Revolution, 1915–1949*. Stanford, Calif.; London: Stanford University Press; Oxford University Press.
Chan, Ying. 2010. "Introduction: The Journalism Tradition." In *Investigative Journalism in China: Eight Cases in Chinese Watchdog Journalism*, edited by David Bandurski and Martin Hala, 1–17. Hong Kong: Hong Kong University Press.
de Burgh, Hugo. 2003. *The Chinese Journalist: Mediating Information in the World's Most Populous Country*. London; New York, NY: Routledge.
Feng Jinsheng (冯金生). 2004. "Who Is Concerned about the Freelance Professionals? (谁来关心自由职业者?)." *Unity Times* (联合时报), Mar. 5, 2, News.
Goldman, Merle. 2002. "A New Relationship between the Intelleculas and the State in the Post-Mao Period." In *An Intellectual History of Modern China*, edited by Leo Ou-fan Lee and Merle Goldman, 499–566. Cambridge: Cambridge University Press.
Goldman, Merle, and Timothy Cheek. 1987. "Introduction: Uncertain Change." In *China's Intellectuals and the State: In Search of a New Relationship*, edited by Merle Goldman, Timothy Cheek, and Carol Lee Hamrin, 1–20. Cambridge, MA: Harvard University Press.
Hallin, Daniel C., and Paolo Mancini. 2004. *Comparing Media Systems: Three Models of Media and Politics, Communication, Society, and Politics*. Cambridge; New York: Cambridge University Press.
Judge, Joan. 1996. *Print and Politics: 'Shibao' and the Culture of Reform in Late Qing China, Studies of the East Asian Institute*. Stanford, CA: Stanford University Press.
Kluver, Randy. 1999. "Elite-Based Discourse in Chinese Civil Society." In *Civic Discourse, Civil Society, and Chinese Communities*, edited by Randy Kluver and John H. Powers, xii, 11–22. Stamford, CT: Ablex.

Lee, Chin-Chuan. 2005. "The Conception of Chinese Journalists: Ideological Convergence and Contestation." In *Making Journalists: Diverse Models, Global Issues*, edited by Hugo de Burgh, 107–126. London; New York: Routledge.

Li Datong (李大同). 2006. *Using News to Influence Today – the Freezing Point Chronicle* [用新闻影响今天 ——《冰点》周刊纪事]. Hong Kong Peaceful and Virtuous Age Publishing Company [香港泰德时代出版有限公司].

Li Qinghua (李庆华). 2004. "Immediately Punishing Malfeasance on the Basis of the Credit Laws Is Not Enough (惩治失信依据不足信用立法刻不容缓)." *China Economic Times* (中国经济时报), Jan. 5.

Liang Qichao (梁启超). 1896. "An Essay on the Benefit of the Press in National Affairs." *Current Affairs* (时务报), Aug. 9.

Liebman, Benjamin L. 2011. "Changing Media, Changing Courts." In *Changing Media, Changing China*, edited by Susan L. Shirk, 150–174. New York: Oxford University Press.

Lin, Fen J. 2010. "Organizational Construction or Individual's Deed? The Literati Tradition in the Journalistic Professionalization in China." *International Journal of Communication* 4:175–197.

Pierson, Paul. 2004. *Politics in Time: History, Institutions and Social Analysis*. Princeton, NJ: Princeton University Press.

Polumbaum, Judy, and Lei Xiong. 2008. *China Ink: The Changing Face of Chinese Journalism*. Lanham, MD: Rowman & Littlefield.

Qian Gang and David Bandurski. 2011. "China's Emerging Public Sphere: The Impact of Media Commercialization, Professionalism, and the Internet in an Era of Transition." In *Changing Media, Changing China*, edited by Susan L. Shirk, 38–76. New York: Oxford University Press.

Shen, Fei, and Zhi'an Zhang. 2013. "Who Are the Investigative Journalists in China: Findings from a Survey in 2010." *Chinese Journal of Communication* 6 (3):374–384.

Tong, Jingrong. 2011. *Investigative Journalism in China: Journalism, Power, and Society*. London; New York: Continuum.

Yin Yungong (尹韵公). 2007. "A Scientific Rethinking of News and Broadcasting During the Sars Period (对"非典"时期的新闻传播的科学反思)." In *China Journalism Yearbook* (中国新闻年鉴), edited by Chinese Academy of Social Sciences News Research Institute (中国社会科学院新闻与传播研究所), 289–290. Beijing: China Journalism Yearbook Publishers (中国新闻年鉴社).

Zhang Ying (张英) and Wu Yi (吴怿). 2005. "Venus: The Price inside the Wall for the Floating Fragrance Outside the Wall [金星: 墙外飘香的墙内价值]." *Southern Weekend* [南方周末], Jul. 28, D28.

7 Pressing back

Introduction

In August 2008, months after having been forced to discipline commentator Chang Ping for a controversial piece, the liberal *Southern Weekend* published a new editorial by him urging that "openness be the rule and secrecy the exception" in government life (Chang Ping [长平] 2008). Just a few months later, in December, the equally feisty *Beijing News* published a story about petitioners to the central government allegedly being detained by police in psychiatric hospitals and "treated" to prevent their complaints from reaching higher-ups.[1]

Three years earlier, in 2005, several letters from top *China Youth Daily* editors excoriating their superiors and party management were "accidentally" leaked onto the Internet and generated a sensation across the media world (Marquand 2005). In late December of that year, a group of over a hundred journalists went on strike to protest the removal of Yang Bin, the editor-in-chief, by top CCP officials (Gill 2005).

This chapter will concentrate on situations similar to the first two contentious incidents, which, I argue, are examples of pushback. I aim in this chapter to explain why the first two incidents should be conceptually separated from the last two and why this distinction is important. Incidents like the last two – the open letters and the strike – move beyond pushback into outright resistance and are the subject of the next chapter.

In Chapter 1, I defined pushback as a form of resistive behavior that takes place when actors privileged by professional or traditional standing oppose power holders or policies in ways that they perceive to be within the boundaries of the permissible, but I did not explain why Chinese journalists might push back. This chapter further refines the concept and lays out its causes and effects.

What is pushback?

The notion of "privileged nonstate actors" is key. While many previous studies have examined resistance behavior among Chinese peasants (e.g., Kelliher 1992; Zhou 1996; Li and O'Brien 1996; O'Brien and Li 2006) or among the working class (Hurst and O'Brien 2002), few have done so from the perspective of those who have a great deal of cultural capital and at least a modicum of political influence.² For journalists, the most obvious way to push back involves writing articles that "play edge ball" (*da cabianqiu* 打擦边求), a ping-pong term that refers to pushing a ball to the very edge of the table. These reporters try not to put the ball out of bounds and so represent a kind of intra-systemic critique of Chinese political life, reminiscent of the acts of Meyerson and Scully's "tempered radicals" (Meyerson and Scully 1995) or what O'Leary has referred to as "guerilla government" (O'Leary 2006). But pushback can take other forms as well, as when Polish journalists under communism, angered by a proposed policy that would allow the government more latitude to jail opposition figures, "sought out specialists to speak against the law by using their positions and expertise in criminology, management, or psychology" (Curry 1990: 190). Chinese journalists, too, speak through "neutral" experts to get controversial opinions in print or get around specific state restrictions. One young reporter in Beijing, for instance, got around a Central Propaganda Department (CPD) requirement not to refer to China's national stadium by its colloquial sobriquet "the bird's nest" by quoting the building's architect using the term (Interview HB24–2).

When journalists publish a sensitive investigative report, quote a controversial but ostensibly neutral expert, or write consistently negative stories – behavior discouraged by China's state media control apparatus – they are likely engaging in pushback.³ For example, a reporter at the *Southern Metropolis News*, a paper that aims explicitly to be the "best in China," (*ban Zhongguo zuihao de baozhi* 办中国最好的报纸), published a story despite the demands of a provincial government bureau to get permission before publication. When the paper went ahead with the publication anyway, nothing came of the matter, demonstrating the paper's ability to carefully triangulate risks (Interview HL08–4B). This type of publication-linked pushback is most visible, though there are myriad varieties, as when Chinese reporters leak stories to the foreign press or lawyers press forward with sensitive lawsuits that may upset governing authorities but do not risk open confrontation. Indeed, lawyers under a thawing authoritarianism may be particularly prone to resistive behavior, echoing Tocqueville's argument that for societies "in which men of law cannot take a position in the world of politics . . . one can be sure . . . lawyers will be very active agents of revolution" (Bell 1997: 66).

But what makes the two stories mentioned in the first paragraph pushback and not simply resistance? Critically, there were no direct repercussions from the two editorials, while the other two cases – the open letters and the strike – ultimately resulted in reporters being fired. But pushback should not be seen as purely from a *post hoc*, potentially tautological perspective. In the case of the first aggressive editorial, it is highly probable that Chang Ping and his editors (correctly) anticipated no state reaction before publication. This conclusion is likely for two reasons: First, although Chang Ping is certainly a controversial media figure, those close to him say he avoids outright challenges to the state⁴ and second, under the editor responsibility system, his editors bear responsibility for what is published and would have also have been sanctioned, fired, or even jailed if Chang's editorial went too far. The second contentious editorial, about abuses of the psychiatric system, has a similar logic. Ultimately, no one at either paper was disciplined for these articles.

In the case of the 2005 strike or the open letters, participants clearly saw both actions as out of bounds before undertaking them, by definition giving them a strongly resistive intent. Strikes, for example, are not legal under Chinese law.[5] Aware of this fact, the would-be strikers locked themselves in a karaoke bar the night before the strike was to take place and refused to allow anyone to leave or make contact with outsiders, to prevent advance knowledge from reaching the CPD and Chinese security apparatus (Interview HB24–2). One open letter, written by *China Youth Daily* editor Lu Yuegang, rhetorically asked if his editor-in-chief thought that ordinary reporters grew up eating "shit" (*shi* 屎), denounced his management style, and opined that "politicians like you ... can cause great damage to the nation" (Lu Yuegang [卢跃刚] 2004), translation by Roland Soong). Even more dangerously for Lu, he recognized that the editor was not acting alone, and explicitly criticized the CCP officials who installed and backed the chief editor, telling them to "strengthen [their] studies" of communist ideology (Lu Yuegang [卢跃刚] 2004). Such a scathing attack is clearly outside the boundaries of the acceptable, and Lu must have had few illusions about this basic fact when writing it. Indeed, he and his direct superior, Li Datong, were ultimately forced from their positions within the paper.

The idea of "playing edge ball" comes up often, and many reporters clearly see their everyday relationship with the state strategically, as a sporting match or a kind of dance of "an old married couple," in which both sides are "neither obsequious nor supercilious" (*bu bei bu kang* 不卑不亢) (Interview HL08–4B). To carry the Ping-Pong analogy further, the two editorials are a clear example of pushback; although the authors hit the ball right to the edge of the table, they did not go out of bounds, nor did they intend to do so. In the case of the strike or the open letters, by contrast, both balls were *deliberately* played far beyond the table, and both cases had serious repercussions for participants.

Pushback also differs in the nature of the claims that participants make. While most claims in China, among the rural population at least, "remain fundamentally reactive" and "hardly ever tak[e] proactive initiatives" (Bianco 1999: 60), the claims of many Chinese journalists are indeed proactive. By appropriating the ability to supervise the Party/state by virtue of their own professional standing, these journalists are in fact implicitly claiming to the right to share one of the fundamental monopolies of an authoritarian state, that of passing judgment. Although taken individually, sensitive articles by bold Chinese journalists might be trivial and contained, taken together they press a proactive claim on the Chinese state. Even more subversively, this claim is based on international (and precommunist Chinese) norms of the proper role of a Chinese journalist, not the norms put forth by the CCP. Hugo de Burgh (2003: 84) has similarly argued that "journalists can now distinguish service to the country from service to the state," but to date, mainstream scholarship on nationalism in the People's Republic has overlooked this important distinction, despite the fact that it has existed in some form at least since the 1980s.[6]

Pushback in context

Because pushback is on a continuum between quiescence and resistance, it has features of both. With quiescence, pushback shares the notion of not challenging elites, even when the relatively powerless are unhappy with their situation. Many journalists fundamentally support China's censorship system, a situation that might be seen by political sociologist John Gaventa, one of the pioneering scholars of quiescence, as strong evidence of reporters' hegemonic domination by the powerful.[7] And yet, unlike Gaventa's thoroughly dominated Appalachian coal miners, Chinese journalists can and do act out to push at the edges of the regime that controls them – often publicly.

Pushback also shares similarities with resistance. While journalists almost never openly challenge the media control apparatus as a whole, they often ignore or chafe at specific restrictions or directives. The editorial mentioned in the opening section, calling as it does for "openness" in government life, is a careful, if not particularly subtle, dig at the information restrictions Chinese journalists face every day. Like this one, many of the claims that pushing back journalists make are proactive, pushing for a change in the status quo. Acts of outright resistance, by contrast, tend to be reactive and to demand a reversion to the way things were before. But there are other distinctions as well, as set out below.

For clarity, it is important to first define "resistance." Hollander and Einwohner have created a useful seven-part typology, with types of resistance varying by whether the acts were intended as resistance and whether they were recognized by targets and/or observers as such (Hollander and Einwohner 2004). Pushback problematizes this dimension, however, since reporters almost always publish sensitive articles with the assumption that the consequences will be minimal or at least mild enough to bear. In other words, pushback is not overt resistance or "behavior that is visible and readily recognized by both targets and observers as resistance and, further, is intended to be recognized as such" (Hollander and Einwohner 2004: 545). Pushback is likely to precipitate overt resistance (like publishing a letter critical of the CCP or going on strike) under circumstances discussed in the next chapter, but because pushback has both ambiguous intent on the side of the journalists and uncertain, *post hoc* reaction on the side of the targets, it cannot be seen as overt resistance. This ambiguity also means that pushback is not covert resistance, defined as "acts that are intentional yet go unnoticed (and, therefore, unpunished) by their targets, although they are recognized as resistance by other, culturally aware observers" (Hollander and Einwohner 2004: 541).

Pushback also differs from some of the most restrictive categories of resistance, strengthening the argument that it falls in a separate domain. McAdam, Tarrow, and Tilly's notion of contained contention has similarities with pushback because reporters' actions and claims do not usually provoke punishment from state authorities. But there is a critical difference because, unlike McAdam et al.'s actors, here the parties are not "previously established actors employing well established means of claim making" (McAdam, Tarrow, and Tilly 2001: 7). Although the political standing of Chinese journalists has certainly improved over the years, the twenty-nine reporters currently languishing in prison (Reporters sans Frontières 2013) conclusively refute the argument that reporters' claim making abilities are "well established." Ultimately, as long as the CCP refuses to quietly relinquish its monopoly on the right to publicly "supervise" or comment on political acts, the media are precluded from contained contention – for now.

Pushback also shares elements of O'Brien and Li's rightful resistance, in particular, by "operating near the boundary of authorized channels" and relying on "mobilizing support from the wider public." However, it differs from rightful resistance in that it does not employ "the rhetoric and commitments of the powerful to curb the exercise of power" (O'Brien and Li 2006: 2). Far from relying, as does rightful resistance, on the state's own guarantees and commitments to force corrective action, pushback involves making claims based on professional or traditional norms separate from and not sanctioned by the state.[8] Finally, pushback should not be confused with James C. Scott's romantic notion that covert resistance among peasants creates the reef on which, perhaps, "the ship of state runs aground" (Scott 1989: 20). Some of these actions, including many of the ones detailed below, have easily identifiable, direct consequences on state policy or control. Moreover, the actors engaging in pushback are relatively privileged,[9] the actions are open for all to see, and the intent is not to directly challenge authorities.

In short, pushback operates between an enforced quiescence and various types of overt resistance, distinctions that Table 7.1 helps draw out.

Causes of pushback

What causes pushback? Traditional political communication theory, whether liberal or critical, often emphasizes the role of market competition in shaping aggressive media action (Shoemaker and Reese 1991). The cross-disciplinary social movement literature, meanwhile, has focused on openings in what it terms the political opportunity structure (POS) as occasions for resistive behavior (McAdam, McCarthy, and Zald 1996; Tarrow 1998).[10] Both answers are partly correct, but the answer is much more nuanced. Although macroeconomic changes in the Chinese economy and society have clearly created the structural conditions necessary for pushback to emerge (Zhao 1998, 2000; Lynch 1999; Borton 2004; Liebman 2005), marketization cannot be seen as proximate cause of pushback.[11] Likewise, while some journalists certainly take advantage of shifting microchanges in the POS in deciding which sensitive articles to pursue and publish, such changes determine the timing, but not the cause, of pushback.

Explaining pushback, take 1: the problem with economic determinism

This project's two methodological parts allow detailed exploration of the micro- and macro-foundations of pushback. The computer content analysis (CCA), in measuring an individual article's *sensitivity* and *negativity*, can determine which structural factors are linked with pushback. An article that is both negative and

Table 7.1 Pushback in context

Name	Basis of claim?	Resistive intent?	Perceived by target as resistance?	Perceived by observer as resistance?	Are claims usually proactive, competitive, or reactive?	Works within existing claim-making system?
Hegemonic quiescence	No claims	No				
Coerced quiescence	No public claims	Perhaps, but stifled				
Pushback	Professional and traditional standing and/or cultural capital	No	Usually not	Ambiguous	Proactive	No
Weapons of the weak	Moral economy, social code, or class-based claim	Yes	No	Yes	Reactive or competitive	No
Contained contention (e.g., protests in a democracy)	Grievances	Yes	Yes, but allowed	Yes	Varies	Yes
Rightful resistance	Grievances and previous promises by the state	Yes	Yes	Yes	Reactive	Spans the boundaries of contained (allowed) and transgressive (not allowed)
Rebellion	Varies, usually grievances	Yes	Yes	Yes	Varies	No

Increasingly rebellious and resistive →

Adapted from Hollander and Einwohner (2004: 544).

sensitive – an investigative report of official corruption, for example – almost certainly represents pushback. Because Chinese press outlets must carefully monitor the political climate before deciding what to publish, publication of a sensitive piece is done consciously and deliberately. By measuring and correlating these sensitive stories to specific structural and individual factors, the CCA allows a macro-level analysis of pushback. Interview data round out the picture by providing the micro-foundations of individual journalists' behaviors.

Traditional liberal theories of the press emphasize the importance of competition in creating a free, aggressive press corps. Hallin and Mancini write that "The traditional interpretation . . . is the view that 'the increasing value of newspapers as advertising mediums allow[ed] them gradually to shake off government or party control and to become independent voices of public sentiment'" (Hallin and Mancini 2004: 203, quoting Altick 1957: 322). This view has hardly disappeared. Lawson, for instance, in research on the Mexican media, argues that "those media which are most exposed to market competition will become free and pluralistic most rapidly" (Lawson 2002: 181). And this view is common among China scholars too. Minxin Pei, for example, has argued that that "the higher the level of marketization, the greater the degree of self-liberalization. Strong market forces [have] reduced the effectiveness of government censorship of the media by multiplying the channels of production and dissemination" (Pei 1994: 155). In short, it is a common view that market competition drives aggressive journalism – and pushback.

Not all hold to this view, of course. But many critics of this "traditional" model of press commercialization still believe that such marketization influences media content. Indeed, critical or Marxist theories of the press argue that that, far from creating journalistic independence, marketization simply transfers control of the press to society's moneyed interests. For example, Herman and Chomsky "start from the assumption that media serve the dominant elite" and argue that "this is just as true . . . when the media are privately owned without formal censorship as when they are directly controlled by the state" (Shoemaker and Reese 1991: 193). This tradition is similar to the Gramscian notion that "media institutions serve a hegemonic function by continually producing a cohesive ideology . . . that serves to reproduce and legitimate the social structure" and ultimately the moneyed interests in society (Shoemaker and Reese 1991: 194; see also Gramsci 1999 [1936]). Ben Bagdikian (1992) has argued that commercial media owners work against the public interest, while China scholar Chin-Chuan Lee has claimed that "the wealthier journalists become, the less politically engaged they are" (Lee 2005: 120). Some media scholars do not go quite as far, but many still find that "largely as a consequence of advertising, papers became increasingly homogenous" (Baker 1994: 41).[12] Starting from a somewhat different theoretical premise, Stockmann (2013) has found that marketized media have similar content to "official" papers like the *People's Daily*, but their commercial appeal makes them more effective at shaping hearts and minds in a direction amenable to the Party/state.

For critical media theorists, the end result is a press "captured" by bourgeois market interests. This end point is very different from liberal scholars' notion of a news media inspired by competition to critique power holders; however, both groups share a common Marxist teleology. For both liberal and critical media theorists, the economic foundation of the press determines its content. Although commercialization of the Chinese newspaper industry is a long-term driver of media change, over shorter periods of time the causality is far from clear.

Working between the extremes of liberal and critical theory, several scholars of the Chinese press have proposed more nuanced relationships between the state, the market, and newspaper content. Yuezhi Zhao, for example, argues that the CCP is now effectively using financial incentives to shape political and economic outcomes for the press, and the results do not necessarily mean that marketized papers will act against the state (Zhao 2000). "I do not equate democracy with the market," she writes (Zhao 1998: 10). Ashley Esarey (2005) makes a similar argument, pointing out that the CCP now uses financial incentives – the very financial incentives enhanced by marketizing reforms – as one among its arsenal of tools designed to keep reporters in line. And Anne-Marie Brady has also carefully argued that although "in a commercialized cultural economy all newspapers and television stations are competing for advertising dollars and subscriptions/ audiences to pay for the cost of production and maintaining well-qualified staff," the CCP is still able to maintain effective control over the media (Brady 2008: 81). Indeed, Brady argues that the Party/state has become even more effective in selling its message in a marketized media that in a state-supported one, despite the impact that commercial pressures tend to have on the industry. Daniela Stockman (2013) makes a similar – and very convincing – argument.

Computer-assisted content analysis

To gauge the various structural factors that affect pushback and other forms of aggressive journalism, I conducted a large-scale, computer-assisted content analysis (CCA), supplemented by data from secondary sources. While CCA is not a new technique, it has never before been applied on this scale to the Chinese media.[13] The tools needed to apply electronic content analysis to Chinese text have been developed only recently, and time and budget constraints limit manual coding of newspaper content to a few hundred or at most a few thousand articles. Perhaps the biggest advantage of using a computerized content analysis is its essentially unlimited scope, restrained only by processing power and data availability. In this study, the scale of the corpus – some 15.4 million words[14] – means that inferences to the larger Chinese newspaper market are reasonable. I chose to perform a CCA because it is the only way to systematically test and measure in a reliable, replicable way the actual content of large numbers of Chinese newspaper reports. Moreover, this approach allows direct measurement of the estimated effects of large-scale variables – newspaper ownership, region, income, and the like – on the day-to-day differences in reporting among different papers. While interviews are critical for analyzing the motivations, training, background, and thought processes of individual journalists and editors, interviews alone cannot hope to capture the macro-scale variables that help shape press coverage over time. The CCA, in other words, allows research on "the forest" rather than just "the trees."

Of course, this method has limitations. Most importantly, CCA is still a blunt instrument, missing the nuance of individual newspaper articles that might subtly praise or criticize government policy in a way not easily observed by a computer. And any article that does not use one of the dictionary's keywords is necessarily ignored by what is essentially a giant word count. It is also important to acknowledge that even twenty-six papers from around China may miss trends happening in smaller regional papers that are not electronically archived or easily accessible.

Despite these issues, however, computer content analysis poses several advantages that outweigh these issues. Chinese newspaper articles are often written in a wooden, predictable form that reduces the advantage of manual coding when compared to less stylized texts. The massive expansion in the number of analyzable newspaper articles greatly increases statistical power. And unlike a human-coded content analysis, CCA does not suffer from reliability issues. Tian and Stewart write, "The process of computer-assisted text analysis can be repeated by other researchers, and, with the fixed algorithms in the computer software, the results should be the same for any researcher with the same text," meaning problems of inter-coder reliability are completely eliminated (Tian and Stewart 2005: 292). In sum, CCA's advantages make it uniquely suited for a study of this type.

Newspaper sampling methodology

The analysis involved first selecting twenty-six newspapers with an eye toward maximizing differences in circulation, geographic region, provincial income, and level of administrative oversight. Note, however that constraints on the availability of newspaper articles and data mean these papers were not randomly selected and do not represent a true random sample of the entire Chinese newspaper market, something difficult or impossible for even Chinese researchers to obtain. Unfortunately, many popular papers – such as most of China's evening papers – could not be included because they either were not in the database or had limited statistical data available. In other words, the sample is potentially biased against the medium-sized commercial presses. The corpus includes articles from the three-year period (2004, 2005, and 2006) so as to minimize short-term temporal aberrations. A full list of newspapers is provided in Appendix A, and the corpus includes newspapers from eleven provinces and the central government; papers with central-, provincial-, and city-level administrative rank; those among China's richest (e.g., Beijing, Shanghai) and among its poorest (e.g., Yunnan, Anhui) provincial-level areas; and papers from all of China's major regions except the northeast and far west. Appendix C lists the tested categories, and Appendix D includes raw results and category means for each of the categories.

From these 26 papers, 20,477 articles were ultimately downloaded, with an aim toward obtaining approximately 900 articles per paper, or 300 articles per paper for each of the 3 years under study. Selection of articles ranged from all of those posted for a particular year to a small fraction of those available, and the statistical results are weighted by likelihood of selection. Various technical issues reduced this number to a final article count of 18,897. These articles were downloaded entirely unsorted from the Eastview online China Core Newspaper Database, a news aggregator similar to Lexis/Nexis. This technique maximized the randomness of the data, but because Eastview apparently practices some sort of newspaper selection and article pre-filtering, it is unclear if this sample is truly random (Fen J. Lin, personal communication). However, the large size of the corpus and the diverse range of papers minimize any bias.[15]

Dictionary construction

After downloading was complete, the next step was to begin building "dictionaries," or lists of terms that are relevant to a certain topical category like sports. In all, twenty categories and twelve subcategories were selected (see Appendix E). In essence, a thematic CCA relies on software that counts the number of relevant terms in the sample of text to be analyzed (Popping 2000). This "dictionary" is in many ways the heart of the enterprise. A dictionary that is very short runs the risk of undercounting relevant articles and serves as a potential source of bias in the results. A dictionary that is very long, however, becomes increasingly onerous to develop, and Zipf's Law (1935) notes that adding rarely used words adds little to the validity of the results.[16] Happily, research suggests that a middle path exists which does not require dictionaries of very large size. Jin and Wong, for example, have found that for Chinese, "a dictionary consisting of only the 500 highest frequency [words] . . . produced as good a retrieval result as using a more complete dictionary with over 100,000 entries" (Jin and Wong 2002: 281). In short, the more than 550 terms (not including the huge sentiment dictionaries) employed here fit the criteria for comprehensiveness.

These dictionaries were mainly constructed automatically, in order to save time, to improve results by capturing hot topics and neologisms and to reduce human bias.[17] This process involved using factor analysis to cluster information by a common, underlying theme. I theorized that words semantically related to one another would appear together in the same newspaper article more often that unrelated words. For example, the words "lawyer" and "courtroom" should appear together more often than "lawyer" and "basketball." Using factor analysis to cluster words in this way is a relatively uncommon, though not unheard-of, technique in text analysis (briefly mentioned, for example, in a footnote in Popping [2000]). So as not to bias the results, the factor analysis dictionary clustering was based on 250 articles that were randomly selected from the larger corpus and discarded once the categories were finished, taking no further part in the content analysis calculations. Moreover, by employing factor analysis, in a certain sense the dictionary construction process was more "objective," with the words themselves coming from a representative sample of the newspapers, not from a preconceived *a priori* list.

After some manual cleanup to remove function words and overly general terms, these 20 categories were supplemented by extremely comprehensive (greater than 20,000 entries) term lists of positive and negative words in Chinese developed by

Taiwanese researchers at the National Taiwan University.[18] These positive and negative term lists allow a gauge of overall newspaper sentiment, albeit one not as subtle as a human would perceive. Finally, three lists of terms deemed sensitive by the government and used in monitoring internet content[19] were also included on the assumption that if terms were sensitive online, they were likely to be so in newspaper articles as well. These sensitive terms lists allowed a further rubric for evaluating sensitive newspaper content.

After the dictionaries were built, all newspaper articles were run separately though Yoshikoder, which is a free content analysis software tool developed by Will Lowe. Thus, the unit of analysis for this portion of the project is an individual article. Proportions were used rather than raw keyword counts to eliminate bias based on differing sample size, and articles were weighted by selection probability in the regressions. The percentage of corpus words that matched dictionary terms was over 20%, though half of this (~10%) resulted from hits on the enormous "positive" and "negative" lists. Category averages, aside from the positive and negative terms lists, ranged from nearly 3% for politics overall to less than .006% for the supportive politics subcategory. Although this might seem small, such percentages are normal for this kind of work (Hassid 2012).

Dependent variable construction

After the raw results were processed, the variable (Sensitivity) was constructed by adding together the Politics-Combative, Corruption, Disasters, Mingan ("sensitive"), Gaoliang ("high level"), and Yanjin ("strictly prohibited") categories. The Politics-Combative list comprises words associated with challenging power holders, such as articles that refer to the 1989 Tiananmen Square massacre. The idea of "challenging" a unitary actor like "the state" is less problematic than it first appears. Kevin O'Brien pointed out the need to disaggregate the state and noted that it "becomes difficult to neatly separate 'challengers' and 'polity members'" (O'Brien 2003: 53) – and this analysis is certainly accurate. To a great extent, however, such "unpacking" is unnecessary here. Because Chinese media outlets are not allowed to conduct original reporting on events or people above their own administrative level, almost all "challenge" is aimed squarely at their own level of government or below. And even when challenging coverage is aimed at lower tiers, media outlets have to be very careful not to alienate powerful officials who can call in favors with higher-ups to chastise the offending publication (HL08–4B). Moreover, although individual negative stories might not challenge the state, if a paper publishes too many of them, trouble results.[20] Even when central authorities tolerate or encourage stories about low-level corruption to serve as a "fire alarm" that something is wrong, publishing too many such stories will bring heat from local or provincial officials (Lorentzen 2014). In short, a hit on the Politics-Combative list – such as an article referring to Taiwan's independence movement – serves as an excellent approximation of challenging the state, at whatever level.

The Corruption category was built around words that are related to corrupt activities, one of the more consistently sensitive topics in contemporary Chinese politics. As with the "challenging the state" idea, this one needs to be broken down a bit. While corruption coverage in general is a sensitive issue, at times, the CCP conducts anticorruption campaigns and urges (or forces) newspapers to print stories praising the leadership for their handling of corruption issues. Thus any individual article exposing corruption is not necessarily pushback – or even sensitive. In aggregate, however, the more corruption issues are covered, the unhappier China's press control apparatus becomes. Indeed, censors specifically read papers to see if "incidents of corruption (*tanwu fubai* 贪污腐败) are being reported too much during a specific time period" (He Qinglian 2004: 17). In this sense, measuring the level of coverage on corruption is a good stand-in for measuring assertive coverage directly, even if some individual cases support the state line. The three-year time frame of this study, too, should "wash out" this type of politically encouraged corruption reporting. And again, all results are relative, not absolute, allowing comparison between papers that report a great deal of this potentially sensitive topic and those that report less.

The Disasters category was based around man-made and natural disaster vocabulary. Although rules and regulations governing disaster coverage have varied over the years, this too has been a consistently sensitive media topic, and indeed the state has recently suggested efforts to further discourage disaster coverage (Duan, Ye, and Wang 2006). The May 12, 2008, Sichuan earthquake may well herald a new day for unrestricted disaster coverage in the Chinese press, but the relatively open disaster coverage in 2008 (coverage that was quickly closed off again) does not mean that such coverage would have been acceptable even two years earlier (or two years later). The last three categories (Mingan, Gaoliang, and Yanjin words) were derived from lists leaked from a major Chinese blog service provider of sensitive terms. In short, the following formula was used:

Sensitivity = Politics-Combative + Corruption + Disasters + Mingan + Gaoliang + Yanjin

Finally, the variable falls on the exponential distribution predicted by Zipf's Law.

Next, the ratio of negative words to total sentiment (Negativity) was evaluated, based on the very extensive lists of negative and positive vocabulary created by researchers at National Taiwan University. This ratio allows evaluation of the general tone of articles, whether critical or supportive.[21] A ratio of negative terms to overall sentiment was used rather than simply the raw proportion of each in an effort to control for articles that were simply highly emotional in tone, without being weighted in either a supportive or critical direction. This method captures articles that use very little sentiment but are still selectively negative. Negativity and Sensitivity are clearly distinct: A simple bivariate correlation demonstrates that the fit between the two is only 0.13, with a miniscule Cronbach's α of 0.03. And finally, it is important to clarify that the unit of analysis in this quantitative analysis is an individual newspaper article, the aim being to test how systemic factors (including journalists' imputed attitudes) affect the production of sensitive news content.

Table 7.2 Dependent variables

Variable name	What the variable represents	How the variable is calculated
Sensitivity	Degree to which article challenges or pushes against the state – at whatever level – by reporting on one of several sensitive topics	Adding together the proportion of words that an article has from the Politics-Combative, Corruption, Disasters, Mingan, Gaoliang, and Yanjin lists
Negativity	Degree of negativity of newspaper article	The proportion of words that an article has from the Negative terms list divided by the total proportion of words than an article has from the Sentiment (positive and negative) terms list

Independent variable construction

Set against these dependent variables are a number of independent and control variables. Among the most important is a newspaper's administrative level, given the simultaneous existence of theories that central papers both get more oversight and that they get less. Testing was done by coding level of government oversight as a dummy variable with Central = 1 and all others 0. Although papers in China actually fall in two ranks below central – provincial and city-level[22] – differentiating between these in coding is problematic. For one thing, market competition statistics and the like are based on provincial level data, which are potentially misleading for lower-ranked papers. And for another, all papers tested are located in provincial capitals, meaning oversight is generally done by both provincial- and city-level authorities. These administrative level data were derived from the official managing bureau's (*zhuguan bumen*) administrative level, information obtained from the *China News Yearbooks (Chinese Academy of Social Sciences News Research Institute* [中国社会科学院新闻与传播研究所], various years). Although some papers normally thought of as local or provincial (e.g., *China Management Daily* [*Zhongguo Jingying Bao* 中国经营报]) are coded as central under this rubric,[23] this approach is more objective than using subjective appraisals of coverage and influence.

Because of its unique history in the modern Chinese press, Guangdong papers were also coded with a separate dummy variable. Given that the modern, commercialized Chinese press system arises mainly from Guangdong's papers (and especially from its capital, Guangzhou), this is the most important regional influence in China. Distance of all papers' main offices from Beijing (in thousands of kilometers) was also included in the regression. This variable was included to separate out the effects of the Guangdong region that are distinct from mere distance from the central government.

Another important factor, marketization, has long been regarded as a critical driver of the changing Chinese press (Zhao 1998, 2000; Lynch 1999; Esarey

2006). It is, however, a tricky variable to operationalize, and so a variety of approaches were taken. First, inspired by a typology introduced by Esarey (2007), I coded newspapers along three dummy variables as being party organ, party commercial, or high commercial. Party organ and high commercial papers are easy to imagine, but the party commercial (PC) category is perhaps somewhat trickier to explain. In brief, this includes papers financed and overseen by major party organs, while still relying on the market for cues and funding. Prominent examples include *Southern Weekend, China Management Daily,* and *Caijing* (the latter not included in this study because of data limitations).

Also included were 2006 provincial per-capita GDP data (China Data Online 2006), market competitiveness calculations, and circulation data. The GDP variable is self-explanatory, but the competitiveness calculations and circulation data require some exposition and caveats. Both these data were all gathered from the respective years of the *Chinese News Yearbooks* so as to minimize the bias potential that comes from picking and choosing circulation numbers from various sources. Although these data are unlikely to reflect a true picture of the Chinese media market, they at least provide a rough estimate of various newspapers' relative circulation statistics. The competition estimates, discussed further below, were occasionally extrapolated from previous years or market averages when only incomplete data were available.

And finally, it is impossible to analyze news content and ignore the reporters producing that content. To this end, the model incorporates an independent variable (IV) that attempts to take quantify the degree of advocacy journalism within each article. Advocacy journalism has two features that make content analysis a particularly appropriate tool for analysis. First, it "tends to give substantial emphasis to commentary" (Hallin and Mancini 2004: 98), a tendency measured among Chinese papers by calculating the proportion of self-reference (e.g., 我, "I"; 我们, "we"; 本人, "I-formal"; etc.) in articles. Such use of first-person vocabulary is much more likely to appear in commentary than in straight news. And second, because advocacy journalism-prone countries like Greece have articles that are "often highly polemical" (Hallin and Mancini 2004: 98), the overall degree of sentiment (positive plus negative proportions) is included in the advocacy journalism calculation as well. The theoretical foundation of coding and measuring advocacy journalism in this way is ultimately derived from Hallin and Mancini's work on different national journalistic styles, which finds that countries like Greece and Italy "retain more of the 'publicist' role that once prevailed in political journalism – that is, an orientation toward influencing public opinion" (Hallin and Mancini 2004: 28). Hallin and Mancini see this attitude prevalent in what they call the "Polarized Pluralist" model of the news, similar to what I call advocacy-style Chinese journalism. Rather than assume that China has a single journalistic style, however, I argue that multiple styles can and do coexist within a single media system.

The end result provides an independent variable that accounts for how much an article falls along the news ethos continuum from "American-style" (low self-reference and sentiment) to "advocacy journalism" (high-self reference and sentiment) news outlook. This IV therefore allows for a rank order of the degree to which newspapers follow either model, a list that is included in Appendix B. It is critical to note that this variable is measuring not the *content* but the *style* of journalism, and presumably of the journalists themselves.[24] There is no *a priori* reason why either the liberal or the advocacy style should have more challenging coverage than the other, making this variable truly independent. This measure is therefore theoretically and statistically distinct from Negativity, with a tiny bivariate correlation of only 0.0077, and a miniscule Cronbach's α of 0.0054, far below the generally accepted 0.7 threshold for demonstrating that two variables are measuring the same underlying concept. Regrettably, measuring the other three types of journalism (Communist, American-style, and workaday) directly from newspaper content proved an intractable problem, and they are not included in the analysis. This measure of advocacy is only a proxy for the underlying phenomenon and attitudes I hope to catch, but in the absence of large-scale interview or survey data with the very journalists who wrote all 18,897 articles in question, it seems a reasonable compromise.

Finally, market competitiveness was calculated with a variant of the Herfindahl-Hirschman Index (HHI) used by the U.S. Justice Department's (DOJ) Antitrust Division for calculating market concentration (Former DOJ employee Amanda Hassid, personal communication). In this case, the reciprocal of the HHI, multiplied by 100, was used so that unlike the original formulation, here higher numbers mean a more competitive market. Because of data limitations, the HHI calculations are estimates, and all numbers reflect provincial rather than potentially more accurate city-based market competitiveness calculations. Ultimately, the fact that market competition level is not statistically significant is itself an important finding and will be discussed further below.

Control variables

Three independent variables were not statistically significant but were included in various iterations of the model as controls. The full tables with these controls are not included because of space constraints but are available from the author. The first is a dummy control for Southern provinces except Guangdong (Anhui, Fujian, Jiangsu, Jiangxi, and Shanghai).[25] This was done to isolate geographic effects and also because southern papers have a reputation for being more assertive.

Second, a standardized measure of the number of reporters per capita was tested in an effort to gauge the networking potential of working journalists. Journalists often evaluate their work not by its commercial impact but upon the response it generates inside the professional media community (Curry 1990). "Not only do reporters tend to cover the same people and stories, but they rely on each other for ideas and confirmation of their respective news judgments," write two influential media scholars (Shoemaker and Reese 1991: 102). If Chinese journalists are developing into a real professional community, it is likely that they tailor their stories – and indeed their whole media approach – based on the feedback they receive from other reporters. In theory, the more journalists exist per capita, the greater the potential for such professional networking.

And third, a related variable is the percentage of journalists with a professional or academic degree (MA or PhD), with figures from the General Administration on Press and Publication (GAPP). This variable was tested to see if more years of schooling translated into measurable differences in content. As formal training is a strong source of socialization, theoretically more journalists with higher levels of training might have produced more professional journalism. None of these proved significant in any tested iteration, and all were subsequently dropped from the final model.

Table 7.3 Independent and control variables

Variable name	What the variable represents	How the variable is calculated
Central (dummy)	Whether paper has central-level administrative rank	Data collected from the *China News Yearbooks*
Party commercial (dummy)	Whether paper is a party paper with commercial tendencies	Talks with journalists and author's judgment
High commercial (dummy)	Whether paper is highly commercialized	Talks with journalists and author's judgment
Guangdong (dummy)	Whether paper is based in Guangdong province	Data collected from the *China News Yearbooks*
Newspaper circulation	Average daily circulation of newspaper	Data collected from the *China News Yearbooks*, standardized
Per-capita GDP	2006 per-capita GDP of province where paper is based	Data collected from *China Data Online* (2006)
Distance from Beijing	Distance of paper's headquarters from Beijing	Distance of paper's headquarters from Beijing, in kilometers, standardized
Advocacy-Style Journalism	Whether individual article represents the mix of personal appeal and highly sentimental language common to advocacy journalism	Proportion of self-reference words + proportion of sentiment words (positive and negative) in article
Market competitiveness	Estimated degree of newspaper market competition province wide, standardized	Reciprocal of the HHI index of market competition; data compiled from various Chinese government sources
Southern (dummy, control dropped from final model)	Whether newspaper is in the historically more liberal South China region	Newspaper is based in Anhui, Fujian, Jiangsu, Jiangxi, or Shanghai
Percentage of reporters with MA/PhD (control dropped from final model)	Proportion of journalists in region with higher degree	Figures available from the GAPP
Reporters per capita (control dropped from final model)	Number of reporters per capita in province, standardized	A compilation of data from various Chinese government sources

Content analysis results

OLS regression results from the computer content analysis, uphold Zhao and Esarey's middle ground by refuting both the liberal and critical orthodoxies in Table 7.4. Note that these results are weighted by article selection probability, because papers with less overall content are oversampled by the selection process. Throughout, I use robust estimated standard errors to help control for heteroskedasticity. A three-level hierarchical linear model (HLM) was also constructed but gave relatively similar results, especially for the advocacy journalism measure, market competition level, and other variables of particular interest. Because these models are harder to interpret and provide no easy goodness-of-fit statistics, I report OLS results instead. Full HLM results are available from the author.

Table 7.5 gives these results with standardized coefficients, to make the results more commensurable. Note that standardized coefficients for dummy variables are not presented, because interpreting them is difficult.

Table 7.4 Regression results (n=18,897)

Independent variables	Dependent variables OLS coefficients (robust estimated standard errors)	
	Sensitivity[a]	Negativity[b]
Intercept	−.0065 (.0019)**	.3638 (.0282)***
Central[c]	.0005 (.0006)	.0146 (.0086)
Party-commercial[c]	−.0020 (.0005)***	.0783 (.0083)***
High-commercial[c]	−.0028 (.0004)***	.0053 (.0075)
Guangdong[c]	−.0010 (.0005)	.1260 (.0050)***
Newspaper circulation ($\log_{10}$ of total yearly distribution)	.0014 (.0002)***	−.0174 (.0047)***
Per-capita provincial GDP (unit = 1000 RMB)	−.00003 (.000007)***	.0011 (.0001)***
Market competition level (modified HHI, unit = 0–1 scale)	.0046 (.0025)	−.1528 (.0380)***
Distance from Beijing (unit = 1000 km)	−.0004 (.0004)	−.0268 (.0050)***
Advocacy journalism (unit = proportion of relevant terms in article, 0–1 scale)	.0773 (.0071)***	−.0166 (.1012)
R^2	0.068***	0.036***

a: Estimated coefficients for change in proportion of sensitive words
b: Estimated coefficients for change in ratio of negative words to total sentiment words
c: Dummy variables – total effect compared with baseline category of "party paper"
*: $p < .05$
**: $p < .01$
***: $p < .001$

Note that results are weighted by article selection probabilities, weighted sum = 20,376.

Table 7.5 Standardized regression coefficients (n=18,897)

Independent variables	Dependent variables Standardized OLS regression coefficients	
	Sensitivity	Negativity
Central[a]	—	—
Party-commercial[a]	—	—
High-commercial[a]	—	—
Guangdong[a]	—	—
Newspaper circulation	.067***	−.057***
Per-capita provincial GDP	−.045***	.099***
Market competition level	.028	−.062***
Distance from Beijing	−.019	−.093***
Advocacy journalism	.211***	−.003

a: Standardized dummy variables are not presented
*: $p < .05$
**: $p < .01$
***: $p < .001$

And finally, Table 7.6 is a more concrete table demonstrating the percent change in the variables moving from lowest to highest observed values, holding other factors constant; dummies are held at zero and continuous variables at their mean. This table is helpful in providing a more accurate real world picture of the total possible effects of each variable:

Far from demonstrating a clear link between market factors and press content, these results demonstrate that a more nuanced approach is preferable. Holding other factors constant, an increase of 1000 RMB (~US$140) in per-capita GDP leads to a very moderate decrease in Sensitivity (−0.00003, or 0.024 words per mean-length article) but an increase in the negative-to-positive-words ratio (0.0011). Richer provinces, then, are associated with less sensitive content but more negative tone. Circulation has a similarly paradoxical effect. It has a moderate statistical impact on Sensitivity (0.0014, or 1.1 words/article) but has a much larger negative correlation with Negativity (−0.0174). In other words, as papers gain higher circulation, their content gets more sensitive but their tone less so.

These findings about the relationship between market conditions and press content are strange enough that they deserve an explanation. After all, the newspaper business certainly *seems* to have cutthroat competition driving coverage forward. One typical reporter at *Southern Metropolis Daily* – an outlet that explicitly aims to be "the best paper in China" (*ban Zhongguo zuihao de baozhi* 办中国最好的报纸) – told me that when she finds a newsworthy event she will sometimes tell other reporters online that she's "bored" and that "nothing is going on" in order to deflect them from the story. At times people get mad about this, she says, but

Table 7.6 Predicted percent change in results, from lowest to highest observed values, holding other factors constant (n=18,897)

Independent variables	Dependent variables predicted approx. % change in statistically significant OLS regression effects, from lowest to highest observed values & holding other factors constant (0 for dummies, mean value for continuous variables)	
	Sensitivity[a]	*Negativity*[b]
Central, compared with non-central	Not significant	+12%
Party-commercial, compared with nonparty-commercial	−18%	+30%
High-commercial, compared with non high-commercial	−18%	Not significant
Guangdong, compared with other provinces	−17%	+53%
Newspaper circulation, observed max vs. observed min	+36%	−14%
Per-capita provincial GDP, observed max vs. observed min	−23%	+35%
Market competition level, observed max vs. observed min	Not significant	−15%
Distance from Beijing, observed max vs. observed min	Not significant	−21%
Advocacy journalism, observed max vs. observed min	+1042%	Not significant

a: Estimated % change in proportion of sensitive words
b: Estimated % change in ratio of negative words to total sentiment words

everyone knows how competitive it is, and sometimes other reporters are competitors first and friends second (Interview HL08–4B).

So what makes the link between market competition and aggressive coverage so tenuous at the systemic level? The most plausible explanation relies on the unique dynamic between state and market in the Chinese news business.[26] The most competitive markets have greater visibility and invite greater state scrutiny, decreasing opportunities for newspapers to slip between the cracks. The state is likely to pay more attention to those media markets that, like Shanghai or Beijing, are larger and more important than others. The CPD simply may not have the time, energy, or inclination to spend much time on newspapers in smaller cities like Hefei or Datong.[27] Or, as Pierre Bourdieu puts it, "One of the paradoxes is that competition, which is always said to be the precondition of freedom, has the effect, in fields of cultural production under commercial control, of producing uniformity, censorship and even conservatism" (Bourdieu 2005 [1995]: 44). Of course, aggressiveness can also sell. *Caijing* magazine, widely regarded as one of China's most daring publications is also very profitable, hauling 181.72 million RMB in advertising money in 2007. This puts *Caijing* at number seven in ad revenue, beaten only by beauty and fashion titles like *Cosmopolitan, Elle, Harper's Bazaar, Vogue China*, and the like (Redl and Simons 2008: 161). But for the media market as a whole, the relationship between market competition and aggressive news coverage is quite tenuous. *Southern Weekend* provides a good example of this phenomenon. A 2007 study conducted by the now-defunct (and banned) Chinese NGO the Open Constitution Initiative (*Gongmeng* 公盟) found that the number of "critical" (*piping* 批评) editorials printed in the popular "Ark Commentary" section (*Fangzhou Pinglun* 方舟评论) increased from 9.8% to 48.5% of total publication from 2005 to 2007 – even as the paper's circulation took a nosedive (Open Constitution Initiative Legal Research Center (公盟法律研究中心) 2008: 4, document on file with author; information about the plunge in circulation from Interview FY22–0A).

It is telling that a 2013 survey I conducted (with a commercial survey firm) of 705 randomly sampled Chinese microbloggers found that increased consumption of Chinese news – whether on the Internet, newspaper, or TV – had no relationship with levels of trust in either the central or local governments (Hassid 2013; see also Tang and Huhe 2014). If the press were increasingly critical toward government, we would expect lower levels of government trust among media consumers, especially those of the relatively free Internet.[28] Even decades of media reforms have not inclined the Chinese press towards systemic criticism of the political system, and the state has kept the press firmly in check. In theory, then, the growing emergence of China's middle class suggests that demand for high-quality news will only increase. In a free society, this demand would put increasing pressure on papers to produce more of what readers want. But China, of course, is unusual, and political pressures ensure that these demands result in a muted response or, at best, careful pushback in the short- and medium-term.

Explaining pushback, take 2: political opportunity structures

These results instead demonstrate the utility of an emphasis on political opportunity structures (POS) to evaluate pushback, for when pushing back – especially when writing sensitive stories – journalists clearly take heed of the political openings available to them. In interviews, reporters often claimed that they were highly attuned to timing and to micro-changes in opportunity for publishing sensitive articles. During the yearly meeting of the National People's Congress (NPC), for example, reporters often hold back on publishing risky articles because they are aware that the media are scrutinized even more closely during these periods (Interview FU17–2; Interview FY22–0A). For example, editors at Guangzhou's *Yangcheng Evening News* (*Yangcheng Wanbao* 羊城晚报) delayed publishing an exposé of forced prostitution at government-run drug rehabilitation clinics because "The National People's Congress, one of the year's most important political events, had opened in Beijing only two weeks earlier. . . . Running a story with such ugly truths at such an inopportune time,"

Bandurski and Hala write, "would mean seriously rocking the boat" (Bandurski and Hala 2010b: 80).

The reporters and editors at *Caijing* magazine, regarded as China's top business publication and one of the country's boldest political news outlets – at least before the 2010 departure of the founder Hu Shuli and much of the staff[29] – were also very careful to time the release of articles with an opportunity to do so safely. Top editors and reporters who worked there in 2007–2008 claimed that the paper had an excellent innate sense of timing, though it seemed to help that the founder and then editor Hu Shuli went to school with many top CCP leaders (Interview GX30–2). By this account, she was able to get a better sense of micro-openings in the political opportunity structure and publish sensitive pieces at a time when others are unable to do so. The fact that *Caijing* reporters (and those from no other paper) beat the CPD's ban on reporting about the existence of avian influenza in China is evidence of this careful timing (Interview HH31–2CZ).

Occasionally, news workers make mistakes about the openings available to them, but even in these cases, they act according to *perceived* openings in the POS.[30] For example, *Beijing News* editor-in-chief Yang Bin was removed after allowing reporting on two corruption cases, including one in Hebei province that highlighted problems with the CCP's "double designation" (*shuanggui* 双规) policy of detention for suspected corrupt party members.[31] This article followed the case of an official under investigation who was beaten to death by authorities while undergoing "double designation" questioning. According to a former employee at the paper, Yang Bin knew the story was sensitive, but the paper ran it because they thought there was space for such a story. Because the "double designation" policy was already under debate by the CCP, Yang Bin and his subordinates thought this "was an opportunity too good to miss" (Interview GM08–2). Furthermore, the reporter and editors involved protected themselves by just reporting the facts and avoiding commentary. Even though this pushback was interpreted by the CCP as resistance behavior and even though Yang Bin was ultimately fired, the publication of the sensitive article was inspired by a sense of political opportunity.

As described in other chapters, many Chinese journalists explicitly aim to "play edge ball." One told me that "of course I have deliberately challenged the government! If you don't, you don't have any readers!" though he has worked within the openings available (Interview HL09–4). The regime of uncertainty discussed in Chapter 1 means that the boundaries are always changing, but again, Chinese publications look for small-scale openings in the POS before deciding whether to publish a sensitive article. An emphasis on political opportunity structures, while certainly having limitations (discussed in the next chapter), is therefore quite useful in predicting the timing of pushback among Chinese journalists.

Indeed, the very regime of uncertainty that the CPD uses to keep most journalists in line fails as a means of control for many of the most self-assured advocate journalists. Because these advocates are driven by a sense of mission and a calling to help China's development – with or without the approval of the CCP – they are often willing to push back against specific policies or state bureaucracies in ways that other journalists would not dare to attempt. As I have described earlier, pervasive surveillance and uncertainty about where the constantly shifting boundaries of the acceptable might currently lie keeps most journalists well back from these boundaries by encouraging a climate of self-censorship. For the bravest advocate journalists who "regard themselves as solo fliers, more willing to stick out their necks" (Bandurski and Hala 2010a: 57), however, the fact that the CPD or other media control organ has not explicitly banned reporting on a topic sometimes offers an opportunity. After all, noted advocate journalist Lu Yuegang has argued that he and his colleagues should remain "professional (*zhiyexing* 职业性) even in the face of danger (*weixian* 危险)."[32]

Through a careful sense of timing and a survey of the political opportunities open to them, such journalists push through stories as sensitive as when *Caijing* founder Hu Shuli (2005) complained in an editorial about the poor media coverage of avian influenza on the Chinese mainland in late 2005. Even though the Chinese government has been quite touchy about reporting the existence of acute communicable diseases ever since the SARS outbreak in 2003, *Caijing* was able to write the editorial because the editors judged the timing with extreme care. In fact, immediately after they broke the news of media cover-ups, the CPD came out with regulations against any further such articles, and any further reporting of avian influenza was essentially closed in the domestic press. The closure of the topic perhaps represented a lost opportunity for the press as a whole but a victory for *Caijing*, whose reporters and editors were able to correctly sense a micro-opportunity that opened and closed very quickly (Interview FY22–0B).

In a sense, such reporters are engaged in a game of chicken with the state media control apparatus. Occasionally, they guess poorly and lose, but far more frequently, they time stories well and push their agenda without negative repercussions to themselves. The very vagueness of the control that is so successful at keeping most journalists well back from the lines is ironically helpful to advocate journalists who wish to write on a controversial story. In a world where uncertainty and "control parables" create the conditions that induce most journalists to self-censor (Stern and Hassid 2012), those few who do not follow the crowd have a small but significantly greater degree of latitude in pursuing aggressive coverage. Unless these advocates terribly misjudge their timing or the sensitivity of their story, they can plausibly claim that no CPD circular or specific state policy bans reporting on a sensitive topic, leaving them free to report.

Explaining pushback, take 3: China's professional journalists

But why do Chinese journalists engage in pushback at all? Why would someone risk "playing edge ball" when "the costs of breaking the rules can be high, . . . [but] in contrast, the rewards for breaking the rules are relatively slight?" (Brady 2008: 81). The answer comes in part from the surprising professionalization of many Chinese journalists many of whom, as we have seen in earlier chapters, have transformed from obedient lapdogs of the CCP into journalists recognizable as such by outside observers. Ultimately, though, it is mostly the advocate journalists who engage in pushback and create the systematic changes so easily visible in the Chinese media.

Advocacy journalism and pushback

As discussed in the previous chapter, advocacy journalism has a long tradition in China and continues to resonate today. Li Datong, whose *Using News to Influence Today – The Freezing Point Chronicle* (2006) has inspired a good deal of discussion and agreement in Chinese media circles, represents this pole most prominently. Li himself specifically points out that reporting on sensitive topics can widen the boundaries of acceptable coverage, writing that "this type of reporting also has another function, which is to gradually increase the sensitivity threshold of those officials who control (*guanzhi* 管制) the media. . . . If they unceasingly see reports that migrate to the edge of what is acceptable, their threshold for sensitivity (*mingan yu* 敏感隅) will gradually increase" (Li Datong [李大同] 2006: 12). Journalists inside the *Beijing News*, one of China's top papers, have discussed this book extensively (Interview GM08–2), and many other reporters have formed their own opinions. Even an editor who said "if the media are too professionalized, it is a problem" agrees explicitly that the news should influence policies (Interview HL09–4), and this view is far from uncommon.

Results from the content analysis back up interview data in suggesting that an advocacy orientation is critical for determining the content of news articles and of challenge to power holders. An increase from no advocacy journalism to perfect advocate journalism – that is, if an article were composed entirely of self-reference and sentiment – predicts an increase in Sensitivity from 0% to nearly 8% of an article's vocabulary but has no statistically significant relationship with Negativity. In more real-world terms, an increase from the observed minimum advocacy journalism (0) to the maximum (0.271, for a 2006 article in *解放军报* [*Liberation Army Daily*]) predicts an incredible 1,042% increase in Sensitivity from 0.002 to 0.023, *ceteris paribus* (holding dummies at 0 and continuous variables at their means). This dramatic increase, with a standardized estimator nearly twice as large as any other estimator for either dependent variable, showcases the power of the advocate journalist orientation to influence sensitive stories.

The results are equally telling on Negativity, where journalistic orientation has no statistically significant effect. As argued earlier, the CPD is unlikely to care as much about small, unimportant media outlets and markets as they do about major, influential ones. But another compelling explanation relies on the fact that, when writing about sensitive issues, even advocate journalists take care to appear unemotional for fear of angering power holders. Hu Shuli sums up this careful approach in a 2009 *New Yorker* profile, saying "we never say a word in a very emotional or casual way, like 'You lied.' We try to analyze the system and say why a good idea or a good wish cannot become reality" (Osnos 2009: 55). This avoidance of negative coverage is common in the Chinese press, especially during sensitive times like the annual meeting of the national legislature. During the leadership transition from Jiang Zemin to Hu Jintao, for instance, "editors had been strictly instructed to report only positive stories" (Brady 2008: 96), and in late 2013, the CPD deputy repeatedly praised the importance of maintaining "positive propaganda" in the press (Cai Fuchao 2013). Ironically, then, negative coverage of "ordinary" issues is often more sensitive than neutral coverage of even "sensitive" issues!

Newspaper articles that follow the advocate professional model of reporter as commentator are far bolder than those that employ the neutrality of American-style journalism. Indeed, the effect on sensitive coverage is significantly higher than for any other variable in the study, demonstrating the importance of the advocacy professional ethos for spurring resistive behavior. This argument perhaps appears at first blush to be a tautology; journalists resist because they are "professional," and they are professional because they resist. But this claim rests on a misapprehension of my argument. The key difference is that I argue that one can be a professional journalist without being at all confrontational with the state. Indeed, a journalist who has undergone advanced training, is aware of ethical requirements, holds a press card, and has a sense of public mission is by definition a professional (Wilensky 1964; Curry 1990; Tumber and Prentoulis 2005). One can therefore be communist with deep conviction in the rightness of the Party and Marxist-Leninist press theory and still develop ethical norms and a sense of public mission as a result of the "professional wave" sweeping the Chinese press. Such a journalist is not, however, likely to be confrontational toward the powerful. By contrast, an advocate journalist goes further, with an aim toward establishing (relative) independence from Party oversight and towards pushing a specific social viewpoint. Although their outspoken beliefs and willingness to delve into commentary might make them anathema in a Western newsroom, these advocate journalists reflect China's unique press history and are most congruent with local conditions. So while a general sense of journalistic professionalism is sweeping across the Chinese press, it is only those few with a commitment to advocacy who tend to be on the front lines of pushing back. A professional press, in short, is not synonymous with a resistive one.

As discussed in earlier chapters, these advocacy journalists find a key distinction between serving "the people" and serving the state, and it is this distinction that lies at the heart of the reason they push back. Prominent former editor Li Datong has been one of the most outspoken news workers in this regard, writing,

> The "spirit of the party" will always trample upon the "spirit of the people," but news itself at the most fundamental level requires [paying attention to] the "spirit of the people." We cannot turn a blind eye to the suffering, hopes, and needs of the people.
>
> (Li Datong [李大同] 2006: 1)

Many are not quite as open or explicit as Li, but this viewpoint seems to be common among China's top journalists.

Although much of the literature on Chinese nationalism has not yet differentiated between love of China and love of the CCP, many advocate journalists do make this distinction. For example, Xu Yihua (Interview HL08–4B), a reporter at a prominent paper, believes part of her journalistic role is to make China a better place, and often this means "supervising" the government. She is strongly engaged in the national project of making China better, and often this requires playing off different levels of government against each other or cultivating relationships with some government bureaus and not others. She and many of her colleagues do so in an effort to expand the political space for reporting and explicitly to help make China a better place. This effort has become easier over the years, in part because pushback from her and colleagues like her has forced the government to respect the media more than it used to. Now, she says, the relationship between the two is almost like "a dance between equals."

For news workers like Xu and Li, the state is often seen as a hindrance toward solving some of China's problems. Those advocate journalists who respect the government and ultimately think the CCP is doing a reasonably good job sometimes feel the need to point out areas of improvement, even in areas that might be sensitive for the Party/state. Many advocate journalists have thus managed to disentangle patriotism and uncritical acceptance of the CCP and, in so doing, have managed to break the Party/state's closely guarded monopoly on the right to comment on political affairs. This change represents a real, long-term shift in power relations inside China, all made possible by advocate journalists who believe it is both their right and duty to point out problems in China's development, even when those problems are the result of sensitive state policies.

Pushback's effects

Although journalists' individual acts of pushback – reporting about the corruption case of the former top party official in Shanghai, for example[33] – are based on the ephemeral events that make up the news, pushback has longer-term effects as well. Most obviously, publication of a sensitive article can at times lead to direct changes in specific Party/state policy. One of the most famous cases concerns the 2003 case of Sun Zhigang, discussed previously. When the *Southern Metropolitan News* broke the case, a national uproar ensued that ultimately led to the end of the national system for detention of migrant workers.[34] Likewise, when Henan TV reported on May 19, 2007, that hundreds of kidnapped children were being held as slaves in brick factories in Shanxi Province, the resulting national outrage prompted investigations and imprisonments of several government officials.[35]

However, these short-term policy changes, momentous though they may be, represent only part of the importance of pushback incidents. Since even before the foundation of the People's Republic in 1949, the CCP has endeavored to retain its monopoly on the right to comment publically on political acts and to ensure that the press remain in the role of a subservient "throat and tongue." Although Mao's statement that "political power grows out of the barrel of a gun" is well known, the party also emphasized the power of the barrel of the pen. Lin Biao, described officially at the time as Mao's successor, claimed, "the gun and the pen (*qiangganzi biganzi*) are the two things to rely on in making revolution" (He 2001: 305), and certainly before the reform era, the CCP made every effort to monopolize the control of both resources. Even today, structural and extralegal impediments the Party/state has imposed mean "all journalists are virtually state employees" (Lee 2005: 117). By pushing their own viewpoint, however, advocate journalists are able to slowly widen the circle of acceptable discourse and (re)assume their place as intelligentsia with the right and responsibility to comment on public affairs. Even if these journalists "play edge ball" for patriotic motives – indeed, *because* they do so – they are still able to slowly nudge sections of the party in directions it wouldn't otherwise want to be taken.

One has to look no further than the case of Zhu Wenna, a reporter who produced an investigative report critical of a local county secretary, to see that journalists have clawed out at least some privileges to comment on or criticize state actions. When the county secretary attempted to have Zhu arrested in Beijing, the press fought back with national media coverage, thundering in editorials that included lines like, "The reporter may choose temporarily to hide away from this wild arrest order. In the long run, however, journalists stand in the sunlight. Public opinion cannot lose, and public opinion will not lose" (Bandurski 2008).

Conclusion

Based on well over a century of Chinese tradition that holds journalists as intellectuals and intellectuals, in turn, as duty-bound to supervise the state, advocacy journalists slowly and carefully challenge the CCP's monopoly on political communication. While Maoism never allowed journalists to serve this role,[36] advocacy journalists – based on a professional orientation spread through formal schooling and journalists' networks – have slowly been seizing it in the reform era, pushing back when the can. Prominent news worker Li Datong explicitly argues that pushback leads to longer-term changes in the Chinese polity:

> This type of [sensitive] reporting also has another function, which is to gradually increase the sensitivity threshold of those officials who mind the media. These sorts of officials are also people, people who received a reasonably good education, and the first time they see a report that "breaks the rules" (*fan gui* 犯规) they may jump up, but the second time, or the third time. . . . If they unceasingly see reports that migrate to the edge of what is acceptable (*zai jinqu bianyuan youzou de baodao* 在禁区边缘游走的报道), their threshold for sensitivity will gradually increase. As the saying goes, if you're used to seeing something, it's no wonder it turns out that way. Under our current system, the scope of news reporting can only "push back" (*tui chulai* 推出来) one step, one article at a time.
> (Li Datong [李大同] 2006: 12, ellipsis in original)

For Li, then, the constant efforts of reporters to stay just inside the limits of the acceptable ultimately expand those very limits. Pushback, then, is ultimately proactive.

And it is this proactive, and simultaneously contained, nature that makes pushback especially interesting. Much attention has been focused on "macro-resistance" patterns – insurgency movements, terrorism groups or revolution – and on "micro-resistance" weapons of the weak. But there has been little illumination of those activities that while not themselves resistive, have clear, long-term influence on the distribution of power within an authoritarian polity. Pushback fills this lacuna. Moreover, as detailed in the next chapter, under the right circumstances those who push back become those who resist outright. In short, although neither necessary nor sufficient for later resistive acts, pushback affects both long-term, large-scale social change and shorter-term, smaller-scale acts of collective defiance.

Notes

1 Hogg (2008) sums up the story in English. The original Chinese language story has been pulled from the Chinese internet, and is no longer available (attempted access, February 17, 2009).
2 Scholarship about the rise of China's homeowners' associations and their protests is a partial exception to this trend, but although homeowners clearly have more money and influence than other groups, they do not have the ability – as journalists do – to mobilize the public square. And such groups tend to be moderate, rather than proactive in their demands (see Cai (2005)). Below, I talk more about the importance of proactive versus reactive action.
3 Because intentionality is an important part of the definition, in these cases I cannot say more than "likely" without more information about the participants.
4 At the time, anyway, according to Interview HL08–4AZ. Currently Chang Ping lives in self-imposed exile in Germany and seems to relish the role of being an outright dissident.
5 The legality of strikes is tricky under Chinese labor law, as they are neither legal nor illegal. The 1982 constitution explicitly removed the right to that existed strike in earlier versions (Weng 1982: 504). In any case, even if strikes are *de jure* legal, they are certainly not allowed in practice. I am grateful for Eli D. Friedman for this analysis (personal communication, June 24, 2009).
6 Noted media expert and activist Sun Xupei, for example, points out that Hu Jiwei, head of *People's Daily* from the late 1970s through the mid-1980s, argued that "Chinese journalists must hold fast to a new principle – while keeping Party leadership of the people our prime consideration, we should honor the people's needs as well" (Sun and Michel 2001: 1).
7 Gaventa (1980) might term this an example of what he calls the third type of power.
8 Though of course they may be sanctioned retrospectively.
9 Though arguably many of Scott's subjects have relatively high cultural capital in their own communities, they certainly do not have the national standing or high socio-economic status of nationally syndicated journalists.
10 For defining works in this vein, see McAdam, McCarthy, and Zald (1996) or Tarrow (1998).
11 This is true in part because it is difficult to know how a single story, even a juicy exposé, is affecting readership – a situation especially true in the pre-Internet era. See also Stockmann (2013) for more on how marketization might lead to more effective content control.
12 He does, however, acknowledge two sentences later that "empirical studies [have] difficulty in finding any significance to competition."

13 Stockmann (2007), Sullivan and Lowe (2010), and Stockmann (2013) are the only examples I am aware of, though all are much smaller.
14 The character count would be even larger, and in total, the text files comprise over 550mb of data.
15 This technique also means that some papers ultimately had more articles downloaded than others. This imbalance does not lead to bias concerns since articles were evaluated not on the absolute number of word "hits" to a keyword list, but on these hits as a proportion of total text size. Although a small sample would indeed have a smaller absolute number of targeted words than would a large sample drawn from the same source, the proportions will not significantly differ. Moreover, for regression analysis purposes, articles were weighted by their probability of selection.
16 Zipf (1935). For example, a dictionary aiming to capture articles related to magicians would do well to include words like "magic" or "illusion" but would get little additional benefit from adding "prestidigitation" or "legerdemain." Moreover, the advent of electronic media has greatly increased the generation of neologisms, and thus even a very large dictionary runs the risk of quickly becoming inadequate.
17 Jin and Wong (2002: 283) note that "if a dictionary were to be constructed manually, it would take months, if not years, before it could be updated. Hence it would be impossible to introduce new works in a timely fashion; yet new vocabulary appears daily . . . on the Internet."
18 The list was provided for me by Ian Johnston and Will Lowe in response to a post I made on the Content Analysis News and Discussion email listserv hosted by the University of Alabama. I am grateful for their assistance.
19 These lists were helpfully provided by Xiao Qiang, director of Berkeley's *China Digital Times* Project.
20 With the exception of the *People's Daily*, the official Party mouthpiece, and perhaps other Party outlets like *Red Flag*.
21 Yoshikoder does allow evaluation of such "sentiment" words within a five-word radius of target vocabulary terms – and thus more sophisticated analysis of tone toward individual topics – but computational requirements and time constraints meant that this facility was not used here. Even analyzing sentiment on a per article basis required hundreds of hours of computer time on a new and sophisticated computer, and therefore the use of this "concordance" function was unfortunately too difficult.
22 County-level papers, once a prominent feature of the Chinese news scene, have all but disappeared over the past decade.
23 This particular paper is sponsored by the Chinese Academy of Social Sciences.
24 If two articles are talking about the same event, their "content" will be coded similarly by the computer. If their use of emotional language differs substantially, however, this will be coded as a difference in "tone."
25 Southwestern provinces like Sichuan and Yunnan were not included, as they are not traditionally thought of as "Southern" Chinese. Shanghai is a bit of a unique case, as it is widely acknowledged among Chinese journalists as having a particularly tightly controlled media market despite its high level of commercialization.
26 Although Rawnsley (2007)'s critiques about the problems of overly state-centric media studies are legitimate, it is clearly too soon to cast the state aside entirely in analyzing the Chinese media sphere.
27 To complicate matters a bit, however, it is worth noting that all newspapers everywhere in China are read by at least a few retired or semiretired party officials who in turn report to higher authorities when they think a transgression has occurred. See He Qinglian (2004: 16–18).
28 Zaller (1992) convincingly demonstrates that when the press presents a united front, audience members tend to follow their lead. Given the evidence here, it seems clear that the Chinese press is not pushing audiences to be more confrontational with the Chinese state.

29 They left to found rival *Caixin*. The split was apparently related to an economic, not political, dispute.
30 For more on the role of perceptions and how they interact with opportunity structures, see O'Brien and Li (2006: Ch. 2) or Koopmans (2005).
31 This policy refers to investigators designating both a time and place for suspects to appear for questioning. As a result of this article, it has become slightly less sensitive to talk about this policy, something one interviewee notes as "progress" (*jinbu* 进步). At one point, there was even a website that allowed readers to track officials targeted by corruption investigations, though that website (http://digest.icxo.com/sp/shuanggui.htm, last accessed November 13, 2008) has now been converted into a far less controversial celebrity entertainment site.
32 Lu Yuegang speaking at the Protecting Investigative Reporters' Legal Consciousness (Diaocha Jizhe de Falü Baohu Yishi 调查记者的法律保护意识) forum, October 27, 2007, China Youth University for Political Science (Beijing).
33 As *Caijing* did in March 2008.
34 See Hand (2006) and especially Liebman (2005) for further details on this case and its repercussions. Overall, this is a clear example of misguided pushback that went too far and was seen as resistance; the top editor at the paper was arrested and his deputies fired soon after in a move that was widely seen as government payback for reporting this and other sensitive cases (Hassid 2008). However, the paper's editorial staff did want to push for policy change (Interview GX30–2), but certainly had no intention of infuriating state authorities enough to result in firings and imprisonment (Interviews ET07–2Z, EU30–3).
35 See www.zonaeuropa.com/20070706_1.htm for an overview.
36 With the short exception of the 1956–1957 Hundred Flowers Campaign.

References

Altick, Richard D. 1957. *The English Common Reader; A Social History of the Mass Reading Public, 1800–1900*. Chicago: University of Chicago Press.
Bagdikian, Ben H. 1992. *The Media Monopoly*. 4th ed. Boston: Beacon Press.
Baker, C. Edwin. 1994. *Advertising and a Democratic Press*. Princeton, NJ: Princeton University Press.
Bandurski, David. 2008. "'Public Opinion Will Not Lose': Chinese Media Heat up over the Attempted Arrest of a Reporter in Beijing." Accessed March 25, 2008. http://cmp.hku.hk/2008/01/08/811/.
Bandurski, David, and Martin Hala. 2010a. "Breaking through the Silence: The Untold Story of the Henan Aids Epidemic." In *Investigative Journalism in China: Eight Cases in Chinese Watchdog Journalism*, edited by David Bandurski and Martin Hala, 35–60. Hong Kong: Hong Kong University Press.
Bandurski, David, and Martin Hala. 2010b. "Undercover Reporting: Ah Wen's Nightmare." In *Investigative Journalism in China: Eight Cases in Chinese Watchdog Journalism*, edited by David Bandurski and Martin Hala, 73–93. Hong Kong: Hong Kong University Press.
Bell, David A. 1997. "Barristers, Politics and the Failure of Civil Society in Old Regime France." In *Lawyers and the Rise of Western Political Liberalism: Europe and North America from the Eighteenth to Twentieth Centuries*, edited by Terence C. Halliday and Lucien Karpik, Chapter 2. Oxford; New York: Clarendon Press; Oxford University Press.
Bianco, Lucien. 1999. "Peasant Revolts from the Pre-1949 Days to the Present." *China Perspectives* 24:56–63.
Borton, James. 2004. "Free Market Generates (Some) Media Freedom." *Asia Times Online*, July 21. www.atimes.com/atimes/China/FG21Ad01.html.

Bourdieu, Pierre. 2005 [1995]. "The Political Field, the Social Science Field, and the Journalistic Field." In *Bourdieu and the Journalistic Field*, edited by Rodney Dean Benson and Erik Neveu, 29–47. Cambridge; Malden, MA: Polity.

Brady, Anne-Marie. 2008. *Marketing Dictatorship: Propaganda and Thought Work in Contemporary China, Asia/Pacific/Perspectives*. Lanham, MD: Rowman & Littlefield.

Cai Fuchao. 2013. "Always Put Emphasis on Positive Propaganda, Consolidate and Grow Mainstream Ideology and Public Opinions – Deeply Study, Implement Guidelines of Comrade Xi Jinpings Important Speech at National Propaganda Ideology Work Conference." *People's Daily* (人民日报), Sep. 25, 7.

Cai, Yongshun. 2005. "China's Moderate Middle Class: The Case of Homeowners' Resistance." *Asian Survey* 45 (5):777–799.

Chang Ping (长平). 2008. "The Public Should Be Public, the Private Should Be Private (公开该公开的, 保密该保密的)." *Southern Weekend* (南方周末), Aug. 27. Accessed November 24, 2008. http://cmp.hku.hk/2008/08/28/1208/.

China Data Online. 2006. Accessed Apr. 30. http://141.211.142.26/eng/default.asp.

Chinese Academy of Social Sciences News Research Institute (中国社会科学院新闻与传播研究所). Various years. *China Journalism Yearbook* (中国新闻年鉴). Beijing: China Journalism Yearbook Publishers (中国新闻年鉴社).

Curry, Jane Leftwich. 1990. *Poland's Journalists: Professionalism and Politics*. Cambridge; New York: Cambridge University Press.

de Burgh, Hugo. 2003. *The Chinese Journalist: Mediating Information in the World's Most Populous Country*. London; New York: Routledge.

Duan Hongqing, Ye Doudou, and Wang Bing. 2006. "Tufa Shijian Yingdui Fa Cao'an 'Tufa Zhengyi' (Sudden Events Response Law Draft Causes Sudden Controversy)." *Caijing (Finance and Economics)*, Jun. 28.

Esarey, Ashley. 2005. "Cornering the Market: State Strategies for Controlling China's Commercial Media." *Asian Perspective* 29 (4):37–83.

Esarey, Ashley. 2006. Speak No Evil: Mass Media Control in Contemporary China. In *A Freedom House Special Report*. Freedom House. http://freedomhouse.org/template.cfm?page=70&release=329.

Esarey, Ashley. 2007. Liberalization without Freedom? An Empirical Analysis of China's Newspapers 1980–2003. Unpublished manuscript.

Gaventa, John. 1980. *Power and Powerlessness: Quiescence and Rebellion in an Appalachian Valley*. Urbana: University of Illinois Press.

Gill, Chris. 2005. "Beijing Paper's Staff Strike after Editor's Removal " *The Guardian*, Dec. 31. www.guardian.co.uk/international/story/0,3604,1675736,00.html.

Gramsci, Antonio. 1999 [1936]. *Selections from the Prison Notebooks of Antonio Gramsci*. Edited and Translated by Quintin Hoare and Geoffrey Nowell Smith. New York: International Publishers.

Hallin, Daniel C., and Paolo Mancini. 2004. *Comparing Media Systems: Three Models of Media and Politics, Communication, Society, and Politics*. Cambridge; New York: Cambridge University Press.

Hand, Keith J. 2006. "Using Law for a Righteous Purpose: The Sun Zhigang Incident and Evolving Forms of Citizen Action in the People's Republic of China." *Columbia Journal of Transnational Law* 45 (1):114–195.

Hassid, Jonathan. 2008. "China's Contentious Journalists: Reconceptualizing the Media." *Problems of Post-Communism* 55 (4):52–61.

Hassid, Jonathan. 2012. "Safety Valve or Pressure Cooker? Blogs in Chinese Political Life." *Journal of Communication* 62 (2):212–230. doi:10.1111/j.1460–2466.2012.01634.x.

Hassid, Jonathan. 2013. "Political Contention on Chinese Micro-Blogs: Motivation and Results." Paper presented at the American Political Science Association Annual Meeing, Chicago, IL, Sep. 1.

He, Henry Yuhuai. 2001. *Dictionary of the Political Thought of the People's Republic of China*. Armonk, NY: M. E. Sharpe.

He Qinglian. 2004. *Media Control in China (Zhongguo Zhengfu Ruhe Kongzhi Meiti)*. New York: Human Rights in China.

Hogg, Chris. 2008. "Locked up for Complaining in China." *BBC News (Online)*, Dec. 10, Asia/Pacific. Accessed February 17, 2009. http://news.bbc.co.uk/2/hi/asia-pacific/7775662.stm.

Hollander, Jocelyn A., and Rachel L. Einwohner. 2004. "Conceptualizing Resistance." *Sociological Forum* 19 (4):533–554.

Hu Shuli. 2005. "Why Must Chinese Press Take a Detour for Virus Info?" *Caijing*, Oct.

Hurst, William, and Kevin O'Brien. 2002. "China's Contentious Pensioners." *China Quarterly* (170):345–60.

Jin, Honglan, and Kam-Fai Wong. 2002. "A Chinese Dictionary Construction Algorithm for Information Retrieval." *ACM Transactions on Asian Language Information Processing* 1 (4):281–296.

Kelliher, Daniel Roy. 1992. *Peasant Power in China: The Era of Rural Reform, 1979–1989, Yale Agrarian Studies*. New Haven, CT: Yale University Press.

Koopmans, Ruud. 2005. "The Missing Link between Structure and Agency: Outline of an Evolutionary Approach to Social Movements." *Mobilization* 10 (1):19–33.

Lawson, Chappell H. 2002. *Building the Fourth Estate: Democratization and the Rise of a Free Press in Mexico*. Berkeley: University of California Press.

Lee, Chin-Chuan. 2005. "The Conception of Chinese Journalists: Ideological Convergence and Contestation." In *Making Journalists: Diverse Models, Global Issues*, edited by Hugo de Burgh, 107–126. London; New York: Routledge.

Li Datong (李大同). 2006. *Using News to Influence Today – the Freezing Point Chronicle (用新闻影响今天 ——《冰点》周刊纪事)*: Hong Kong Peaceful and Virtuous Age Publishing Company (香港泰德时代出版有限公司).

Li, Lianjiang, and Kevin O'Brien. 1996. "Villagers and Popular Resistance in Contemporary China." *Modern China* 22 (1):28–61.

Liebman, Benjamin L. 2005. "Watchdog or Demagogue? The Media in the Chinese Legal System." *Columbia Law Review* 105 (1):1–157.

Lorentzen, Peter L. 2014. "China's Strategic Censorship." *American Journal of Political Science* 58 (2):402–414.

Lu Yuegang (卢跃刚). 2004. An Open Letter to Zhao Yong, Secretary of the Standing Committee of the Chinese Communist Youth League (致中国共产主义青年团中央书记处常务书记赵勇的公开信). *China Youth Daily* (中国青年报). Translated and available at www.zonaeuropa.com/20040725_1.htm (accessed March 10, 2009).

Lynch, Daniel C. 1999. *After the Propaganda State: Media, Politics, and "Thought Work" in Reformed China*. Stanford, CA: Stanford University Press.

Marquand, Robert. 2005. "Chinese Media Resisting Party Control." *Christian Science Monitor*, Aug. 26, Asia Pacific. Accessed September 1, 2006. www.csmonitor.com/2005/0826/p01s04-woap.html.

McAdam, Doug, John D. McCarthy, and Mayer N. Zald. 1996. "Introduction: Opportunities, Mobilizing Structures, and Framing Processes – toward a Synthetic, Comparative Perspective on Social Movements." In *Comparative Perspectives on Social Movements:*

Political Opportunities, Mobilizing Structures, and Cultural Framings, edited by Doug McAdam, John D. McCarthy, and Mayer N. Zald, 1–20. Cambridge; New York: Cambridge University Press.

McAdam, Doug, Sidney G. Tarrow, and Charles Tilly. 2001. *Dynamics of Contention*, Cambridge Studies in Contentious Politics. Cambridge; New York: Cambridge University Press.

Meyerson, Debra E., and Maureen A. Scully. 1995. "Tempered Radicalism and the Politics of Ambivalence and Change." *Organization Science* 6 (5):585–600.

O'Brien, Kevin J. 2003. "Neither Transgressive Nor Contained: Boundary-Spanning Contention in China." *Mobilization* 8 (1):51–64.

O'Brien, Kevin J., and Lianjiang Li. 2006. *Rightful Resistance in Rural China*, Cambridge Studies in Contentious Politics. New York: Cambridge University Press.

O'Leary, Rosemary. 2006. *The Ethics of Dissent: Managing Guerrilla Government*, Public Affairs and Policy Administration Series. Washington, DC: CQ Press.

Open Constitution Initiative Legal Research Center (公盟法律研究中心). 2008. 2005–2007 China Media Freedom Survey Report (2005–2007 年中国新闻自由观察报道). Open Constitition Initiative (公盟).

Osnos, Evan. 2009. "The Forbidden Zone." *The New Yorker*, Jul. 20, 54–61.

Pei, Minxin. 1994. *From Reform to Revolution: The Demise of Communism in China and the Soviet Union*. Cambridge, MA: Harvard University Press.

Popping, Roel. 2000. *Computer-Assisted Text Analysis*, New Technologies for Social Research. London; Thousand Oaks, CA: Sage Publications.

Rawnsley, Gary D. 2007. "The Media and Democracy in China and Taiwan." *Taiwan Journal of Democracy* 3 (1):63–78.

Redl, Anke, and Rowan Simons, eds. 2008. *2008 China Media Yearbook and Directory*. Second ed. Hong Kong: CMM Intelligence (HK) Ltd.

Reporters sans Frontières. 2013. "China." Accessed January 22, 2013. http://en.rsf.org/report-china,57.html.

Scott, James C. 1989. "Everyday Forms of Resistance." In *Everyday Forms of Peasant Resistance*, edited by Forrest D. Colburn, 3–33. Armonk, NY: M.E. Sharpe.

Shoemaker, Pamela J., and Stephen D. Reese. 1991. *Mediating the Message: Theories of Influences on Mass Media Content*. New York: Longman.

Stern, Rachel E., and Jonathan Hassid. 2012. "Amplifying Silence: Uncertainty and Control Parables in Contemporary China." *Comparative Political Studies* 45 (10):1230–1254. doi:10.1177/0010414011434295.

Stockmann, Daniela. 2007. "Propaganda for Sale: The Impact of Newspaper Commercialization on News Content and Public Opinion in China." PhD dissertation, Political Science, University of Michigan.

Stockmann, Daniela. 2013. *Media Commercialization and Authoritarian Rule in China*, Communication, Society, and Politics Series. New York: Cambridge University Press.

Sullivan, Jonathan, and Will Lowe. 2010. "Chen Shui-Bian: On Independence." *China Quarterly* 203:619–638.

Sun, Xupei, and Elizabeth C. Michel. 2001. *An Orchestra of Voices: Making the Argument for Greater Speech and Press Freedom in the People's Republic of China*. Westport, CT: Praeger.

Tang, Min, and Narisong Huhe. 2014. "Alternative Framing: The Effect of the Internet on Political Support in Authoritarian China." *International Political Science Review* 35 (5):559–576. doi:10.1177/0192512113501971.

Tarrow, Sidney G. 1998. *Power in Movement: Social Movements and Contentious Politics*. 2nd ed, *Cambridge Studies in Comparative Politics*. Cambridge; New York: Cambridge University Press.

Tian, Yan, and Concetta M. Stewart. 2005. "Framing the Sars Crisis: A Computer-Assisted Text Analysis of Cnn and Bbc Online News Reports of Sars." *Asian Journal of Communication* 15 (3):289–301.

Tumber, Howard, and Marina Prentoulis. 2005. "Journalism and the Making of a Profession." In *Making Journalists: Diverse Models, Global Issues*, edited by Hugo de Burgh, 58–74. London; New York: Routledge.

Weng, Byron. 1982. "Some Key Aspects of the 1982 Draft Constitution of the People's Republic of China." *The China Quarterly* (91):492–506.

Wilensky, Harold L. 1964. "The Professionalization of Everyone?" *American Journal of Sociology* 70 (2):137–158.

Zaller, John. 1992. *The Nature and Origins of Mass Opinion*. Cambridge; New York: Cambridge University Press.

Zhao, Yuezhi. 1998. *Media, Market, and Democracy in China: Between the Party Line and the Bottom Line*. Urbana: University of Illinois Press.

Zhao, Yuezhi. 2000. "From Commercialization to Conglomeration: The Transformation of the Chinese Press within the Orbit of the Party State." *Journal of Communication* 50 (2):3–26. doi:10.1093/joc/50.2.3.

Zhou, Kate Xiao. 1996. *How the Farmers Changed China: Power of the People, Transitions – Asia and Asian America*. Boulder, CO: Westview Press.

Zipf, George Kingsley. 1935. *The Psycho-Biology of Language; An Introduction to Dynamic Philology*. Boston: Houghton Mifflin Company.

8 Beyond pushback[1]

Introduction

Previous chapters have demonstrated how and why journalists would choose to push back, but occasionally Chinese media workers enter the realm of outright resistance. When journalists ignore repeated warnings to tone down coverage,[2] go on strike,[3] or publish extremely aggressive open letters criticizing their direct bosses and the CCP,[4] they have deliberately moved beyond the boundaries of the acceptable and into the "red zone" of behavior unacceptable to China's censorship apparatus. In so doing, such journalists are leaving the relative safety of pushback and are directly – and intentionally – challenging parts of the Chinese party state. Naturally, such behavior has consequences. Most journalists who resist the state outright quickly find themselves thrown out of a job, kicked from the profession entirely, or even imprisoned.

Why would journalists brave such punishments when the odds of success are low and other, safer means of changing policy are available? Why, in other words, might reporters decide that pushback is inadequate and that more direct measures are called for? In this chapter, I point toward the importance of explicit grievances, rather than a general professional orientation, as key toward sparking outright resistance. Specifically, the evidence presented here from general interviews and two case studies suggests that grievances can inspire action when they are one) related to interference with everyday routines (what Snow et al. [1998] call "disruption of the quotidian"); 2) have a specific, visible target or targets; 3) can be easily framed as a moral rights claim to maximize external support; and 4) when actors are already engaged in pushback. When power holders engage in behavior that fits these conditions, outright resistance is more likely.

This chapter relies mainly on case studies of two events, the *Beijing News* strike in late 2005 and the open letters penned in 2004 and 2005 by *China Youth Daily* editors Lu Yuegang and Li Datong. Data about these cases come from published news stories in China and the West, more detailed accounts published in Hong Kong and elsewhere, and interviews with many of the major participants. In particular, the account of the *China Youth Daily* letters relies on Li Datong's first-hand account from inside the paper, published as a book in Hong Kong (Li Datong [李大同] 2006). Together with more general interview data, these case studies allow an in-depth look at what happens inside progressive Chinese news organizations when many of the employees are angered. An overview of the strike and open letters follows. Supplementing these two full cases is a mini-case based on newsroom protests – and a threatened strike – that happened at *Southern Weekend* in early 2013.

Case one: the *China Youth Daily* open letters[5]

Background

Founded in 1951, *China Youth Daily* (CYD) is the official mouthpiece paper of the Communist Youth League, the CCP's equivalent for young people.[6] Since then, but especially since the reform era began, the paper has had a reputation for pushback through interesting and aggressive reporting, especially when compared to other official papers. One of the CYD's most popular sections has been the weekly *Freezing Point* (*Bingdian Zhoukan* 冰点周刊) supplement, which has published a number of sensitive articles over the years. These included the first major domestic press story on AIDS villages in Hebei province; an article on Lin Zhao, an early communist who was unfairly branded a rightist by the party and killed during the Cultural Revolution; and one that criticized China's textbooks for slanted coverage of World War II at around the same time the Chinese foreign ministry was criticizing Japan for similar behavior. Although this latter piece ultimately precipitated the Central Propaganda Department's (CPD) decision to temporarily shutter the supplement for "viciously attacking the socialist system" (Pan 2006), an internal, informal market survey in 2004 revealed that similar instances of pushback had already made the brand new *Freezing Point* the "nucleus of the paper's competitiveness" (Li Datong [李大同] 2006: 8).

This competitiveness resulted largely from the paper's culture of relative independence from the party and a tradition of internal hires for the top editorial positions. This situation changed in 1998 when, for the first time in the forty-seven-year history of the paper, Li Xueqian was made top editor despite having had no experience running a newspaper (Li Datong [李大同] 2006: 3). Indeed, the fact that the CCP moved him from the leadership ranks of the CPD into the editor-in-chief role suggests that party leaders wanted *China Youth Daily* under more direct political control. Ultimately, the appointment of Li Xueqian represented the first salvo in a fight between the CPD and the paper's editorial staff.

The fight begins

Throughout this period, CYD – and many other party papers in China – were losing circulation and money to the extent that "mainstream papers were marginalized and marginal papers had become mainstream" (Li Datong [李大同] 2006: 3). Although appointed by the CCP as an outsider, Li Xueqian moved to strengthen the financial position of the paper by announcing a joint venture with the Jade Bird Group (*Beida Qingniao Jituan* 北大青鸟集团),[7] which would allow the paper to combat declining margins and become a top national political and economic newspaper. In return for its huge 100 million RMB (US$16.5 million) investment, Jade Bird would take over the CYD's circulation, advertising and day-to-day management (Li Datong [李大同] 2006: 2). Although the paper's staff members were enthusiastic about the plan, the CCP was not and was instead worried that, rather than speaking for the Communist Youth League (and CCP), the paper would instead "speak for capital" (*wei ziben shuohua* 为资本说话) (Li Datong [李大同] 2006: 3).

To combat this potential loss of control, Secretary of the Youth League Zhao Yong gave a May 24, 2004, speech at CYD headquarters telling the reporters and staff members that they are a party organ (*jiguan bao* 机关报) responsible only to the Youth League and CCP, not the market. Using Mao-era rhetoric, he claimed that, along with the military's "gun barrel" (*qiang ganzi* 枪杆子), the paper served as part of the "pen barrel" (*bi ganzi* 笔杆子) of party support, acting as if little had changed from the paper's founding in 1951. Even more risibly from the reporters' viewpoint, Zhao then pointed to recent resignation of Indian Prime Minister Vajpayee as an example of what happens when the government fails to properly "guide public opinion" (*yulun daoxiang* 舆论导) apparently not realizing that India is a democratic country without press censorship (Li Datong [李大同] 2006: 5–6).

Far from consolidating control over *China Youth Daily*, Zhao's speech was seen as so out-of-touch that it alienated many of the news workers forced to attend. In response to what he saw as hectoring interference in the paper's internal affairs, Lu Yuegang, the vice-editor of the *Freezing Point* section, decided to privately confront Zhao by writing him an angry letter and "severely scold this little bureaucrat" (Li Datong [李大同] 2006: 6). Lu wrote his letter several weeks after the Zhao speech and posted it on CYD's internal website, though he did not himself release it publicly.

Lu Yuegang's "An Open Letter to Zhao Yong, Secretary of the Standing Committee of the Chinese Communist Youth League" (Lu Yuegang [卢跃刚] 2004) was originally written for an audience inside the paper only and, as such, does not demonstrate as much tact or civility as might be expected in a public statement. In a remarkably harsh tone, Lu not only attacks his speech but also Zhao Yong personally:

> You [Zhao Yong] said before you finished talking that you definitely wanted to have a "heart-to-heart talk" (*tan xin* 谈心) with everyone. We also want to have a heart-to-heart talk with you. But what kind of talk will this be? Do you think those of us listening to you grew up eating shit (*shi* 屎)? Do you secretly think that the intellect of your audience is so low that we cannot distinguish between a "heart-to-heart talk" and a "reprimand?" You represented the Youth League Secretariat when you demanded that the leadership ranks of the China Youth Daily "strengthen [their] studies [of Communist ideology]," but it is the Youth League Secretariat, and you especially, who need to "strengthen [your] studies" even more.
>
> (Lu Yuegang [卢跃刚] 2004)

Although intended to be more or less private, the letter was quickly leaked by colleagues inside the paper who were sympathetic to Lu's agenda. After the mentions in several international press stories, Lu himself became a bit of a cause célèbre and a poster-child for what appeared to many foreign journalists as an example of China's loosening press strictures.[8]

The party responds

Although it took a week for Youth League officials to respond, on July 15, 2004, Zhao Yong's office sent a "response and verdict" (*dingxing jielun* 定兴结论) to the paper calling the open letter a "serious political error" that touched on "sensitive topics" and was a "typical case of [bourgeois] liberalization" that has "been exploited by hostile outside powers" (*jingwai didui shili* 境外敌对势力). Ultimately, this "response and verdict" called on Lu Yuegang to "bear responsibility" for the "negative influence and consequences" that the letter supposedly produced, but did not otherwise clarify what would happen to Lu (Li Datong [李大同] 2006: 7). According to Lu's editor and friend Li Datong, the Youth League did not initially press for Lu's dismissal or any further immediate consequences for at least three reasons. First, the matter had already attracted international press attention, and League officials were worried that dismissing Lu would make the story even bigger. Second, Lu had an ally inside the League, head of the Political Bureau Wang Zhaoguo, who pressed for a weaker punishment for Lu in a memo to others inside the League. And third, Lu had too many other allies inside the paper and out, and the CCP and Youth League were apparently worried that his removal would touch off further embarrassing difficulties in maintaining press control (Interview ET09–2A). In addition to shedding light on the empirics of this case, these reasons also have theoretical interest as well, demonstrating both the sensitivity of Chinese power holders to international press coverage and the importance of having elite allies.[9]

As a true advocate journalist, however, Lu was not satisfied with simply escaping further punishment. Indeed, the "response and verdict" handed down by Zhao Yong and the Youth League secretariat infuriated him further, in part because Lu (by his own reckoning) had not violated any law or CCP regulation. And so, "boiling with rage" (*nubuke'e* 怒不可遏), Lu drafted a further 11,000-character response to the League's "response and verdict," delivered it personally to League officials, and gave copies to friends at the paper (Li Datong [李大同] 2006: 9). Lu did offer a note of conciliation, however, promising that if the League did not further retaliate, he would neither give further interviews to the foreign press nor defend his original open letter. At the same time, however, Lu told his friends that if any "accident" (*buce* 不测) were to befall him, his friends were to publicize his second letter. There was no further response from the League or CCP for six weeks, and the matter seemed at an end.

The battle is joined

The Youth League Secretariat, however, was biding its time. Rather than strike at Lu individually, a response that might cause the matter to escalate further, the

League decided to simultaneously take on the paper's entire editorial staff by coming up with a policy that would affect them all. And so, on September 1, 2004, the internal website of the paper posted a new policy requiring that all editors have their names removed from the paper, making editorial contributions anonymous. No reason for the policy was offered. Although this tactic would serve to slowly reduce the profile – and thus the safety – of rebellious editors like Lu, it backfired as a low-publicity way to retaliate.

Rather than ensuring a quiet and eventual removal of Lu and his supporters, this move immediately collectivized the dispute. At a stroke, the CYD's entire editorial staff was dragged into the dispute as the paper attempted to take away the "right," given years earlier, of having their contributions acknowledged. As such, the League was attempting to change the day-to-day work habits of the paper's editorial staff in what amounted to a "disruption of the quotidian." Previous scholarship has indicated that such a disruption is likely to cause collective action and unrest (Snow et al. 1998; Chen 2000).

Unrest ensued. In addition to numerous comments on the paper's internal website questioning the reason for this policy change, the proposal also rallied many of the editors around the points expressed in Lu's original letter. In other words, far from isolating Lu, the League's new policy had encouraged the other editors to offer support to his original incendiary claims and rhetoric. Li Datong writes that Lu "was not acting for himself, but for *China Youth Daily* and the rights of the whole Chinese news community. Now the retaliation on him became a retaliation on our whole group, and we had no choice but to fight off this frontal assault" (Li Datong [李大同] 2006: 9).

One of the most interesting challenges to this policy came from Lu's boss, Li Datong, who posted a response on the paper's internal website entitled "Isn't the Right to Sign One's Name Fundamental to Those Working in the News Industry?" (*Shumingquan Shibushi Chuanmei Congyerenyuan de Yixiang Jiben Quanli?* 署名权是不是传媒从业人员的一向基本权利?). This posting relies on seven principal arguments: 1) a claim that not publicly naming editors is not in the government's interest because otherwise it will be more difficult to figure out who is responsible for political and other mistakes; 2) reporters' professional ethics and procedures create the right to be named; 3) the current system is the only way for editors to get recognition and fame; 4) this right has existed since the mid-'80s, and other government-run press outlets like China Central TV (CCTV) identify their editors; 5) getting rid of the naming system doesn't make economic sense, since famous reporters and editors are the paper's major resource; 6) a *reductio ad absurdum* argument – if Lu Yuegang were a reporter, would the state now be abolishing this right for all reporters as well?; 7) Li raises the question about whether the Youth League even has the right to eliminate the editor naming system, and if so, under what authority and according to what reasons? Although Li presents this multipronged challenge to the new policy, he is careful not to question press control in general or to attack Zhao Yong personally. And some of these arguments are more theoretically interesting than others. In the analysis section of this chapter, below, I will concentrate on numbers two, three, and seven.

After other editors posted their own letters of support for Li and Lu, the paper's editor, Li Xueqian, withdrew the policy. The editors had won. By banding together, they had, not only beaten back a challenge to their authority, but also saved one of their colleagues from further retaliation. Li Datong writes that he had never heard of a victory like this inside this or any paper, and it prepared him for the possibility of future changes and victories as well. Social science literature suggests that when subordinates collectively win against power holders, they are emboldened by the victory and more likely to attempt such action again (McAdam 1989). The change in consciousness this first victory produced meant that the editors were beginning to discover their strength, something that made future confrontation more likely, not less.

Round two

The leadership of the Youth League was apparently – and understandably – quite unhappy with this outcome, ordering the replacement of editor-in-chief Li Xueqian shortly thereafter. In his place, the League and party-appointed Li Erliang (no relation), someone widely seen as more closely representing the interests of the CCP and Youth League (Li Datong [李大同] 2006). And the new editor Li acted quickly, proposing a policy in mid-2005 that would tie employees' compensation to how favorably senior officials viewed their articles. This policy would determine bonus payments to reporters and editors based mainly on whether their articles were praised or criticized by higher officials. For example, if an article appeared as one of the top three most popular in each month's readers' survey, it received 50 points, but if it was praised by higher Party/state officials it would receive from 80 to 300 points and lose as much if criticized (Li Datong [李大同] 2005). Because bonus payments are often the bulk of reporters and editors' salaries (Esarey 2005), this proposal would for the first time tie news workers' pay directly to the official reception their stories received. In short, this was a bold and transparent attempt to control the writers and editors at CYD through their pocketbooks.

Unsurprisingly, this plan did not sit well with CYD news workers. Li Datong, again spoiling for a fight, posted a long and scathing letter on the paper's internal website claiming that the plan would "enslave and emasculate and vulgarize the *China Youth Daily,*" though Li was "not so naïve as to think that this is a product of [the editor's] personal will. It goes without saying that [the editor] is an executor" (Li Datong [李大同] 2005). Although Li wrote the letter alone, it was quickly leaked to others in a form of collective action. "'We had to move quickly, before they [the CPD] started blocking it,' recalled one senior editor" who was among those responsible for publicizing the letter (Pan 2006).

Echoing the similar Lu Yuegang letter of a year earlier, the uproar at the paper and online ultimately doomed the "points for pay" plan. Despite the harshness of their comments, however, neither editor was thrown in jail or removed from his job. Li Datong and Lu Yuegang's own prominence and the paper's high profile were important reasons that the CCP moved slowly and deliberately in chastising the two men. Initially the two were not disciplined because of a threat by other journalists to strike if the CPD did so, thus turning this protest into collective action, albeit briefly (Interview ET09–2A).[10] The two journalists' aggressive behavior did not end there, however. When *Freezing Point*, the section Li edited, published an article by a controversial historian challenging the official interpretation of the Chinese Civil War, the CPD decided it was finally time to strike back. In February 2006, party officials demoted both Li and Lu to a backroom "research" section of the paper and temporarily shuttered *Freezing Point*. When it relaunched five weeks later, it did so without either Li or Lu, its crusading editors (Spencer 2006). Even with a prominent public stature and the backing of colleagues, then, journalists can only push the government so far before facing serious consequences. Nonetheless, the case of the *China Youth Daily* open letters has interesting theoretical implications that are drawn out in the analysis section of this chapter below.

Case two: the strike at the *Beijing News*

Background

The *Beijing News* was founded in 2003 as a joint venture between the staid, central government-run *Guangming Daily* and the commercially successful Southern Newspaper Group (*Nanfang Baoye Jituan* 南方报业集团), publisher of well-regarded papers like the feisty *Southern Weekend* (Interview GM08–2). On paper, the match benefitted both companies. *Guangming Daily* ("*Guangming*") has a valuable central-level administrative rank but as China's poorest major publisher is chronically short of cash (Interview HH20–2), and the Southern Newspaper Group ("Southern") has plenty of money but China's newspaper administration rules make it difficult for it to obtain a publication number[11] or expand outside of its base in Guangdong province (Interview GX31–2). *Guangming* thus gained a potentially lucrative source of revenue, and Southern, a high-profile presence in Beijing. Although Southern initially contributed most of the staff and investment, *Guangming* received 51% of the new paper's shares, giving it ultimate voting control (Interview GX31–2).

Southern staff initially dominated the day-to-day running of the paper (Interview GX31–2) and quickly turned the *Beijing News* into one of the most influential papers in Beijing (Brady 2008: 75). Coming from the generally more open and aggressive Guangdong newspaper market, the Southern editors and staff ran the *Beijing News* very differently from the way *Guangming* was run. At the paper's helm was Yang Bin, a former Southern employee who encouraged a number of sensitive and controversial stories. These included a report on official corruption in early 2005 (Interview GX31–2), a story on demonstrations in Hebei province by landless farmers, and a piece on pollution in Northeast China's Songhua River (Reporters sans Frontières 2006). Although these stories sold papers and at times even influenced national policy, they did not sit well with either CPD officials or *Guangming* executives, who were used to a much more politically pliant newsgathering operation. Ultimately, the different risk tolerance and work styles of the Southern and *Guangming* staff created chronic tension, on at least one occasion leading to a fistfight between rival reporters in the newsroom itself (Interview GX31–2). In short, although the paper was beginning to be commercially successful, this success masked deep structural problems within the company.

An editor goes too far

Throughout Yang Bin's tenure as editor-in-chief, *Guangming* and CPD officials grew increasingly dissatisfied with the *Beijing News*' aggressive coverage, and over time, it became clear that they would be unable to control Yang (Interview GM08–2). The final straw was when Yang allowed reporting on two corruption cases, including a story by veteran reporter Luo Changping that highlighted problems with the CCP's "double designation" (*shuanggui* 双规) policy of detention for suspected corrupt party members in Hebei province.[12] This piece followed the case of an official under investigation who was beaten to death by authorities while undergoing "double designation" questioning. According to a former employee at the paper, Yang Bin knew the story was sensitive but ran it anyway because he and Luo thought there was enough political space for such a story. Because the policy was already under debate by the CCP, Yang and his subordinates thought this "was an opportunity too good to miss" (Interview GM08–2). Furthermore, the reporter and editors involved protected themselves by just reporting the facts and avoiding commentary. And the article has had a real policy impact, making public discussion of the "double designation" policy less sensitive, an effect one interviewee notes is "progress" (*jinbu* 进步) (Interview GM08–2). Indeed, at one point there was even a "double designation" website that allowed readers to track officials targeted by corruption investigations.[13]

The strike

In spite of – or perhaps because of – this policy success, power holders were not amused, and in late December 2005, they acted. Soon after the article on the "double designation" policy appeared, the CPD and *Guangming* ordered Yang Bin and several of his deputy editors, all originally from Southern, to be removed and replaced by *Guangming* employees (Soong 2005). The removal of editorial staff is fairly common at Chinese papers, which normally carry on business as usual after such an event. However, what happened next at the *Beijing News* was unprecedented: "Reporters stopped filing articles . . . after Mr. Yang was moved aside, employees told Associated Press. Some reports suggested that up to a quarter of the paper's 400 editorial staff walked out" (Gill 2005). One unnamed reporter quoted in the foreign media talked about the first moments after the dismissals:

> The announcement of [deputy editor] Sun Xuedong's dismissal caused a great deal of turmoil among the staff. Seven of my colleagues spontaneously

downed tools in protest and left the office. Others meanwhile thought it was the end of the newspaper and tried to rescue copies. Sun asked all the journalists to go back to work at once. One of the strikers replied: "It's out of the question. That would be like being a traitor."

(Reporters sans Frontières 2006)

News workers at the paper tell a dramatic tale in which over a hundred people, mostly staff originally from Southern, hugged each other and cried in the newsroom before meeting to discuss the events (Interview HB24–2). Ultimately, they decided to go on strike to protest the decision, an action that is not legal under Chinese labor law. Worried that if CPD officials got wind of the planned strike they would try to stop it in advance, or that some of the participants would back out before it began, the meeting participants decided to lock themselves inside a karaoke parlor and prevent each other from leaving (Interview HB24–2). Ultimately, about 70% of the editorial staff struck (despite the newspaper report above claiming only 25%), divided into 50% who were die-hard Yang Bin supporters and 20% who could have gone either way but were persuaded – or forced – to go along (Interview GM08–2).

Perhaps because of the secrecy measures the participants implemented, the strike apparently took the CPD by surprise, but foreign media had thorough coverage, including interviews with several of the participants. Foreign and Chinese journalists found out about the strike either through a posting on influential blogger Michael Anti's website or through their own personal networks (Interview GM08–2). Many of the reporters who went on strike are advocacy journalists, an orientation that has given them experience with pushing the boundaries of the acceptable and one that likely makes them more willing to directly challenge the state. For example one *Beijing News* journalist said to an Associated Press reporter about Yang Bin, "He asked us to be responsible, accurate, and true. He is a model for me, and a man with high standards. I would hope that someday I could be like him." One reporter went further:

> We were happy with our paper and the idea we had. But now the editor is leaving and the idea will leave with him. I am very sad," said a journalist who spoke with foreign reporters despite the presence of security officials and a warning that she could lose her job.
>
> (Marquand 2006)

Even some *Beijing News* journalists not on strike gave sympathetic support to the strikers. For example, a picture widely interpreted as showing support for the strikers appeared in the paper on the strike's second day. The picture, apparently taken from the newspaper offices, shows a flock of birds with poetic caption reading "the lead bird guides its flock through the upper air, and although the sky is neither clear nor sunny, the birds still fly toward the distant objective they carry in their hearts" (Kang Yafeng [康亚风] 2005). Such coverage strongly implies the presence of advocate professionals willing to challenge state actors on an issue they feel strongly about.

Although the strike only lasted two days, both sides agreed to a face-saving measure whereby Yang Bin was still removed from his post but the deputy editors retained their jobs and the *Guangming Daily* received less control than originally announced. The strikers had thus obtained a partial victory, an impressive result under China's draconian media control apparatus. The strikers' victory, however, proved temporary. Rather than attempting to remove the strikers *en masse*, the CPD and *Guangming* simply slowly replaced them over time with *Guangming* officials, who dominate the day-to-day affairs of the paper (Interview GX31–2). The result was (for a time) a more supine product that lost much of its previous influence and reputation as a crusading newspaper (Interview HB24–2), and ironically was not a large source of revenue for cash-poor *Guangming* (Interview HH20–2). Nonetheless, the incident so embarrassed propaganda officials, and the paper proved so hard to control, that both the Southern Group and *Guangming* were forced to sell, and the paper was taken over directly by the Beijing Propaganda Department in late 2011 (Interview ML2–2).

Despite its ultimately disappointing outcome, the strike was a watershed for many of the advocate professional participants, who have since met at the same karaoke bar every year to reminisce and relive the dramatic events (Interview HB24–2). And finally, the walkout of senior staff indicates a strong level of commitment to their editor and their journalistic ideals. It is certainly no accident that by all accounts the paper was full of advocate professionals or that many of them chose to go on strike when their grievances reached fever pitch. As one anonymous *Beijing News* journalist wrote after the strike,

> We are not against society. . . . We only want to say and do right on each and every concrete issue. To change things one bit at a time. . . . Now that we are living in this dispiriting darkness, we realize we cannot just work for that bit of salary. Ideals are where self-respect lies.
>
> (Anonymous 2006)

Supplemental case: the *Southern Weekend* strike that wasn't

Early in 2013, the Chinese news world and foreign press were rocked by newsroom protests and a threatened strike at *Southern Weekend*, a newspaper full of advocate journalists and one that has constantly tested boundaries in the past. Traditionally, *Southern Weekend* published a "New Year Address" (*xinnian tekan* 新年特刊) early each year to make a general political or social point or speak to some aspect of national affairs. Unlike most censorship in China, the address is always approved in advance by top paper officials and members of the Guangdong provincial Propaganda Department. Consequently, the address is carefully written and rewritten by some of the paper's most senior reporters and editors, and it goes through multiple rounds of checks before imprimatur is granted. Although burdensome, this process was at least consistent and had become an annual tradition.

The 2013 address initially looked like it was following the same process. After Xi Jinping, China's incoming president, announced that the Party/state would be emphasizing a new policy of shared prosperity known as the "Chinese Dream" (*Zhongguo Meng* 中国梦), it was natural for the paper's staff to pen their New Year editorial on some of the goals and challenges of this new approach.[14] In particular, the Address was to be called "The Chinese Dream, a Dream of Constitutional Government" (*Zhongguo Meng, Xianzheng Meng* 中国梦, 宪政梦), which would have (carefully) placed the paper in the middle of an ongoing sensitive political discussion on the appropriateness of constitutionalism in China (BBC News 2013b). Their initial approach was to write a carefully worded editorial supporting the new "China Dream" policy, but noting uncontroversially that "achieving the dream will be difficult." In due course the editorial was approved, and the reporters and editors involved all left on their annual holiday leave (Interview MH26–2).

The address that eventually was published on January 3, 2013, however, had little resemblance to the one that staff had written. Indeed, while the responsible reporters and editors were out of the office, the Guangdong Propaganda Department stepped in and rewrote it wholesale, toning down its message and introducing numerous embarrassing mistakes. Crucially, the censorship officials did not change the supposed authorship of the address, leaving the "writers" angry and embarrassed to be associated with what they saw as an inferior product. This sort of tinkering had happened before, with one journalist earlier astonished to see his name attached to a published article that was 75% different from the one he had penned (Interview MH26–2). Although not a common practice, this type of censorship was a consistent sticking point for many in the newsroom, who were then often made even more frustrated by reader responses accusing them of official "ass kissing" (*pai mapi* 拍马屁) (Interview MH26–2).

The editorial staff, furious at this latest attack on their autonomy, released an official statement online condemning the changes and demanding both an official investigation into the violation of their journalistic professional rights and the restoration of deleted staff microblog accounts (BBC News 2013b). After this statement, many journalists and intellectuals from China and outside the country demonstrated their support for *Southern Weekend* online, with a few going so far as to demand the resignation of Guangdong propaganda chief Tuo Zhen (BBC News 2013b). At the same time, sister paper *Southern Metropolis Daily*[15] and several others published statements of support, as did journalism students at Nanjing University, Sun Yat-sen University, Beijing Foreign Studies University, and elsewhere.[16]

In the following days, support built inside and outside the paper for more dramatic action, in part spurred by the CCP's infuriating official response that "[s]o-called censorship does not exist in China, and the Party and government protect the freedom of the press according to the law."[17] This popular anger at the Party/state culminated in a gathering of protesters outside the *Southern Weekend* newsrooms in Guangzhou and Beijing – protests that received a great deal of international press attention (e.g., Johnson 2013). One famous Chinese writer and blogger, for example, brought a bottle of expensive Maotai liquor to the newsroom to show his support (Interview ML2–2). The incident even briefly turned into collective action for journalists around the country, as several papers resisted a call to publish an editorial condemning the *Southern Weekend* staff for their intransigence (BBC News 2013a).

At the same time, many inside the paper, especially among the younger staff, were urging that reporters go on strike to protest the issue (Interview ML2–2). Older editorial staff, however, urged caution; this cautious approach, coupled with a lack of internal organization, caused the strike demands to quickly die down. Interestingly, the paper's internal censor – an elderly former propaganda official who helped liaise between the paper and the Propaganda Department – was one of the most vocal calling for the strike, and in the event's aftermath, he was removed from his position at the paper. As other studies have found, it seems a united group under a determined leadership is helpful for pushing resistance forward (Zoller and Fairhurst 2007; Li and O'Brien 2008). As in the other examples, the fact that reporters were engaging in pushback long before the New Year's Address incident was critical in spurring them forward in this case. The internal culture of the paper and the commitment of many reporters there to "play edge ball" meant that when grievances reached a fever pitch, many were ready to throw caution to the winds and engage in contentious action. Although the strike did not, in fact, happen, the incident showcases the clear links between prior pushback and future resistance.

The theoretical payoff

But why does this matter theoretically? Does the fact that some individual Chinese journalists or papers get rambunctious from time to time merely add another wrinkle to previous theories of contentious politics? Other than recognizing that media groups do not always act at the behest of the state, what can this behavior tell us about contentious politics more generally? How is this all related to pushback? In answering these questions, China's contentious journalists can help shed fresh light on venerable theories and provide some new testable propositions at the same time.

First, this behavior suggests that the recent effort by the most prominent theorists of political process theory (PPT) to revise its micro-foundations by moving away from overly structural arguments is laudable. In its earlier incarnations, PPT relied on "the conviction that most political movements and revolutions are set in motion by social changes that render the established political order more vulnerable or receptive to challenge" or, in other words, changes in the political opportunity structure (POS) (McAdam, McCarthy, and Zald 1996: 8). Elements of the POS have included "1) The relative openness or closure of the institutionalized political system; 2) The stability of that broad set of elite arguments that typically undergird a polity; 3) The presence of elite allies, and 4) The state's capacity and propensity for repression" (McAdam, McCarthy, and Zald 1996: 10).

Realizing that purely structural approaches to PPT can approach tautology – evidence for changes in the POS are usually determined *post hoc* after an effective social movement – these scholars have moved toward recognizing the importance of perceptions that mediate actors' interactions with the POS. "Rather than look[ing] upon 'opportunities and threats' as objective structural factors," McAdam, Tarrow, and Tilly increasingly "see them as subject to attribution" (McAdam, Tarrow, and Tilly 2001: 43). Indeed, this chapter's emphasis on individual acts of journalistic resistance itself falls into the "analysis of smaller-scale causal mechanisms" that these scholars have turned toward (McAdam, Tarrow, and Tilly 2001: 24). And although grievances are not specifically mentioned, these PPT scholars have hinted at their importance when they recognize the need to both "explain how people who at a given point in time are not making contentious claims start doing so" and indeed "to explain what sorts of actors engage in contention" (McAdam, Tarrow, and Tilly 2001: 34).

The cases presented here do indeed support the efforts of PPT scholars to move away from a purely structuralist approach.[18] The strike of most of the *Beijing News* senior staff, for example, does not fit neatly into the original, unmodified POS explanation. On none of McAdam, et al.'s (1996) original four factors were any objective changes evident that might encourage the emergence of a new, brief social movement. For example, even by strict Chinese standards, the political system at the time of the strike was not particularly open – especially for journalists. In addition, building on McAdam, Tarrow, and Tilly's (2001) enhanced allowance for the role of perception, it is clear that, at least in the case of the letter writers Li and Lu, the principal actors involved did not perceive an "objective" opening in the opportunity structure and seem to have been motivated more by exasperation than any sense of an enhanced possibility of success (Interview ET09–2A). These news workers' perceptions, and the ultimate state reaction against them, make clear that this was not a case of pushback but of outright resistance. And during cases of outright resistance, journalists generally throw caution to the winds and aim to move beyond the boundaries of the acceptable.

It would be a stretch to claim any sort of "objective" opening at all in the Chinese media, which at the time was experiencing a well-publicized crackdown on wayward newspapers (Kristof 2005), especially those that concentrated on political reporting (Interviews ER29–0, FY01–0, and GL09–0). Indeed, seventy-nine newspapers were closed by the central government in 2005, with the CPD vowing to "severely crack down on illegal publications" (South China Morning Post Staff 2006). In other words, during the very time of both the *Beijing News* strike and open letters at *China Youth Daily*, the CPD was visibly and publicly cracking down on wayward elements of the Chinese press. Such a scenario makes it very unlikely that the participants in both events saw objective political openings.

But the current media tightening extends beyond these arguably informal measures, as Beijing has also pursued increasingly onerous legal restrictions. Regulations issued by the General Administration on Press and Publication (GAPP, now the State Administration of Press, Publication, Radio, Film, and Television [SAPPRFT])[19] in late 2005, for example, require that a newspaper's publication permit be revoked if "the newspaper publication quality fail[s] to reach the prescribed standard over a long period of time" or if it "fails to improve after being investigated and penalized" (Chang, Wan, and Qu 2006: 459). Neither the "prescribed standards" nor the "long period of time" is further specified, and the vague wording of these regulations is no accident. Again, these regulations came in effect around the time of the open letters and *before* the *Beijing News* strike. In short, these examples demonstrate that, even in such inauspicious circumstances, resistance is possible; this conclusion reinforces the importance of PPT scholars' recent moves away from a purely structural explanation of contention and protest.

Towards a synthetic theory of grievances?

The key questions, then, are what motivated journalists to engage in contentious, collective action despite the lack of an obvious political opening? And why did their protests take the form they did? Why not simply push back and stay (relatively) safe? For preliminary answers, the literature on grievances and repertories is helpful. The empirical evidence from these cases within the Chinese news media implies that grievances alone can often be enough to spark contentious action, though probably only when other criteria are also met. Evidence from the media and elsewhere in Chinese public life suggests that grievances can inspire action when they are 1) related to "disruption of the quotidian" (Snow et al. 1998), 2) have a clear personal target or targets, 3) potential actors can seize the moral or symbolic high ground, and 4) actors are already involved in pushback.

Kahneman and Tversky (1979) discovered decades ago that in general people are much more sensitive to potential losses than to potential gains, and this loss aversion is a key insight of what they term prospect theory. While people are indeed motivated to action by the possibility of gains, in general they are more highly motivated to avoid losing what they already have, an insight Snow et al. build upon with their theory of how social movements begin. "The kind of breakdown most likely to be associated with movement emergence," they argue, "is that which penetrates and disrupts, or threatens to disrupt, taken-for-granted, everyday routines and expectancies" (Snow et al. 1998: 2). While journalists face constant challenges from superiors and the central government, low pay and social prestige, danger from irate targets of investigative stories, and an overwhelming desire to change jobs (Wang Zhuoqiong 2005), this sort of "everyday" pressure only rarely turns into contentious social action.

Even when journalists are threatened *en masse*, as with the public media crackdown of 2005, they tend to merely grumble about it,[20] but when reporters at individual papers are threatened with a disruption of their everyday routine – as in the cases above – they are much more likely to react against power holders. In the case of Li Datong and Lu Yuegang's *China Youth Daily* open letters, both rebelled against changes in the day-to-day running of the paper. Those journalists and editors at the *Beijing News* who went on strike did so to protest the removal of their editor and the sudden, heavy-handed interference by the CPD and their *Guangming* colleagues and bosses. Snow et al. argue "it is not exploitation or deprivation per se that is unsettling to the peasant, but actual or threatened disruptions of the peasants' subsistence routines" (Snow et al. 1998: 10), and the evidence from the media suggests this analysis can be extended to "public professionals" as well (Stern and Hassid 2012).

This disruption of the quotidian is, however, necessary but not usually sufficient to produce collective action. Feng Chen, in an analysis of labor strikes at failing state-owned enterprises (SOEs), argues that the bankruptcy of an SOE was not by itself enough to induce worker ire in most cases: "The motivation [to strike] increases if they believe that their economic plight is exacerbated by managerial corruption at the workplace" (Chen 2000: 42). In other words, the workers need a visible target. And Snow et al. agree, claiming that accidents tend to encourage collective action when they "can be attributed to human negligence and or error rather than to natural forces or 'acts of God'" (Snow et al. 1998: 7). Or, as one downtrodden worker in the 1970s American South put it after he lost his job, "I had to hate somebody. Hatin' America is hard to do because you can't see it to hate it. You gotta have somethin' to look at to hate" (Terkel 1980: 201).

Evidence from the Chinese news media further supports this conclusion. Despite the fact that seventy-nine newspapers were closed in 2005, collective action by the reporters involved remains rare. In the specific incidents described above, there was always a specific target or targets that mobilized collective action. Both Li Datong and Lu Yuegang, for instance, wrote letters directly to the CCP-appointed editor-in-chief in protest of policy changes. The *Beijing News* strike is a little more general, but Southern workers had the easy, visible target of the Guangming group editors called in to replace them. One reporter quoted in the foreign press said "All day, Mr. Chao, a very conservative envoy from *Guangming Ribao*, tried to restore order among us in the name of the Chinese Communist Party. Without success" (Reporters sans Frontières 2006). Indeed, the strikers specifically targeted Guangming when "a petition denouncing Mr. Yang's dismissal and the handover of control to more conservative editors was circulated among staff" (Gill 2005). While liberal editors are replaced all the time in the Chinese press, they are not usually replaced by representatives of the very organization that ordered their replacement in the first place. Thus having a general "disruption of the quotidian" or threatened subsistence routines are necessary but not usually sufficient – there often must be a concrete and easily visible target for collective action.

Next, contentious collective action is also encouraged by the easy employment of moral symbolism to frame and legitimate the nascent movement. Hurst and O'Brien (2002) point to examples of protest without an obvious individual target, but their work highlights the importance of a moral element to inspiring collective action. In their study, pensioners, raised in the Maoist context of proletarian dictatorship and the "iron rice-bowl," believe their moral rights are violated when their pensions are not paid. The "radiant past" of the Mao years (imagined and real) and the government's own rhetoric both give them an easily employable symbolic weapon they can use to legitimate their protests.

Similarly, collective action by the media is often made in reference to a moral compass defined by the official views of the ruling CCP and international journalistic practice. In response to *China Youth Daily* editor-in-chief Li Erliang's announcement that reporter pay was to be tied to the political reception of their articles, Li Datong wrote:

> The core of these regulations is that the standards for appraising the performance of the newspapers will not be on the basis of the media role according to Marxism. It is not based upon the basic principles of the Chinese

> Communist Party. It is not based upon the spirit of President Hu Jintao about how power, rights, and sentiments should be tied to the people. It is not based upon whether the masses of readers will be satisfied. Instead, the appraisal standard will depend upon whether a small number of senior organizations or officials like it or not.
>
> (Li Datong [李大同] 2005)

Here, Mr. Li is criticizing the plan on the basis that it is opposed to Marxism and "the basic principles of the Chinese Communist Party" or, in other words, is immoral even in reference to the CCP's own standards.

Interestingly, and unlike O'Brien and Li's rightful resistance, journalists also base their claims on international press standards, not just the CCP's own rhetoric. Li Datong writes,

> The public letter was written as criticism from one individual to another, but the responsibility of an editor is to the public as a whole according to professional standards. Therefore canceling the rights of editors to have their names on articles must also be done according to reasons governed by professional standards.
>
> (Li Datong (李大同) 2006: 8)

Similarly, "The freedom of the press should be guaranteed as before. Pressure is unacceptable," one reporter in the *Beijing News* strike was quoted as saying,[21] despite the obvious fact that in practice, freedom of the press has never been "guaranteed" in China at all. Employing this type of language may indeed be merely a cynical tactic, but it is tactic not always available. While "retirees' protests in China display elements of moral economic resistance" (Hurst and O'Brien 2002: 360), reporters' moral claims are not restricted to an urban underclass and indeed seem to be a common feature of many Chinese collective action incidents, arguably related to what Tilly and Tarrow call "standing claims" (Tilly and Tarrow 2007: 82).[22]

And finally, outright contention seems more likely when actors have already been involved in pushback. It is certainly no accident that both papers have high concentrations of advocate journalists, including "authority-baiting" *Beijing News* editor Yang Bin (Gill 2005). Moreover, McAdam's work on the consequences of activism suggests that it can leave participants "attitudinally more disposed and structurally more available for subsequent activism" (McAdam 1989: 758). Although pushback is certainly far from comparable to the intense activism that characterized the subjects of McAdam's research, it does seem likely that journalists who spend their days trying to advance policy, often against authorities' interest, will be predisposed to challenge the state more directly when they feel such action warranted. One of the more common phrases I heard from these journalists was "those on top have policies, and those on the bottom have countermeasures" (*shang you zhengce, xia you duice* 上有政策,下游对策). The implication is that advocate journalists spend much of their normal working time trying to wiggle around various state policies, and this orientation almost certainly makes further activism more likely when grievances reach a breaking point.

Echoing scholarship arguing past activism makes future activism more likely, news workers who push back seem predisposed to moving toward outright resistance when sufficiently aggrieved. This conclusion is in contrast with the "conservative perspective" suggesting that "subordinates' 'ritual rebellion' and satirizing of authority constitutes a 'safety valve' for their frustrations and tensions" (Rodrigues and Collinson 1995: 743). Instead, empirical work in a Brazilian telecom company, for example, has suggested that by sensitizing subordinate classes to the possibilities of resistance, such borderline unacceptable behavior seems to make employees more rebellious (Rodrigues and Collinson 1995).

The "near strike" at *Southern Weekend* also incorporates many of the elements that spurred previous journalistic resistance. The regular routine of the *Southern Weekend* newsroom was disrupted; perfidious propaganda officials presented a clear target. The aggrieved staff used moral language and engaged in an appeal to their professional rights, and of course *Southern Weekend* journalists are among those most likely to be pushing back on a day-to-day basis. So why was there no strike? The difference between this case and the two that did actually result in outright resistance comes down to a lack of leadership and unity in the newsroom. While younger workers in this case might have been willing to lose their jobs, such a course did not appeal to older staff over what was seen to be a relatively minor affront. Instead, rather than striking, the *Southern Weekend* staff presented the Propaganda Department a formal demand for more autonomy. Although the censorship authorities initially agreed to some of the demands, once the popular pressure had passed and the newsroom agitation had died, the reforms came to nothing (Interview ML2–2). With many of their colleagues urging caution, even the most firebrand youngsters were dissuaded from crossing the line into clearly unacceptable behavior. The fact that they came so close, however, demonstrates the power of this combination of factors into spurring mass action.

Conclusion

Not only has previous scholarship on social movements in China overlooked the media's relationship with the emergence or development of such movements, this scholarship has also downplayed the extent to which journalists are sometimes contentious actors themselves. This revelation has both an empirical and theoretical payoff, not only shedding light on the phenomenon of China's contentious reporters, but also providing evidence for the renewed importance of grievances in studies of movement emergence. Results from the press and elsewhere suggest that collective action is most likely to arise when groups are faced with subsistence crises or "disruptions of the quotidian" have a specific target or targets to blame, are able to call upon a moral or symbolic claim as a legitimating factor, and are already engaged in resistive behavior.

Notes

1. Sections of this chapter are adapted from Hassid (2008).
2. As apparently happened with Chen Jieren, the former editor of *The Public Interest Times* (*Gongyi Shibao*), who was eventually fired for ignoring warnings about sensitive reporting for some time (Interview FH21–0; http://zonaeuropa.com/20060210_2.htm).
3. As with the *Beijing News* (*Xin Jing Bao*) in late 2005. See Gill (2005).
4. Something Lu Yuegang and Li Datong, both formerly of *China Youth Daily*, did. See (Li Datong [李大同] and Lu Yuegang [卢跃刚] 2006; Marquand 2005).
5. Unless otherwise noted, details about this case are taken from Li Datong [李大同] (2006). Li was the head of the paper's *Freezing Point* (*Bingdian Zhoukan* 冰点周刊) supplement and had worked at the paper for years as a journalist and editor, and much of his 2006 book is concerned with this incident. Translations are mine.
6. www.cyol.net/2001/50baoqing/gb/baoqing/2000–12/26/node_799.htm, accessed April 16, 2009.
7. This is a large corporation affiliated with and apparently spun off from China's prestigious Peking University.
8. Marquand (2005) mentions it, for example, although this article was written more than a year later. Coverage at the time was provided by prominent blogger Roland Soong at EastSouthWestNorth, with the full text of the letter available at www.zonaeuropa.com/20040725_1.htm.
9. Of course, neither of these points is new, but they do confirm the "boomerang" theory of international press coverage put forth by Keck and Sikkink (1998) and validate importance of elite allies emphasized by O'Brien and Li (2006).
10. Interview ET09–2A. However, this is not to imply that everyone at CYD agreed with Li and Lu's handling of this situation. One senior editor told me that she thought they had both gone too far and did not support their actions (Interview HB20–2).
11. Publication numbers (*kanhao*) are parceled out twice a year by the GAPP (and successor agency SAPPRFT) and are difficult to obtain. All legal publications must have one. See Redl and Simons (2008: 62).
12. This policy refers to investigators designating both a time and place for suspects to appear for questioning.
13. See http://digest.icxo.com/sp/shuanggui.htm, last accessed June 19, 2009. The site has since changed.
14. For more on the "China Dream" see www.theasanforum.org/xi-jinpings-china-dream-same-bed-different-dreams/.
15. http://epaper.oeeee.com/A/html/2013–01/05/content_1787486.htm.
16. www.cna.com.tw/News/FirstNews/201301060042–1.aspx.
17. http://hk.aboluowang.com/2013/0105/276760.html#.Unr_gJSSAjg.
18. Though naturally these cases neither represent nor are intended to represent the same sort of thoroughgoing quantitative review that characterizes most of the early PPT scholarship.
19. Chapter IV, Article 53, paragraphs (2) and (1), respectively, of the *Regulations for the Administration of Newspaper Publication* promulgated by the GAPP on September 30, 2005, as Decree No. 32.
20. One interviewee, for example, asserted at the time that the large majority of Chinese journalists "hated [*hen*]" the Hu Jintao administration (Interview ER29–0), though this is impossible to verify.
21. Yahoo! News, via Kodo News, at http://asia.news.yahoo.com/051229/kyodo/d8eq4a6g4.html, accessed March 2006, but now apparently offline.
22. These are claims that "say the actor belongs to an established category within the regime and therefore deserves the rights and respect that members of that category receive" (Tilly and Tarrow 2007: 190).

References

Anonymous. 2006. "Eastsouthwestnorth: From inside Beijing News – Part 1." [Blog]. www.zonaeuropa.com/20051230_2.htm.

BBC News. 2013a. "The CCP Forces Reprints of the 'Global Times' Editorial, but Media Resistance Beckons (Zhonggong Ling Zhuanfa Huanshi Sheping Meiti Duikang Youzhao 中共令转发环时社评 媒体对抗有招)." *BBC News*, Jan. 8. www.bbc.co.uk/zhongwen/simp/chinese_news/2013/01/130108_china_global_times.shtml.

BBC News. 2013b. "Online, *Southern Weekend* Organizes a Statement of Resistance to the 'Killed Manuscript' (Wang Chuan Nanfang Zhoumo Cai Bian Renyuan Kangyi 'Bi Gao' Shengming 网传南方周末采编人员抗议"毙稿"声明)." *BBC News*, Jan. 3. www.bbc.co.uk/zhongwen/simp/chinese_news/2013/01/130103_china_nanfang_newspaper.shtml.

Brady, Anne-Marie. 2008. *Marketing Dictatorship: Propaganda and Thought Work in Contemporary China, Asia/Pacific/Perspectives*. Lanham, MD: Rowman & Littlefield.

Chang, Jesse T. H., Isabelle I. H. Wan, and Philip Qu, eds. 2006. *Chinas Media and Entertainment Law*. Vol. 2. Hong Kong: TransAsia.

Chen, Feng. 2000. "Subsistence Crises, Managerial Corruption and Labour Protests in China." *China Journal* (44):4–63.

Esarey, Ashley. 2005. "Cornering the Market: State Strategies for Controlling China's Commercial Media." *Asian Perspective* 29 (4):37–83.

Gill, Chris. 2005. "Beijing Paper's Staff Strike after Editor's Removal." *The Guardian*, Dec. 31. www.guardian.co.uk/international/story/0,3604,1675736,00.html.

Hassid, Jonathan. 2008. "China's Contentious Journalists: Reconceptualizing the Media." *Problems of Post-Communism* 55 (4):52–61.

Hurst, William, and Kevin O'Brien. 2002. "China's Contentious Pensioners." *China Quarterly* (170):345–60.

Johnson, Ian. 2013. "Test for New Leaders as Chinese Paper Takes on Censors." *The New York Times*, Jan. 7, A4. www.nytimes.com/2013/01/07/world/asia/chinese-newspaper-challenges-the-censors.html?_r=0.

Kahneman, Daniel, and Amos Tversky. 1979. "Prospect Theory: An Analysis of Decision under Risk." *Econometrica: Journal of the Econometric Society* 47 (2):263–292.

Kang Yafeng (康亚风). 2005. "Time: Yesterday. Place: Yong'an Road Number 106 (Shijian: Zuori. Didian: Yong'an Lu 106 Hao时间: 昨日。 地点: 永安路106号)." *Beijing News* (新京报), Dec. 30. www.zonaeuropa.com/20051230_2.htm.

Keck, Margaret E., and Kathryn Sikkink. 1998. *Activists beyond Borders: Advocacy Networks in International Politics*. Ithaca, NY: Cornell University Press.

Kristof, Nicholas. 2005. "A Clampdown in China." *The New York Times*, May 17, Editorial/Op-Ed. www.nytimes.com/2005/05/17/opinion/17kristoff.html?hp.

Li Datong (李大同). 2005. A Letter to China Youth Daily's New Editor-in-Chief Li Erliang on the New Methods for Evaluation at China Youth Daily (Jiu Zhongguo Qingnian Bao Xin de Kaoping Banfa Zhi Li Erliang Zongbianji de Xin 就中国青年报新的考评办法致李而亮总编辑的信). *China Youth Daily* (中国青年报).

Li Datong (李大同). 2006. *Using News to Influence Today – The Freezing Point Chronicle (Yong Xinwen Yingxiang Jintian – Bingdian Zhoukan Jishi* 用新闻影响今天 ——《冰点》周刊纪事): Hong Kong Peaceful and Virtuous Age Publishing Company [香港泰德时代出版有限公司].

Li Datong (李大同) and Lu Yuegang (卢跃刚). 2006. "Joint Statement of Li Datong and Lu Yuegang toward the Developing State of Affairs on the Stopped Publication of Freezing Point (*Li Datong, Lu Yuegang Bingdian Tingkan Shitai Fazhan de Lianhe Shengming* 李大同、卢跃刚对《冰点》停刊事态发展的联合声明)." [Blog]. www.zonaeuropa.com/20060218_2.htm.

Li, Lianjiang, and Kevin O'Brien. 2008. "Protest Leadership in Rural China." *China Quarterly* 192:1–23.

Lu Yuegang (卢跃刚). 2004. An Open Letter to Zhao Yong, Secretary of the Standing Committee of the Chinese Communist Youth League (Zhi Zhongguo Gongchanzhuyi Qingniantuan Zhongyang Shujichu Changwu Shuji Zhao Yong de Gongkaixin 致中国共产主义青年团中央书记处常务书记赵勇的公开信). *China Youth Daily* (中国青年报).

Marquand, Robert. 2005. "Chinese Media Resisting Party Control." *Christian Science Monitor*, Aug. 26, Asia Pacific. Accessed September 1, 2006. www.csmonitor.com/2005/0826/p01s04-woap.html.

Marquand, Robert. 2006. "China Ratchets up Control on Expression." *Christian Science Monitor*, Jan. 3, World – Asia/Pacific. www.csmonitor.com/2006/0103/p06s01-woap.html.

McAdam, Doug. 1989. "The Biographical Consequences of Activism." *American Sociological Review* 54 (5):744–760.

McAdam, Doug, John D. McCarthy, and Mayer N. Zald. 1996. "Introduction: Opportunities, Mobilizing Structures, and Framing Processes – Toward a Synthetic, Comparative Perspective on Social Movements." In *Comparative Perspectives on Social Movements: Political Opportunities, Mobilizing Structures, and Cultural Framings*, edited by Doug McAdam, John D. McCarthy, and Mayer N. Zald, 1–20. Cambridge; New York: Cambridge University Press.

McAdam, Doug, Sidney G. Tarrow, and Charles Tilly. 2001. *Dynamics of Contention*, Cambridge Studies in Contentious Politics. Cambridge; New York: Cambridge University Press.

O'Brien, Kevin J., and Lianjiang Li. 2006. *Rightful Resistance in Rural China*, Cambridge Studies in Contentious Politics. New York: Cambridge University Press.

Pan, Philip P. 2006. "Leading Publication Shut Down in China: Party's Move Is Part of Wider Crackdown." *The Washington Post*, Jan. 25, A15. www.washingtonpost.com/wp-dyn/content/article/2006/01/24/AR2006012401003.html?referrer=emailarticle.

Redl, Anke, and Rowan Simons, eds. 2008. *2008 China Media Yearbook and Directory*. 2nd ed. Hong Kong: CMM Intelligence (HK) Ltd.

Reporters sans Frontières. 2006. "Restless Journalists at Beijing News Kept under Close Surveillance." Accessed June 24, 2009. www.rsf.org/Restless-journalists-at-Beijing.html.

Rodrigues, Suzana B., and David L. Collinson. 1995. "Having Fun? Humor as Resistance in Brazil." *Organization Studies* 16:739–768.

Snow, David A., Daniel M. Cress, Liam Downy, and Andrew J. Jones. 1998. "Disrupting the 'Quotidian': Reconceptualizing the Relationship between Breakdown and the Emergence of Collective Action." *Mobilization* 3 (1):1–22.

Soong, Roland. 2005. "Eastsouthwestnorth." [Blog]. www.zonaeuropa.com/200512brief.htm.

South China Morning Post Staff. 2006. "79 Newspapers Fall Victim to Cultural Crackdown." *South China Morning Post*, Jan. 19. Accessed January 29, 2006. www.asiamedia.ucla.edu/article.asp?parentid=37371.

Spencer, Richard. 2006. "Protest Editor Sent to 'Research Room.'" *The Telegraph*, Feb. 27. Accessed June 6, 2007. www.telegraph.co.uk/news/main.jhtml?xml=/news/2006/02/27/wchina27.xml&sSheet=/portal/2006/02/27/ixportal.html.

Stern, Rachel E., and Jonathan Hassid. 2012. "Amplifying Silence: Uncertainty and Control Parables in Contemporary China." *Comparative Political Studies* 45 (10):1230–1254. doi:10.1177/0010414011434295.

Terkel, Studs. 1980. "C.P. Ellis – Why I Quit the Klan." In *American Dreams: Lost and Found*, edited by Studs Terkel, 200–211. New York: Pantheon.

Tilly, Charles, and Sidney G. Tarrow. 2007. *Contentious Politics*. Boulder, CO: Paradigm Publishers.

Wang Zhuoqiong. 2005. "Four in Five Reporters Want to Change Jobs." *China Daily*, Nov. 8. www.chinadaily.com.cn/english/doc/2005-11/08/content_492251.htm.

Zoller, Heather M., and Gail T. Fairhurst. 2007. "Resistance Leadership: The Overlooked Potential in Critical Organization and Leadership Studies." *Human Relations* 60 (9):1331–1360.

9 Chinese journalism in the Internet age

This book is mainly about the newspaper industry, but the Internet is clearly moving to a position of increasing prominence in Chinese public life. By 2012 nearly half the Chinese population – 538 million people – were online, the majority through their cell phones (China Internet Network Information Center [CNNIC] 2012). Although still heavily censored, the Internet has given many Chinese unparalleled access to news, current events, and other relevant public information. Indeed, in many ways, the Internet is Mainland China's very first "public sphere," a place where netizens can (virtually) meet, discuss opinions, and even organize collectively.[1] Although the demographics of Internet users tend to skew male, highly educated, and urban,[2] never before in Chinese history have such a high percentage of the population had the ability to *publicly* comment on, critique, or satire events and people. Because the relative openness of the Internet is new for many, online activities seem to have

> made a more substantial political impact than in some democratic countries. For example, in China, nearly 80 percent of people think that by using the Internet they can better understand politics, compared with 43 percent in the United States, 31 percent in Japan and 48 percent in South Korea.
>
> (Zheng 2008: 118)

Given that Chinese have had only highly circumscribed ability in the past to engage in public political discussion,[3] it is hardly surprising that Internet access has had a transformative impact on Chinese political life. Indeed, one author argues that the Internet's relatively unrestricted space for consumption and communication has "alone ensured the loyalty of this generation to the Chinese state so far" (Jiang 2012: 47).

This is not to say that the Internet represents a Wild West where anything goes and speech is unregulated. China runs the world's most sophisticated Internet censoring apparatus, blocking sensitive domains and those that might be commercial competitors to domestic services, conducting IP filtering, and passing a host of regulations that ensure websites self-censor their content (MacKinnon 2009). This formidable system is apparently backed by up to 2 million paid monitors, who read posts in real time and flag challenging content for deletion (Agence

France-Presse 2013). Although on major breaking events the censors can be temporarily overwhelmed, this system ensures that content that could foment problems for the Party/state is quickly removed.[4] Nonetheless, there is clearly far more space for dissent online than has ever been possible in the traditional media.

Two of the major scholarly books on the Chinese Internet – Zheng (2008) and Yang (2009) – recite a litany of cases in which online public activism has encouraged the Chinese Party/state to change law or policy. Although the Sun Zhigang case, discussed in Chapter 1, is perhaps the most famous, it is by no means unique. For example, when organized crime boss Liu Yong had his execution set aside by Liaoning province's highest court, there was a "massive public response, decrying the higher court's reprieve" (Zheng 2008: 124). Intense popular pressure in 2003 encouraged the Supreme People's Court to hear its very first criminal appeal and to uphold Liu's original death sentence. In another case, student Liu Di (writing under the pseudonym "Stainless Steel Mouse" [*buxiugang laoshu* 不锈钢老鼠]), imprisoned for her online activism and held on charges of "being detrimental to state security," was freed without trial after an online and international uproar (Zheng 2008: 126).

Online activism can affect local officials too. For example, when Shaanxi farmer Zhou Zhenglong claimed in late 2007 to have a photo of the endangered South China tiger, a picture that was "allegedly authenticated by a team of experts commissioned by the local government," netizens quickly discovered the photo was copied from a traditional Chinese New Year painting (Yang 2009: 115–116). With comments like "This is such a huge lie. A big country like this cannot authenticate a photograph" and "The public demands the truth of the matter," online opinion quickly swung against local Shaanxi officials who had helped perpetrate the hoax (Yang 2009: 117). As a result of online uproar, the officials involved were fired, a rare punishment for local government. What these examples demonstrate is that the Chinese Party/state, at all levels, is much more susceptible to public pressure than many observers realize (Hassid and Brass 2015). Practically the only possible source of legal public pressure in contemporary China is Internet opinion, and we should not be surprised to learn how effective netizens (online citizens, or *wangmin* 网民) can be in shaping Chinese law or policy when organized around a hot-button issue.

Down in the trenches of the newspaper industry, the Internet's impact has been no less momentous. As in the West, news has been available online for free since the mid-to-late 1990s, but only since about 2011 have many newspapers started to see an impact on their bottom line. Compared to the United States and other Western countries, this shift started quite late; even as late as 2010, many Chinese newspapers still saw increasing print circulation, leading some to discount the Internet's financial impact. However, the delay was not a pardon but a reprieve, and in recent years daily newspapers – especially Party papers – have been hit hard financially. Follow-up interviews conducted in Guangzhou and Beijing in 2013 suggest that introduction of Sina Weibo (微博), Sina's wildly popular microblog (weibo) service in late 2009 was a key catalyst in hurting daily newspaper revenues. Magazines and weekly periodicals that provide more in-depth coverage have been less affected, perhaps because, as one editor noted, "140 characters is enough to convey who, when, and where – but not why" (Interview MH21–4).

Most journalists have belatedly realized that online media presents a competitive threat to their reporting and employers. Just as in the West, the emergence of new media has intensified the pressure on traditional journalists to produce more rapidly in the 24-hour news cycle. As traditional news outlets are attempting to establish their online presence, journalists are forced to work faster and change their work routines to compete. Highly respected business magazine *Caijing*, for example, can publish a news story in its print edition ten to fourteen days after the event – at the fastest. To compete with a frenetic news cycle, they have begun concentrating on general trend pieces and re-examining past events (including sensitive ones) to provide more in-depth coverage. A March 2013 issue, for example, ran a cover story about the 2012 downfall of Chongqing police chief Wang Lijun, one of the most sensitive stories of the previous year (Xu Qianchuan [徐潜川] 2013). Enough time had passed that the editors felt safe in implicitly criticizing the CCP for allowing the concentration of so much power in the hands of one relatively junior official. Even though Propaganda Department officials did in fact criticize the magazine, the issue went ahead as planned, and no serious negative repercussions resulted (Interview ML1–2Z). Sensitive, interesting, and relevant – but not time-sensitive – stories like this one help *Caijing* resist the pressure that a 24-hour news cycle brings to magazine readership.

Increased pressure on traditional publications is especially brutal in an era where Beijing and many local governments are pushing toward further consolidation in the publishing industry, apparently with an eye toward easing their regulatory and censorship burdens (Zhao 2008). Authorities in the north-eastern province of Liaoning, for example, started a trial in April 2010 whereby papers that fell below 3% of total circulation would be "punished," with the paper in the "last place eliminated through competition (*mowei taotai* 末位淘汰)" (Tang Xujun [唐绪军] and Zhuo Hongyong [卓宏勇] 2011: 42). Similar restrictions do not apply to the Internet media.

The different censorship pressures faced by online editions further complicate this process. Many editors of the online versions of traditional media are constantly called upon to remove or revise content, monitor readers' comments, and generally act as a proxy censor for the Party/state. This pressure on such workers is especially acute because of "the complete absence of clear-cut rules for deciding whether or not to delete an online post" (Zhang Lei 2010). Or, as one website developer put it, "The criterion of sensitivity depends on many aspects such as the political environment, the website's background, size and location, as well as the different understandings of Web masters," many of which change day-to-day (Zhang Lei 2010).

But the future for print reporters is not entirely bleak. A number of interviewees argue that the Internet has already enhanced their media operations by letting them learn about public reactions to their reports, thus helping to improve content and increase readership. In the past, it was very difficult to gauge readers' reactions to individual stories; the Internet has made doing so easy. The Internet's feedback systems – including page views, direct reader comments, and retweets – allow journalists an accurate appraisal of audience interest in their work for the first time, discouraging them from writing boring official boilerplate.

Moreover, many reporters have strong confidence that the Internet increases demand for "professionals," those who are able to process large amounts of information and accurately report on it. For example, Lin Jun (Interviewee HL9–4), an editor with *Southern Weekend*, argues that the Internet is certainly hurting newspaper advertising revenue, but in the long run, it will strengthen the position of the news media. Internet information is suspect, he argues, and there will always be a role for professional journalists to play a truth-seeking gatekeeper role, even if economic losses occur in the short term. Moreover, journalists who work for the state or CCP-sponsored papers are even less worried. As a journalist at *China Environment News* (*Zhongguo Huanjing Bao* 中国环境报), a paper run by China's Ministry of the Environment, notes, such official bodies will always need propagandizing journalists, whether online or off (Interview HH12–2).

This gatekeeper role is especially important given the profusion of rumors and fake information on the Internet and *weibo* in particular.[5] Because initial reports online are often wrong, the more diligent sort of journalist will check the veracity of online stories before publishing them. In a 2010 survey, investigative reporters list providing "verifiable information to prevent the spread of rumors" as one of their most important tasks (Shen and Zhang 2013: 379), but many ordinary journalists are not so diligent. Thanks to China's large number of lazy, overworked, or dishonest reporters (see Chapter 4), however, many stories in the traditional media simply reprint online rumors. One *Southern Weekend* editor told of a traffic accident in Guangzhou allegedly involving the son of a high official (known in Chinese as a *fu er dai* [富二代] or "rich second generation"). The driver was apparently involved in an illegal street race during which he struck and killed several pedestrians. Such accidents seem to be quite common in China and often involve high-performance (and very expensive) cars unavailable to the general population. Assuming that this case involved such a car, microblogs quickly lit up with speculation and outrage about the privileges accorded to the children of high officials, and several mainstream media outlets followed suit. Only after thorough investigation did the *Southern Weekend* reporters discover that the malefactor was driving an ordinary Hyundai and that his family's annual income was around 40,000 RMB (US$6,000), placing him solidly in the middle class. Even after this discovery, many *weibo* writers and mainstream journalists – apparently more interested in sensationalism than truth – continued to give credence to the earlier false story. In short, the gatekeeper role is real but potentially limited.

Another positive role for the Internet is that it can help open and even democratize the process of selecting "newsworthy" stories for investigation and publication. One longtime *Southern Weekend* editor estimates that before 2005, for example, 10%–20% of initial story ideas came into the newsroom by mail, a similar percentage by direct phone calls to reporters, and only 5%–10% came from the Internet (with the balance collected by reporters' personal and professional contacts).

By 2013, however, at least 70% of story ideas at the paper come from monitoring the Internet (Interview MH21–4Z). Rather than relying on the networks of experienced journalists – networks that are potentially biased toward government sources and official news announcements – editors can now select stories based on their national or regional importance or reader interest. In other words, the Internet potentially decreases the well-established newspaper bias toward reporting mainly on government happenings and discounting many nonpolitical events of social importance (Cook 2006). In China, this represents a huge shift.

The Internet also allows journalists to "spill news," a phenomenon in which those who are unable to publish sensitive stories themselves share them with colleagues at other publications (Hassid and Repnikova, forthcoming; Repnikova 2014). Given how wired the profession is, it is much easier to share juicy tidbits than it might have been in an earlier era. A stratified survey I conducted of randomly selected Chinese Sina Weibo users in August 2013 (n=705), for example, revealed that 94% of regular users also used a QQ message account, a figure that is likely to be even higher for journalists. All journalists have mobile phones, many blog, and most are highly connected to their colleagues and friends. In other words, physical distance no longer poses much of a barrier to sharing locally forbidden news. This practice of circumventing local restrictions by passing news to colleagues in other jurisdiction (known in Chinese as *yidi jiandu* [异地监督]) was officially banned in the mid-2000s, following the complaints of local authorities, but it still prevails in practice (Bandurski and Hala 2010; Liebman 2011).

Aside from revealing many new stories, some interviewees also claim that the Internet has improved state transparency, at least in limited areas. For example, transcripts of the highly publicized trial of former Chongqing Party boss Bo Xilai were posted in near real-time on *weibo*, allowing millions of netizens a peek inside China's notoriously secretive judicial system. This openness was even officially trumpeted; one CCP journal crowed that the trial "displayed China's confidence: the confidence of the rule of law; confidence of the facts; confidence of the ability to distinguish right from wrong" (Wong 2013). Whether such changes are permanent is debatable, but in countless examples, the Internet has helped journalists and the general public find information that was previously unavailable.

Although many local authorities are not thrilled about China's increasingly open governance, the central government has made increasing efforts to improve official transparency in the Internet age. In 2007, after years of local experiments, the central-level State Council approved China's Open Government Information Regulation (*zhengfu xinxi gongkai tiaoli* 政府信息公开条例), to be implemented by May 1, 2008. The regulation, designed to combat bureaucratic secrecy, in theory forces local governments to default to releasing nonsensitive information to the public instead of keeping it proprietary. Although the regulation's success has been decidedly mixed, in many locales it has resulted in a wealth of information that journalists can use for investigative reports. A major 2012 story in *The New York Times* about the lavish wealth of Premier Wen Jiabao's immediate family was based entirely on public documents, many available online a result of the regulation (Barboza 2012). And domestic journalists, lawyers, and others have taken advantage of the new openness, especially regarding environmental data (Mol, He, and Zhang 2011).

Many journalists also believe that once a potentially sensitive news item has attracted enough attention online, it becomes fair game for publication in the mainstream media. A good example followed the crash of a train on China's vaunted high-speed rail line outside the city of Wenzhou in 2011. Although the politically powerful railway ministry tried to *literally* cover up the incident by quickly burying the crashed train, immediate coverage on Sina's Weibo (微博) microblogging service made silence impossible (Wines and LaFraniere 2011). Within minutes of the crash news was spreading online, and the 10 million *weibo* posts; 90,000 Internet forum messages; and 53,000 blog posts appearing over the next five days made the crash an impossible story for the traditional media to ignore. Ultimately, one scholar estimates, such sustained public interest led the traditional media to publish nearly 18,000 stories on this single accident. (Sun Xupei [孙旭培] 2013: 1). In the pre-Internet era, such an outpouring of coverage and journalistic investigation would likely have been impossible.

The Internet should not be seen in isolation

Although powerful, dramatic examples like the aftermath of the Wenzhou train crash can obscure the fact that the Internet should not be seen in isolation from other Chinese media (Hassid 2012). Many of the most influential cases of online activism that scholars point to either had their origins in the traditional media or were "discovered" by mainstream journalists. In the Liu Yong gangster death penalty case, Zheng acknowledges that "local state media did report angry popular sentiments" that were amplified online (Zheng 2008: 124). The case of the "paper tiger," similarly, was discussed in the traditional media, most notably by *Southern Metropolis Daily* reporter Tan Renwei (Yang 2009: 116, fn. 53). Even the most celebrated cases of Chinese Internet activism, like the Sun Zhigang incident discussed in earlier chapters, often began in the traditional media. Although the Internet ultimately provided the public pressure forcing Beijing to eliminate the internal detention system, reporters from *Southern Metropolis News* broke the story initially in a boundary-pushing effort that later led to the jailing of senior editors (Hand 2006: 185). "The Internet amplified and expanded the dissemination and public discussion of the Sun Zhigang incident," one scholar writes, rather than creating the pressure from scratch (Hand 2006: 137).

The traditional media, then, helped shape nearly all of the most prominent examples of Chinese online activism. In many cases, the Internet has distributed and magnified a story that appeared earlier in print or on television. Despite an Internet penetration rate approaching 70% in Beijing by 2009, the city still has 173 print publications,[6] and nearly 40% of televisions are switched on at any one time (Sun Xupei [孙旭培] 2013: 2). Indeed, a survey of *weibo* users (n=705) I conducted in late 2013 revealed that even among this highly wired subset of the Chinese population, more than 60% still read the newspaper and more than still 70% watch TV news at least a few times a week.

And both *weibo* users and the traditional media still greatly privilege exposure topics' exposure in newspapers and on TV. Based on *Caijing* magazine's analysis of nearly 290,000 Sina Weibo posts on the forty-eight separate feeds of five major media conglomerates, Table 9.1 demonstrates just how frequently the media cite each other's stories day-to-day, with papers of the Southern group being the most prolific at reprinting others' work (especially stories from *People's Daily*). Interestingly, *People's Daily* and the Xinhua News Agency seem mostly to reprint each other's' stories, probably because such news has already been carefully vetted and represents no political risk.

Although this table does not demonstrate how often *weibo* users reprint stories from the traditional media, it is clear that newspapers and TV still greatly matter in disseminating news, especially with a combined 289,365 *weibo* items posted during 2012 by these 5 media organizations alone. To date, however, scholars have tended to look at the Internet in isolation from other media. Rather than conceiving of online opinion as *sui generis*, however, I argue that the "emerging" and "traditional" media should be seen as a complex feedback system, where developments in one often affect the other. China has over 600 million Internet users, but this still represents less than half of the country's gigantic population. Most Chinese, then, do not get their news online. When the traditional media break or amplify a story, especially if the news outlet has national reach, the information potentially reaches millions of non-Internet users. This fact alone means that scholarly concentration on the unrepresentative Internet population to the exclusion of the traditional media is missing at least half the story.

The gatekeepers

Traditional news outlets also have another important role to play for netizens – that of gatekeeper. With literally millions of potential news stories, comments, and discussions on the Internet, it is difficult for people to know what information to trust. When a traditional news outlet verifies[7] and publishes an online story, the reputation of the news outlet attaches to the story, giving much more credence to

Table 9.1 Approximate number of article reprints in mainstream media Weibo feeds

Media source using reprints	Media source being reprinted					
	Southern Group	Caijing	People's Daily	Xinhua	CCTV	Total reprints
Southern Group	500	1,400	2,100	1,750	65	5,815
Caijing	250	750	700	550	600	2,850
People's Daily	50	0	500	175	0	725
Xinhua	0	160	25	400	0	585
CCTV	10	80	80	80	100	350

Data from *Caijing* Magazine (Vol. 350, March 18, 2013), p. 91, based on analysis of 289,365 Sina Weibo posts made during 2012. These counts are estimated from the original figure.

its claims. Traditional news outlets serve as gatekeepers, providing at least a modicum of assurance that stories with their imprimatur are genuine and newsworthy. China's major Internet portal sites – Sina, Sohu, Netease, and others (collectively the *menhu* 门户) – also play this role in China, anecdotally to a much greater extent than in the United States. However, portals are legally barred from having their own newsgathering operation and must instead reprint stories that have already been published elsewhere (Interview FU27–2). In short, the newspapers often serve to verify and guarantee the authenticity of online news.

Outside of their employers, journalists also serve another gatekeeping function, directly posting stories to their blogs and trading information with each other and with other netizens. Although evidence here is limited to data from a small-scale (n=24), informal survey I conducted in 2008, interview data, and personal observations, journalists seem highly wired and have an active Internet presence. Of the fifteen respondents who answered the question, for example, eleven, or nearly three-quarters, have their own blog. This is dramatically higher than the population at large.[8] More substantively, about half post at least several times a week, most often (re)posting news reports or news commentary. Although the small size of the survey makes it difficult to draw substantive conclusions, the evidence is supplemented by interview data. One of my interviewees, for instance, became a reporter because he started reading the blogs of famous reporters while he was still in school and now has one of his own (Interview HH05–2A). Another reporter has two separate blogs, one which is open to family and friends where she posts personal information and the other a work blog where she post stories her paper does not allow her to publish because they are too sensitive (Interview GM14–2B). This latter arrangement seems particularly common among Chinese journalists, especially advocate professionals. And these reporters do use them; during China's 2008 severe winter storms, for instance, many news workers turned to the blogs of local reporters and citizens to learn about the true situation on the ground rather than relying on official reports (Interview HH05–2A). Indeed, so many Chinese news workers blog that state news agency Xinhua has in the past specifically disallowed its employees from having one (Interview HE24–2). Clearly more research should be done in this area, but preliminary evidence and impressions point to the fact that many of the online gatekeepers are current or former news workers, further strengthening the argument that the Internet should be seen as working in concert with the other media, not as a separate and unique political realm.

Conclusion

The Internet is an increasingly important part of Chinese life, and incidents exposed online often spur the authoritarian government into action. Indeed, the CCP has proven surprisingly responsive to online opinion, often resolving "incidents" quickly and ruthlessly, even compared with some democracies (Hassid and Brass 2015). What is also clear, however, is that the Internet does not work on its own but functions as a crucial part of China's media ecosystem. Often a small paper will report on a sensitive incident that would have passed unnoticed in previous decades but is now picked up by netizens. Once the incident becomes prominent online, the large traditional media outlets feel secure enough to report, creating a cycle of more online commentary and ultimately perhaps encouraging the state to act. Although the Internet serves as a crucial outlet for Chinese public opinion and allows millions of ordinary citizens their first opportunity to discuss public affairs, it does so only in conjunction with the traditional media. In sum, the Internet is a major player in the Chinese media, and it has brought systemic and irreversible changes to the Chinese political system. But the Internet has not superseded the importance of traditional media outlets – nor is it likely to anytime soon.

Notes

1 I use the term public sphere advisedly, aware of the very different context under which Habermas (1989) argues it developed in early modern Europe.
2 56% of Internet users are male, more than 50% are 30 years old or younger, and these are heavily biased to university students, according to the China Internet Network Information Center (CNNIC) (2013: 17–18).
3 Perhaps the only quasi-legal way for Chinese citizens in the past to do so has been through posting "big character posters" (*da zi bao* 大字报) on public walls, a form of speech which has played a critical role in Chinese politics at various points in the past. Their legality varies by time period, however, and although in 1978 the right to post them was enshrined in the Chinese Constitution, this right was removed in 1980.
4 King, Pan, and Roberts (2013) argue that the CCP tolerates some level of dissent online but quickly moves to silence any attempts at collective action. The evidence from China's censorship directives themselves, however, demonstrates that the state at all levels takes criticism seriously as well, and often works to have it removed (Xiao Qiang and Ashley Esarey, personal communication, April 2013).
5 Rumors, even quite implausible ones, are rampant on the Internet. In the aftermath of the 2011 Japanese tsunami and subsequent meltdowns at the Fukushima nuclear plants, thousands of panicked Chinese citizens flocked to stores to purchase iodized salt in the mistaken belief – spread online – that this salt would protect them from radiation-induced thyroid cancer. In 2008, during a research trip to Chongqing just days after the nearby Sichuan earthquake, I personally saw the impact false information can have. While I was there, rumors spread online and through SMS that another quake was imminent, leading tens of thousands of people to sleep in the streets. Earthquakes, of course, cannot be predicted in this way, and sleeping in the streets is not very likely to be safe.
6 Internet penetration numbers are likely significantly higher in subsequent years, though the number of print publications is probably down (Chinese Academy of Social Sciences News Research Institute [中国社会科学院新闻与传播研究所] 2010: 638 & 662).
7 Though given the corruption of Chinese journalists, information is sometimes published completely unverified, or plagiarized directly from websites.
8 Of the 25% of the Chinese population who accessed the Internet, only about 23.5% had a blog at the time, according to (China Internet Network Information Center [CNNIC] 2008: 40). Both figures have climbed substantially since then.

References

Agence France-Presse. 2013. "Two Million Monitoring Internet in China: State Media." *Global Post*, 5 Oct.
Bandurski, David, and Martin Hala. 2010. "The Kingdom of Lies: Unmasking the Demons of Charity." In *Investigative Journalism in China: Eight Cases in Chinese Watchdog*

Journalism, edited by David Bandurski and Martin Hala, 61–72. Hong Kong: Hong Kong University Press.
Barboza, David. 2012. "Billions in Hidden Riches for Family of Chinese Leader." *The New York Times*, Oct. 25, Global Business. www.nytimes.com/2012/10/26/business/global/family-of-wen-jiabao-holds-a-hidden-fortune-in-china.html?pagewanted=all&_r=0.
China Internet Network Information Center (CNNIC). 2008. Statistical Survey Report on the Internet Development in China (Zhongguo Hulianwangluo Fazhan Zhuangkuang Tongji Baodao 中国互联网络发展状况统计报告). CNNIC.
China Internet Network Information Center (CNNIC). 2012. Statistical Survey Report on the Internet Development in China (Zhongguo Hulianwangluo Fazhan Zhuangkuang Tongji Baodao 中国互联网络发展状况统计报告). CNNIC.
China Internet Network Information Center (CNNIC). 2013. The 31st Statistical Survey Report on the Internet Development in China (Di 31 Ci Zhongguo Hulianwangluo Fazhan Zhuangkuang Tongji Baodao 第31次中国互联网络发展状况统计报告). CNNIC.
Chinese Academy of Social Sciences News Research Institute (中国社会科学院新闻与传播研究所). 2010. *China Journalism Yearbook* (*Zhongguo Xinwen Nianjian 中国新闻年鉴*). Beijing: China Journalism Yearbook Publishers (中国新闻年鉴社).
Cook, Timothy E. 2006. "The News Media as a Political Institution: Looking Backward and Looking Forward." *Political Communication* 23 (2):159–171.
Habermas, Jürgen. 1989. *The Structural Transformation of the Public Sphere: An Inquiry into a Category of Bourgeois Society*. Cambridge, MA: MIT Press.
Hand, Keith J. 2006. "Using Law for a Righteous Purpose: The Sun Zhigang Incident and Evolving Forms of Citizen Action in the People's Republic of China." *Columbia Journal of Transnational Law* 45 (1):114–195.
Hassid, Jonathan. 2012. "Safety Valve or Pressure Cooker? Blogs in Chinese Political Life." *Journal of Communication* 62 (2):212–230. doi:10.1111/j.1460–2466.2012.01634.x.
Hassid, Jonathan, and Jennifer N. Brass. 2015. "Scandals, Media and Good Governance in China and Kenya." *Journal of Asian and African Studies* 50 (3):325–342.
Hassid, Jonathan, and Maria Repnikova. Forthcoming. "Why Chinese Print Journalists Embrace the Internet." *Journalism: Theory, Practice and Criticism*.
Jiang, Ying. 2012. *Cyber-Nationalism in China: Challenging Western Media Portrayals of Internet Censorship in China*. Adelaide: University of Adelaide Press.
King, Gary, Jennifer Pan, and Margaret Roberts. 2013. "How Censorship in China Allows Government Criticism but Silences Collective Expression." *American Political Science Review* 107 (2):326–343.
Liebman, Benjamin L. 2011. "Changing Media, Changing Courts." In *Changing Media, Changing China*, edited by Susan L. Shirk, 150–174. New York: Oxford University Press.
MacKinnon, Rebecca. 2009. "China's Censorship 2.0: How Companies Censor Bloggers." *First Monday [Online]* 15 (2).
Mol, Arthur P.J., Guizhen He, and Lei Zhang. 2011. "Information Disclosure in Environmental Risk Management: Developments in China." *Journal of Current Chinese Affairs* 40 (3):163–192.
Repnikova, Maria. 2014. "Investigative Journalists' Coping Tactics in a Restrictive Media Environment." In *Chinese Investigative Journalists' Dreams: Autonomy, Agency and Voice*, edited by Marina Svensson, Elin Saether and Zhi'an Zhang, 113–132. Lanham, MD: Lexington Books.
Shen, Fei, and Zhi'an Zhang. 2013. "Who Are the Investigative Journalists in China: Findings from a Survey in 2010." *Chinese Journal of Communication* 6 (3):374–384.

Sun Xupei (孙旭培). 2013. Getting through the 'Two Fields of Public Opinion' (打通"两个舆论场"). Hebei University. Unpublished manuscript, on file with author.

Tang Xujun (唐绪军) and Zhuo Hongyong (卓宏勇). 2011. "Keyword Two: 'Stopping Mechanism': Allowing the Resource of Publication Numbers to Start Circulating (Guanjianci Er 'Tuichu Jizhi' Rang Kanhao Ziyuan Liudong Qilai 关键词二 "退出机制": 让刊号资源流动起来)." In *Blue Book of China's Media* (传媒蓝皮书), edited by Cui Baoguo (崔保国), 42–43. Beijing: Social Sciences Academic Press (社会科学文献出版社).

Wines, Michael, and Sharon LaFraniere. 2011. "In Baring Facts of Train Crash, Blogs Erode China Censorship." *The New York Times*, Jul. 28, Asia/Pacific. www.nytimes.com/2011/07/29/world/asia/29china.html?_r=1&scp=1&sq=weibo&st=cse.

Wong, Edward. 2013. "China Debates Effect of Trial's Rare Transparency." *The New York Times*, Sep. 3, A3, Asia/Pacific.

Xu Qianchuan (徐潜川). 2013. "Wang Lijun's 'Inheritance' (Wang Lijun 'Yichan' 王立军 "遗产")." *Caijing* (财经), Mar. 18, 56–73.

Yang, Guobin. 2009. *The Power of the Internet in China: Citizen Activism Online*. New York: Columbia University Press.

Zhang Lei. 2010. "Publish and Be Deleted." *Global Times English Edition*, Feb. 25. Accessed 2/28/2010. http://tinyurl.com/y9nztvu.

Zhao, Yuezhi. 2008. *Communication in China: Political Economy, Power, and Conflict, State and Society in East Asia*. Lanham, MD: Rowman & Littlefield.

Zheng, Yongnian. 2008. *Technological Empowerment: The Internet, State, and Society in China*. Stanford, CA: Stanford University Press.

10 Conclusion

This book has aimed at surveying the landscape of activism by Chinese journalists, examining how, when, and why professional Chinese news workers decide to enter the treacherous political fray. Activism by journalists is hardly new, but it does seem to be entering a new phase of importance in the People's Republic. Although a pervasive climate of uncertainty and other structural mechanisms keep most journalists' behavior in check, a few intrepid souls – mostly advocate journalists – manage to nudge CCP policy in unexpected directions.

These journalists share a common understanding of their place in Chinese political life, one based heavily on the mores and outlook of their profession. Professions, whether public (e.g., journalism and law) or nonpublic (e.g., medicine and engineering), play an increasingly important role in the Chinese polity. Professionals do not face a smooth road to political importance, however, and must overcome institutional and behavioral roadblocks. Pervasive corruption is among the most important of these obstacles, creating public outrage and preventing professional unity. When, despite all the obstacles, professionals do push back, they aim to advance the envelope of acceptable political action from the inside, achieving maximum leverage with minimum risk. Sometimes, though, power holders push journalists too far, and when these news workers feel their livelihoods are threatened, they tend to move from the relative safety of pushback into the maelstrom of outright resistance to Chinese power holders.

In the sections below, I will recap each of these arguments in turn, situating them in the social science literature while drawing out implications for China and elsewhere. I then advance an agenda for future research, drawing out specific hypotheses that follow from my conclusions. And finally I draw out some implications for China's political, economic, and social future and look at how these lessons may be applied elsewhere as well.

Uncertainty: obstacle and opportunity

Although long a topic in international relations (Downs and Rocke 1995; Fearon 1997; Powell 1996), the study of uncertainty is still in its early stages for most comparativists. Works like Lisa Wedeen's *Ambiguities of Domination* (1999) have pointed to uncertainty as a critical element in some authoritarian governments' efforts to control their citizens. In highlighting the importance of uncertainty in controlling the Chinese media, I hope to move the study of Chinese repression beyond simply calculating the number of cracked skulls or imprisoned journalists. As in other countries,[1] the Chinese government hopes to induce *internal* control – having people control their own behavior – rather than relying on expensive and inefficient *external* control. This desire for internal control may well be universal among modern governments,[2] but too little previous work in political science has taken it seriously as an effective, cheap, and ubiquitous control mechanism.

Even if not deliberate,[3] the use of this uncertainty to control the behavior of journalists and other public professionals fits with the CCP's general pattern of policy experimentation and pragmatism. The central Party's penchant for results rather than dogmatism and China's decentralized policy implementation together mean that the country does not have one media policy but dozens or even hundreds. Because each level of administration has its own local propaganda department with varying levels of tolerance (Lee, He, and Huang 2007), and because actual monitoring of press content is often done nonsystematically by retirees or pensioners (He Qinglian 2004: 14–16), the press environment changes from place to place, region to region, and even seasonally. The dynamic and mercurial nature of this press control system makes it difficult for news workers to anticipate changes in policy and discourages most from pushing the boundaries of the acceptable.

But this system has positive effects for news workers as well. Because nearly every local press market in China is a potential laboratory for political or economic innovation, changes often spread quickly when they are seen to work. The rise of the "metro" paper – one more attuned to the cultural and political sensitivities of its urban audience than its less nimble party competitor – is a direct result of the experimentation allowed by this local laboratory culture. And in what David Bandurski from the University of Hong Kong's China Media Project has dubbed "Control 2.0," China's censorship organs seem to be shifting from reacting to breaking news toward agenda setting and proactively framing events (Bandurski 2008). Like many market innovations, this new, less invasive form of control seems to have bubbled up from below, with local propaganda departments in southern China employing "hitmen" to write stories lauding local officials rather than simply suppressing negative news (Zhang Yanlong 2008).

Finally, this regime of uncertainty means that those journalists brave enough to risk sanctions can take advantage of the shifting political space for publication to work on aggressive or sensitive pieces. Those who push back are aware of micro-variations in political timing and can seize on power holders' statements or actions as an excuse to spur publication of stories that just days earlier would have been unacceptably aggressive. Reporters at *Caijing*, for example, sat on a story about the outbreak of avian influenza in China until they felt the timing was auspicious. Immediately after the story broke, the Central Propaganda Department (CPD) restricted any further news reports on the subject, but *Caijing* escaped unscathed (Interview FY22–0B). Sometimes even the most seasoned news workers misjudge timing, but for those brave enough to attempt gaming China's shifting political winds, the regime of uncertainty can offer opportunities as well as limitations. As one journalist writes, "Very few media outlets and journalists practice investigative reporting. We prefer pushing the limits . . . and we always do it until we can push no more" (Repnikova 2014: 115, ellipsis in original).

The utility of the pushback concept

Although pushback is relatively common in China, and likely elsewhere as well, theoretical treatment of it and similar kinds of behavior is rare. Analyzing how reporters "play edge ball" is difficult given the ambiguous and ever-changing environment in which they work. More generally, scholarly treatment of similar kinds of behavior in China and elsewhere is "a highly complex task" given the necessarily "disguised and subterranean nature of many of these resistance practices" (Rodrigues and Collinson 1995: 740). The notion of pushback avoids some of these problems by recognizing the highly contingent nature of resistive activities. By focusing both on the *intent* of Chinese journalists skirting the line and on how their actions are *perceived*, I hope to avoid a "one-size-fits-all" approach to theory building.

Concentrating on news workers' intent alone is a tricky business; memories are fallible, and those caught making trouble often profess – or, indeed, believe – in their own purity of mind. Likewise, relying exclusively on the *post hoc* perceptions of pushback targets or third parties runs dangerously close to tautology. Such a definition, classifying an act as either pushback or resistance based entirely on power holders' reaction, is equally unsatisfactory. By combining the two elements, however, I hope to advance a definition that is both mindful of actions' individual context and robust enough to be applied outside a Chinese context.

In arguing for increased attention to acts that are between quiescence and resistance, I am answering Zoller and Fairhurst's call for "views of behavior that can simultaneously be reproductive and resistance," that evaluate "both overt and covert forms of resistance, including the politics of ambiguity," and that provide a "view of how emotion and reason intertwine" (Zoller and Fairhurst 2007: 1341). The concept of pushback fills this gap by concentrating on acts that are intended to change the policies or behavior of power holders without challenging the foundations of the Chinese political system. Indeed, those professionals engaging in pushback often seek to support or even strengthen the CCP's rule in China but feel that the Party/state sometimes needs a nudge in the right direction. In providing this nudge, most of these public professionals are deliberately seeking nonchallenge to the regime's power structure. Although those who push back seek to avoid challenging the regime, the long-term effects of this behavior have a potentially transformative effect on the Chinese political system, a point I will expand upon below.

Pushback and social movement theory

Despite significant differences between pushback and social movements, the dearth of literature on similarly ambiguous behavior has encouraged reliance on the social movement's literature for theoretical foundations. Definitions of social movements vary, but Burstein et al. provide a typical one: "organized, collective efforts to achieve social change that use noninstitutionalized tactics at least part of the time." By "noninstitutionalized," they mean "activities that (1) are not part of the formal political process and (2) are intended to be disruptive (whether they are legal or illegal)" (Burstein, Einwohner, and Hollander 1995: 278). Although many of the resistive actions discussed in other chapters are clearly noninstitutionalized, Chinese news workers who push back generally lack formal organization and at times have contradictory goals or strategies. Collective action, too, is rare.

Given these key differences, the increasing phenomenon of pushback by Chinese news workers is best thought of not as a social movement itself but as a potential spawning ground for future social movements. Like a nebula that makes future star formation more likely, the spread of noncommunist, and especially advocate, professional ethos is likely to increase pushback – and potentially outright resistance – throughout the Chinese media. Although conventional social movement literature has some utility in this context, it is helpful not to overstate the similarities between this literature and the Chinese case. Critically, the majority of social movement studies and much of the theorizing concerns Western, and especially American, contexts. Many of the early, influential studies were based on the American civil rights movement (Eyerman 1989: 532). But even seminal works like Tarrow (1989) and Tilly (1995), who present on contemporary Italy and early modern Great Britain, respectively, still assume an open, democratic political system generally tolerant to popular challenge.

The relatively closed, authoritarian Chinese regime complicates earlier notions of "insider" and "outsider" challenge. The existence of pushback in a nether region between "contained" and "transgressive" contention suggests that reliance on these terms is unhelpful toward advancing truly comparative – not merely Western – social science. Although pushback indeed "operates near the boundary of authorized channels," it differs from O'Brien's concept of "boundary-spanning contention" in that those pushing back generally do not employ "the rhetoric and commitments of the powerful" (O'Brien 2003: 53), relying instead on traditional standing and professional mores to justify action. The dynamics of the Chinese media and studies of other public professionals[4] suggest that a strict dichotomy between those legally allowed to engage in political activity and those banned from the political sphere serves as a blinder to other forms of liminal political action. Such a view glosses over the important realm of activists who stand outside the formal political system while still socially or culturally empowered to comment on and engage with political forces.

Why does the CCP allow pushback?

Why does the CCP risk allowing bold reporters to push back and publish sensitive stories that might embarrass various levels of Chinese officialdom? Why not simply implement a Soviet-style prepublication censorship apparatus, especially as the Chinese copied the Soviet media system wholesale in the years after 1949? There are at least four likely reasons: 1) the regime of uncertainty is cost-effective;

2) it increases the credibility of Chinese news at home and abroad; 3) allowing minimal media freedom can help the central government monitor problems in the periphery; and in a related point, 4) the relatively decentralized Chinese state has overlapping and conflicting lines of authority that allow bold reporters to work between the interstices of the system, exploiting gaps and playing power holders against one another. I will expand each of these arguments in turn.

As an alternate model to China's current system, the Soviet Union's press control apparatus relied on prepublication censorship and approval by Glavlit, the main press control organ. Interestingly, the head of Glavlit claimed that this preapproval system was a "more efficient and less 'painful' method" than was *post-hoc* censorship, which he claimed was "'essentially punitive' and 'totally inapplicable' to newspapers, television, and radio broadcasts, [and] he decidedly did not favor confiscating, destroying or altering publications that had already been typeset" (Murray 1994: 59). Where Glavlit was a huge organization, employing 70,000 censors and with "an elaborate internal structure" (Murray 1994:58), the Chinese CPD is less than .05% the size (Brady 2008: 20), more nimble, and almost certainly cheaper to operate.

Lower expenses aside, the relative sprightliness of the Chinese system also has other distinct advantages. Compared with the USSR's onerous system of prepublication censorship, the Chinese censorship apparatus allows much quicker media response to changing events. After the 2008 Sichuan earthquake, for example, the Chinese press was on the scene and reporting live very soon thereafter, and this quick response dramatically increased the Chinese media's domestic credibility, at least initially.[5] The gulf between China's disaster coverage, especially over the past few years, and the glacial response of the Soviet press to the 1986 Chernobyl nuclear accident, for example, is huge. By allowing relatively free on-the-spot reporting, the CCP ensures that the domestic media superficially resembles respected international media, potentially keeping fewer Chinese from taking the trouble to circumvent restrictions on access to foreign news while simultaneously increasing China's soft power abroad. Given that journalists in contemporary China still self-censor, the CPD has hit upon a strategy that is simultaneously more responsive and more effective than the Soviet model, especially in the era of the 24-hour news cycle.

A third reason the CPD likely allows some pushback is to help the central state monitor conditions and compliance at the local level. It is well known that local Chinese authorities often conceal negative information from superiors or subvert central directives, strong evidence that Beijing is not always aware of what happens locally (O'Brien and Li 1999). Reporters are well aware of this phenomenon, too, and the center encourages media to root out local corruption – up to a point (Interview ET02–3). Sometimes even diligent reporters have trouble investigating local conditions. One environmental journalist, for instance, has noted the tendency of officials to be "mute" (*kouya* 口哑) when he investigates local problems, even when sent by his central-level paper.

In the 1980s, media scholar Sun Xupei used the same argument to urge for greater press freedom, writing that "The existing structure of China's bureaucratic system does not provide the right to combat misguided policies. . . . Consequently, the Chinese media can do serious harm" (Sun and Michel 2001: 4). Peter Lorentzen has argued that local protests can serve as a "fire alarm" to higher-ups to alert them to local problems and that central-level authorities are unlikely to know about such events without reasonably accurate and timely media reports. Beijing, he argues, allows "incomplete censorship" to simultaneously provide this vital information while not allowing so much negative news that it might cause instability (Lorentzen 2014). Egorov, Guriev, and Sonin (2009) advance a somewhat similar argument, though their evidence from China is somewhat inaccurate. This sloppiness aside, their macro-conclusion that "resource-poor dictators" allow freer media in an effort to control lower-level bureaucrats does seem plausible in China as well.[6] This system works especially well because reporters for agencies like Xinhua often write sensitive stories for "internal reference" only. This means such stories can alert higher-level authorities to problems without the knowledge of the general public.[7]

And finally, pushback happens in China in part because the Party/state apparatus is so vast and fragmented that a total crackdown on aggressive media reporting is nearly impossible to implement. Unlike the centralized Soviet system, policy implementation in Communist China has always been relatively decentralized, even under Mao.[8] Although the state has attempted regulations making aggressive reporting more difficult – including forcing journalists to exclusively write about their own local geographic area[9] and at their paper's administrative rank or below – such restrictions are often ignored in practice with few consequences (Interview HL8–4B). The multiplicity of Party/state agencies at all levels of the bureaucratic hierarchy means that journalists can often play off different levels of administration against one another. For example, one reporter from a Guangzhou-based paper ignored the request from a provincial-level government bureau to get advance approval on a story she was running because she had backing from an even more important bureau. When her paper ran the story without further consultation, she was mildly reprimanded but otherwise unaffected, even after disobeying a direct state agency request (Interview HL8–4B). Sometimes reporters can go even further in directly taking advantage of their place in the Party/state hierarchy. One editor claimed that the Chinese press actually has more "power" (*quanli* 权利) than the American press because in a sense most Chinese reporters, as official government employees, represent the Party/state. When journalists from a paper like the *People's Daily* or even the *Southern Daily* goes to talk to someone like a "county head" (*xianzhang* 县长), they can claim with some justification to represent a higher administrative level and sometimes even tell local state officials what to do (Interview HL8–4AZ). Given the fragmented state of the administrative hierarchy and the positive benefits that Beijing gets from an imperfectly controlled press, the central state is likely to conclude that a total crackdown on reporters' pushback is both impractical and counterproductive.[10] So pushback continues.

From pushback to resistance

In the move from pushback to outright resistance, news workers travel beyond the pale of acceptable political action into a realm explicitly forbidden by the powerful. Resisting journalists have few illusions about how activities such as strikes or aggressive open letters will be received by their targets and are often resigned to punishment before beginning the offending acts. Such workers, then, are decidedly *not* taking advantage of openings in the political opportunity structure for their activism. Instead, they are goaded beyond endurance to act out their frustrations despite nearly certain punishment. While a reliance on political opportunity structures is useful in explaining the timing of pushback, in cases of outright resistance, a turn toward examining grievances is more theoretically fruitful.

The cases of the *China Youth Daily* open letters, the *Beijing News* strike, and the protests at *Southern Weekend* detailed in the Chapter 8 suggest that grievances are likely to inspire political action when potential actors' everyday lives, and especially their economic livelihood, are disrupted, when targets are clear, and when the language of a moral cause is easily deployable. Note that I am not arguing that these three conditions are either necessary or sufficient to cause resistance behavior – leadership and conscious framing clearly play a role as well[11] – but these three elements certainly seem to make resistance more likely. Although developed in a Chinese context, evidence from abroad also suggests the utility of this formulation.

For example, when Soviet officials objected to the vice-presidency – specifically required by statute – of activist journalist Stefan Bratkowski at the Moscow meeting of the International Organization of Journalists (IOJ) and invited a rival group of Polish journalists instead, it created a battle between Polish journalism and state officials. Curry notes, "This displacement was an issue worth fighting about for them even though the IOJ, as a Soviet-based organization, offered little concrete gain and no real prestige in Poland itself or in the West." They engaged in the battle, instead, because their "defiance was a reflection of their desire to play their professional roles of communication and orientation" (Curry 1990: 231). In other words, the actions of Polish and Soviet officials 1) disrupted the set routines of Polish journalism by barring the attendance of activist journalists at the conference, 2) created the easily visible targets of specific Polish and Soviet officials, and 3) allowed the deployment of moral language targeted at professional rights, and together inspired dramatic solidarity among most Polish journalists and against state power holders. This and other defiance against the state ultimately left the journalists' union "one of the few organizations explicitly attacked for 'threatening the interest of the security of the state'" (Curry 1990: 236).

Evidence also exists outside the authoritarian regimes of the last thirty years. For example, the Boston Tea Party, one of the iconic incidents of early American history (and now again in the political spotlight via the so-called Tea Party movement), also fits the pattern. In May 1773 the British government passed the Tea Act in an effort to shore up the flagging finances of the state-sponsored British East India Company, increase state revenue, and "confirm Parliament's right to tax the colonies" (Knight 2003: 132). The Tea Act directly threatened American merchants' illegal and lucrative smuggling of Dutch tea, and outraged colonists already angered by previous taxation efforts (Labaree 1964: 102). There was a highly visible target, too: Massachusetts governor Thomas Hutchinson had refused to allow untaxed tea to be returned to Britain and had written letters arguing that colonists' liberties should be further curtailed. Claiming that the British crown was infringing on their liberties, hundreds of colonists threw 90,000 pounds of tea into Boston Harbor and further inflamed both British and American public opinion (Knight 2003: 132). Especially coming after years of previous pushback, often in the form of contentious lawsuits by radical American colonists like Samuel Adams, the attack on the economic livelihood of (illegal) tea smugglers, ease in deploying moral language, and a highly visible target made the Boston Tea Party a clear case of resistance spurred by specific grievances.

The importance of the professions

Although not an element of late eighteenth-century American resistance, in contemporary China and around the world the professions – especially public professions like law and journalism – have become critical in shaping political action. Sociologist Pierre Bourdieu has written that "political subversion presupposes cognitive subversion, a conversion of the vision of the world" (Bourdieu and Thompson 1991: 127–128), and powerful professions ultimately provide this "cognitive subversion." Although I have argued that Chinese journalism is hardly monolithic, groups of news workers within the four professional orientations I describe share Peter Haas's criteria for belonging to an "epistemic community." Many advocate journalists, in particular, have "a shared belief or faith in the verity and the applicability of particular forms of knowledge or specific truths" (Haas 1992: 3). In the case of some advocates, these shared truths are relatively simple. First, they tend to believe in taking up the traditional mantle of a Chinese intellectual, a view that entitles them to critique and comment on affairs of state and to educate the public at large about "correct" policies and opinions. Many also further hold that their job is to "supervise" the Party/state, especially in terms of protecting the interests of "the people" in general or vulnerable social groups (*ruoshi qunti* 弱势群体) in particular.

As members of an epistemic community, such advocate journalists have the potential, increasingly realized, to be a powerful force in Chinese public life. Peter Haas notes that as the world becomes increasingly complex, the state's need for information and advice increase accordingly. In general, "epistemic communities are one possible provider of this sort of information and advice" (Haas 1992: 4), a trend further strengthened by the fact that the very nature of the news profession is to gather and disseminate information and analysis. As the Chinese government looks toward the media to provide ever more information and interpretation, the role of the advocates, especially those organized in institutionalized and semiformal networks, is likely to increase proportionally. Even (or perhaps especially) under authoritarianism, the central state must turn to a professionalized media to provide it with information about the actions of local authorities. To ensure that this information is reliable, it is in Beijing's interest to encourage an accurate, professional, and politically neutral media. Given the resonance that the traditional role of Chinese intellectuals has for many contemporary journalists, the Chinese government is likely to get the first half of its wish – greater professionalization – while being unable to avoid an increasingly networked, organized, and activist media. It is ultimately the nature of the Chinese news media as an epistemic community and as a profession that makes such a fate likely.

Lawyers, like journalists, are *public* professionals, or "those whose jobs offer a platform (courts for lawyers, the media for journalists) to attract public attention and broadcast opinions" (Stern and Hassid 2012: 1232). But what about the *nonpublic* professionals? What of those doctors, engineers, accountants, and architects who are members of a well-defined profession but whose job does not entail public action? These professions have also gained prominence in recent years, especially as China has turned to technocratic solutions for many social, economic, and political problems. Indeed, although the percentage has declined in recent years, several current members of the Politburo Standing Committee, China's highest governing body, are engineers by training, and in years past, up to 100% of them were as well (Cheng 2009: 18). As the professions gain prominence and coherence in China – a process helped along by foreign exposure, training, and direct influence – even the nonpublic professions are likely to be more assertive on areas that affect them directly. In turn, this makes it likely that state-employed professionals will act according to their own professional training and code of conduct rather than in the interests of their Party/state employers.[12] In other words, increasing pushback is might come from other professions as well, though it will likely be less public and more narrowly targeted at areas of specific technical competence compared with journalists' rather broadly resistive behavior.

Corruption's corrosion

This rise of increasingly politically mobilized professions is not inevitable, however. Perhaps the greatest institutional obstacle to a professional, united, and activist news media is corruption. And the corruption of the Chinese news world is often epic. Hundreds of journalists routinely line up to receive "gag fees" (*fengkoufei* 封口费) after industrial or mining accidents, sometimes representing the most trusted names in Chinese news. Indeed, journalists from central-level radio, television, and newspapers are even more likely to be corrupt because they can take advantage of their position in the administrative hierarchy and the greater negative publicity a story by their employer would generate (Interview HH12–2). For some industrialists, even paying hundreds of reporters hundreds of dollars apiece is cheaper than making basic safety upgrades or improving worker training. Business reporters routinely play the stock market while writing stories to promote the stocks they own and make a quick profit, to the point of collectively organizing across papers to increase the positive "bump" on a stock from news stories (Interview GX30–2). Others try to blackmail companies with negative information, asking for as much as 300,000 RMB (~US$50,000) at a time (Interview GM05–2). Journalists and editors hire their friends or relatives to be reporters without any training or aptitude, further encouraging cronyist behavior (Interview HL9–4). Such corruption even extends into the media control apparatus, with some companies or powerful individuals having officials from the local propaganda department call a paper to kill a story rather than pay the journalists off. For this reason, "mine owners often get chummy with propaganda department officials, and then when a problem happens, tap this resource to unilaterally shut things down, regardless of official policy" (Interview GM08–2).

And with growing competition in the Chinese economy, some reporters think that corruption is increasing. In part, this is because there is simply more money to go around, but more importantly, as new companies are started, they often pay reporters to promote positive stories about them in an effort to get noticed (Interview ET08–2). This blurring of the lines between news media and public relations is very common. But although news workers know that such behavior is problematic and that taking bribes is wrong, "the vast majority do it anyway while aspiring for a system in which it isn't necessary" (Interview HL6–4).

Reporters' corruption – especially when they know better – therefore serves as a systemic block to further professionalization of the news media. The central state, for its part, seems to be of two minds about media corruption. On the one hand, state organs like the State Administration of Press, Publication, Radio, Film, and Television (SAPPRFT) and party-affiliated organizations like the ACJA exhort against corrupt activities and shame journalists publicly caught breaking the rules. On the other hand, however, the Party/state seems to encourage further corrupt actions because it makes the job of policing and controlling the media somewhat easier. When news workers cross a political line, charging them with corruption is an easy and believable way to ensure their silence.[13] This policy works even better if the accused journalists are actually guilty of corrupt behavior; the media's systemic corruption means that such charges are often true.

When the CPD forces an unwilling professor to offer bribes to journalists attending his press conference (Interview HH23–2), at a minimum controlling corrupt journalistic behavior is not at the top of its agenda. Moreover, some of its directives strongly imply that the CPD itself is corrupt or at least in collusion with those who are. The fact that papers are not allowed to report on corruption in their local areas too regularly is evidence of this conclusion, as is the fact that one interviewee provided me with a CPD directive banning coverage of poor mobile phone service. A sudden increase in dropped calls hardly seems like a political issue, and it is reasonable to conclude that the (state-controlled) mobile phone companies bribed or otherwise pressured CPD officials to ban coverage for purely economic reasons. In the end, the systemic corruption of Chinese media workers makes professionalization – of all types – less likely and keeps the media pliant. Writing about single-party rule in Mexico in the 1980s, Susan Eckstein argues, "The regime, in particular, thrives on corruption. For decades, such everyday defiance of the law enhanced the regime's stability; all groups had some stake in noncompliance with rational-bureaucratic rules" (Eckstein 1989: 42–43). Activists who stick to their principles and rock the boat are a threat to everyone; those at the top of the pile fear for their position and those at the bottom resent and mistrust colleagues who will not "play by the rules." A similar dynamic is at work in China.

Advocacy's short-term consequences

Whether working online or in print, all Chinese journalists face significant political, economic, organizational, and behavioral barriers to advocacy. What is surprising, then, is not that China has so few advocates but so many. Even this powerful handful can promote immediate, dramatic political and social consequences. The most famous remains the Sun Zhigang incident, discussed more fully in Chapter 2, where pressure from a report by advocate journalists spread online and forced Beijing to ditch its decades-old system of detention for internal migrant laborers. Equally dramatic, however, was the 2007 exposure by a local television reporter of hundreds of kidnapped children being used as slaves in Shanxi brick factories (Zhu Zhe 2007). This Dickensian "black kiln" incident galvanized online opinion and ultimately led to the disciplining of ninety-five mostly lower-level officials even as the local scion of a CCP official in charge of one of the kilns received only a nine-year sentence (Ni 2007). Despite this leniency and charges that many of the officials disciplined were scapegoats, having ninety-five Party/state officials punished was a major victory for public opinion, and the outrage led to hundreds of children being freed.

In another prominent example, Huang Yuhao, a reporter from the *Beijing News*, reported on local officials in Shandong and elsewhere forcibly committing petitioners for government redress to psychiatric institutions (Canaves 2008).[14] Reports like this, republished in other papers and spread online, have increased pressure to end this practice. Although there has been no change in official policy, exposing the abuse of the psychiatric detention system to public scrutiny represents a step forward. Advocate journalists, especially when they push back with sensitive stories about corruption or misconduct, can instigate real policy change in the PRC, even under a government often systematically unresponsive to public opinion.

Advocacy's longer-term consequences

The longer-term implications of the rise of the advocates are perhaps more consequential. These journalists have strong parallels to Meyerson and Scully's "tempered radicals," individuals within American organizations "who identify with and are committed to their organizations, and are also committed to a cause, community, or ideology that is fundamentally different from, and possibly at odds with the dominant culture of their organization" (Meyerson and Scully 1995: 586). Many of these reporters feel a tension between their belief in moving China forward and the everyday restrictions the CCP and their own news organizations impose on their work. Being committed to working within the system while simultaneously trying to change it has consequences for reporters and the media system as a whole. One former *Southern Weekend* reporter sums up this attitude, claiming that "being a reporter is impossible in China," in part because press restrictions make it difficult for reporters to push policy changes (Interview ET02–3). Ultimately, such tempered radicals "experience tensions between the status quo and alternatives, which can fuel organizational transformation" (Meyerson and Scully 1995: 586). This is because "change often comes from the margins of an organization, borne by those who do not fit well" (Meyerson and Scully 1995: 586).

In the Chinese media, advocate journalists assume this role. As patriots with an interest in China's development, they are likely to be at the vanguard of many of the structural changes in Chinese communication now and in the future. People like Hu Shuli, founder and former head of *Caijing* are slowly changing the balance of political power in China. Advocates like her are simultaneously (re)assuming the complementary roles of being "professional" journalists and traditional Chinese public intellectuals. Both roles allow them to discuss and critique the Party/state in ways never before allowed. These advocates, then, are slowly crumbling the CCP's jealously held monopoly to comment on, and ultimately criticize, public affairs. As this monopoly disappears, China is likely to become a more pluralist, open society. This pluralism is necessarily limited to the elite – neither advocate journalists nor officials tend to believe that "the public" should enter debates directly – but it is a step forward and certainly moves beyond the CCP's recent, highly vaunted claims that it is expanding "intra-party democracy" (Lin 2004). The fact that those who push back tend to do so nationalistically makes it even more difficult for the CCP, an organization at pains to burnish its nationalist credentials, to fight their rise. It is the advocate journalists and other public professionals carefully prodding the Party/state forward that will likely lead to slow but steady changes in the Chinese political landscape.

Future research

I have pointed to the need for research that sees the Internet and traditional media as an interrelated system, but this is far from the only area that deserves more scholarly attention. An explicit investigation of how public issues originate and propagate online would tell us a great deal about the functioning of China's public sphere. I hypothesize that journalists have a key role to play in this process, with most working informally or unofficially – not on behalf of their employers – to spread knowledge through their personal networks. Mapping the flow of information in these networks and in the Chinese news environment as a whole would provide tremendous insight into the daily functioning of the Chinese polity.

The professions, too, are an understudied area in China. To date, relatively little work has examined the potentially changing role of even "public professionals" like journalists or lawyers in shaping Chinese policy,[15] let alone on the nonpublic professions. As Peter Haas has written, "control over knowledge and information is an important dimension of power" (Haas 1992: 2), and as the world complexifies, we should expect that those who have this control, and especially members of the professions, will gain in influence. Specifically, Haas's work points to the importance of "epistemic communities," those networks "of professionals with recognized expertise and competence in a particular domain and an authoritative claim to policy-relevant knowledge within that domain or issue-area" (Haas 1992: 3). However, the power of professions is necessarily circumscribed in

China, held in check by the overweening authority of the Party/state. Although the Chinese policy-making process seems to have become more technocratic over the past decade, it is clear that political considerations trump purely technocratic solutions in most areas.[16]

Influential research in the 1970s and 1980s examined how "professional commitment" clashes and interacts with "organizational commitment" (Wallace 1993), and this work has relevance in the Chinese context, where professionals are potentially torn between their commitments to their professions and their Party. Despite foundational research arguing that professionals have greater commitment to their professions than organizations, it seems clear that "the early belief that professional and organizational commitments are inherently conflicting ... is not at all supported" by meta-analysis and more recent empirical findings (Wallace 1993: 339). It is therefore unlikely that professional status alone will spur most professionals into increasing conflict with the Chinese Party/state. This unlikelihood increases when professional organizations are weak, as with journalists' thoroughly co-opted All-China Journalists' Association (ACJA) or lawyers' equally politically hamstrung All-China Lawyers Association. Even if Chinese lawyers rank "political rights as more important than economic ones to a similar degree as people in Sweden, Australia, and the United States," the lack of a strong coordinating body that ensures a universal professional ethos seems likely to hamper any potential "lawyer-led rights revolution" (Stern 2013: 212). For the nonpublic professions – engineers, architects, city planners, doctors, dentists, and so on – the immediate possibility of bold political action seems even more remote. And this possibility is even more remote considering that NGOs and other groups that in many Western countries take a confrontational approach to the state tend in China toward a cozy rapprochement with power holders.[17]

Advocate journalists provide an interesting counterpoint, as much of their professional identity is based upon challenging the Party/state or at least giving it a bit of a nudge. Professions are not monoliths; internal difference in *beliefs and content* matter a great deal. As I have argued in previous chapters, there are at least three "flavors" of professional journalist in China, aside from the arguably nonprofessional workaday reporters. In the West, the profession of journalism is often poorly institutionalized and often does not serve as a foundational unifying element for its practitioners (Tumber and Prentoulis 2005). With the profession so divided in China, it is clear that it is more fruitful to analyze different versions of Chinese journalism rather than make a claim for the profession as a whole. While communist professionals are unlikely to create the conditions that demand more of power holders, advocate professionals will continue to do so as members of a "loyal opposition." After all, "demonstrating that the true correlation between professional and organizational commitment is positive does not necessarily mean that there is no tension between the two commitments" (Wallace 1993: 346). Advocate journalists, committed *both* to their profession and the success of the CCP, act upon these dual ties to carefully maneuver China into the future.

Corruption remains a thorny area of the social sciences. Although numerous definitions exist,[18] most boil down to a variant of U.S. Supreme Court Justice

Potter Stewart's famous "I know it when I see it" dictum. But while hundreds of studies tally corruption's systemic causes (e.g., Lü 2000; Shleifer and Vishny 1993) or effects (e.g., Rose-Ackerman 1999); argue over whether a certain level of corrupt activity is helpful for development (Mauro 1995); or discuss the best ways to stamp it out (Behn 2001), few scholars have tackled the corrosive effects of corruption on the corrupt themselves. Corruption, like censorship, has a very real political effect on news workers. China's serious corruption may actually provide greater short-term political stability by creating a class of professionals whose supplemental income from illegal or unprofessional activities gives them a vested interest in preserving the status quo. Future research is needed to flesh out the understudied political implications of corruption for elites in China and elsewhere, both on the systemic and individual level.

I have highlighted uncertainty as a key element in China's media control regime, but its use is hardly restricted to Chinese journalists. There is evidence, for instance, that the CCP uses it to control lawyers as well (Stern and Hassid 2012). I predict, however, that its use as a cheap and effective control mechanism extends beyond Chinese professionals into other social groups and countries. Uncertainty has a flip side as well, providing pushback opportunities for those willing to push the envelope of acceptability. I encourage others to look at actions by "tempered radicals" (Meyerson and Scully 1995) who have loyalty to the system but want to change it from the inside. I hope to complicate the binary distinction between political "insiders" and "outsiders," by focusing on groups simultaneously committed to the system and to reform. Often these relatively elite groups can achieve greater change than those who resist outright, and I predict that (once scholars take a look) pushback will emerge as a common feature of many polities.

The Chinese future

Predicting the future is always a risky business, but evidence from China and models from around the world can help sketch out what the future might bring. China's future is, of course, dependent on the decisions its top leaders make. The leadership transition in late 2012 from Hu Jintao to Xi Jinping has spawned endless analysis about the intentions and capabilities of the incoming administration. Will Xi be a bold reformer, in the model of Deng Xiaoping, or will he favor adherence to the status quo and a far more gradual pace of change, *à la* Hu Jintao? This is clearly an important question, and the colossal – and unexpected – democratizing reforms that Chiang Ching-kuo instituted in Taiwan in the mid-1980s demonstrate the power that a determined leader can have in changing national direction (Gold 1986).

The question of what kind of leader Xi and his colleagues will be is an important one, but making predictions of this kind is folly. Instead, we can look toward the systemic factors pushing the media and polity and make some tentative suggestions for possible outcomes. Most importantly, it is clear that the CCP wishes to remain in power. All major reforms are assessed against this benchmark, and Deng Xiaoping's exhortation to consider "stability above all else" (*wending yadao yiqie* 稳定压倒一切)remains in full force. Barring an unexpected revolution or a Chiang Ching-kuo like reformer, the short and medium term is likely to look much like the past.

Looking toward the future, the example of Mexico has particular relevance. Mexico's Institutional Revolutionary Party (Partido Revolucionario Institucional, PRI) maintained its authoritarian, single-party rule for over seventy years despite a (state-led) capitalist economy, ties to the U.S., and a system of regular (though not free or fair) elections. Under the PRI, a confluence of interests between media owners and the regime ensured political quiescence even in the absence of a formal censorship system (Lawson 2002: 28–31). Given the pervasive cronyism in all aspects of Chinese life, it seems likely that even if the CCP were to slowly remove formal political restrictions from the press, media barons will continue to push allegiance to the Party to serve their own interests. Moreover, the commercialized media and the official press provide mostly the same news content, but the public finds the commercialized outlets overwhelmingly more trustworthy because of their image and somewhat more negative tone (Stockmann 2013). In other words, even if the Chinese government were to take a more hands-off approach to controlling the press, the end result might be a population *more* supportive of its authoritarian government (Stockmann 2013). In sum, dramatic changes over the short and medium term in the content of the Chinese media are unlikely.

Far more likely is a gradual pushing of boundaries around specific issues, leading to slow accompanying reforms in the Chinese political system. In Mexico, as is likely to happen in China, a more aggressive press preceded and helped cause political liberalization, not the other way around. Chappell Lawson argues that there are several broader lessons that can be drawn from the Mexican experience:

> First, political liberalization is not the sole or even the most important ingredient in media opening. Second, market-oriented reform tends to encourage competition between media outlets and thus stimulates change in coverage. Third, the emergence of a new cohort of journalists with different norms and visions can play a potent role in transforming the media (especially the print media). Fourth, the impact of technological innovation and foreign penetration, though undeniable, appears to be rather modest.
>
> (Lawson 2002: 181)

All these conclusions apply to China as well, with a caveat on point two. As I have argued in earlier chapters, market-oriented reform has driven long-term changes in the Chinese press, but over the short and medium term, the impact of marketization is much more muted. The third point has wide congruity with the increasing impact in China of "media professionalism," and especially an advocacy orientation spreading among journalists. And the fourth point meshes well with my earlier argument about the Internet's impact, which is best seen as working together with the traditional media to bring change and not as a disruptive element on its own.

Taking together the arguments of previous chapters and the Mexican example, we can sketch out a likely future for China and its media. Political change is likely to come slowly, driven in part by advocate journalists looking to help their country by solving the specific, often embarrassing, problems that the CCP would rather ignore. These advocates work to "play edge ball" and proactively push back over issues they feel are safe but near the edge of acceptability. Over time, these small changes and the "two steps forward, one step back" cycle of media boundary-pushing can add up to have real impact and increase public pressure for systemic change. In Mexico, increasing coverage of scandals and sensitive topics led to gradual regime delegitimation, a process that is perhaps underway in contemporary China.

The Internet will clearly play an important role in this process, but it will do so in conjunction with the traditional media, not as a strategic competitor. The traditional media's role as gatekeeper, source of authority, and news provider to the hundreds of millions of offline Chinese ensure that it will continue to have relevance even in the Internet age. As individual Internet services gain prominence in turn – search engines, blogging, social media, and now microblogging – they attract much Western media and scholarly attention. Each new service is trumpeted in the West as finally being "the one" that will bring democracy to China. As the boldest early adopters join each new service, users may have a period of initial high hopes and great impact. Yet all such services are victims of their own success. Popularity brings a reversion to the mean and an influx of users who are less bold and more strongly committed to the status quo (Hassid 2013). Moreover, an Internet service that is popular enough to have political and social impact invariably attracts the attention of China's censorship authorities, ensuring that the content of each new thing resembles that of the ones that have come before. The Internet as a whole is clearly transformational, bringing the opportunity for millions of people to participate in public debate like never before in Chinese history. But I am skeptical that any one particular Internet service will have revolutionary impact, and I argue that it important to consider the Internet as just one element in a complex media ecosystem.

Finally, it is important to note that even gradual media transformation can backfire and create problems for China and its people. The traditional media already have a degree of bias against reporting issues in the countryside, discussing these issues about as much as the arts and far less than issues of business and finance, despite the fact that nearly 50% of China's population is still rural (see Appendix D). The Internet, however, is far worse in its discussions of these issues, with blogs discussing rural and agricultural issues about 90% less frequently than newspapers, and microblogs even less (Hassid 2013). Chinese netizens are more urban, better educated, and richer than the Chinese population as whole (China Internet Network Information Center [CNNIC] 2014), and we should certainly expect a degree of urban bias in their discussions. What is alarming is the degree of bias, and the seriousness with which the central state often takes the claims and complaints of these (overwhelmingly urban) netizens (Hassid, forthcoming).

It is easy to imagine a future in which the CCP becomes increasingly responsive to the concerns of the "haves" – the relatively prosperous urban dwellers – while ignoring the pleas of the "have-nots" in the countryside. Urbanites increasingly have a "voice" option either online or via the traditional media, and the Party has taken great pains to ensure their continuing support.[19] Those in the countryside, by contrast, increasingly only have an option to "exit," escaping their poverty by joining the migrant exodus to the cities (Hirschman 1970). This process will likely exacerbate social tensions and continue to worsen China's already epic inequality.[20] With social instability – including protests and even riots – on the rise (Yu Jianrong and Yu Debao 2008), it is possible that the countryside might become a powder keg lit by any slowdown in China's meteoric economic rise and a media unable or unwilling to take rural residents' problems seriously. The best case scenario for China's future, it seems to me, looks like Mexico's recent past: A moderately aggressive media (led by advocate journalists) creates pressure over time that leads to moderate, though meaningful, political reform. The worst case scenario, however, has a dysfunctional, chaotic countryside that remains ignored by China's urban-centered, brittle, and relatively weak central government, all abetted by a simultaneously sensationalist and circumscribed media. In both cases, the media have an important role to play. For China's sake, we should hope the advocates win.

Notes

1. Such as Communist-era Yugoslavia. See Drakulic (1993).
2. Foucault (1977) certainly argues that it is, claiming that modern governments have moved from external control to internal control, creating populations that govern themselves. Etzioni (1965) makes a similar argument about the relative effectiveness of internal versus external control. At a minimum it is a very old strategy, as Padgett and Ansell (1993) demonstrate in their study of the rise of the Medici in fifteenth-century Florence.
3. And again, evidence seems to indicate that it is, but it is too early to claim a definitive answer
4. For example, Rachel Stern's work on Chinese environmental lawyers. See (Stern 2013).
5. See, for example, http://chinadigitaltimes.net/2008/06/zhang-qi-will-the-earthquake-transform-china/.
6. For example, they argue that during the 2002–2003 outbreak of sudden acute respiratory syndrome (SARS), "in the absence of free media, incentives for lower-tier bureaucrats to provide sufficient effort and transmit necessary information to higher levels proved inadequate." They then contend that orders banning coverage on SARS originated from the Central Propaganda Department, apparently not realizing that the CPD is a *central*, not local-level, agency. See Egorov, Guriev, and Sonin (2009: 646).
7. Wang Jun, a reporter for *Outlook Weekly*, discusses this system in Polumbaum and Xiong (2008: 24).
8. For contemporary legacies of Maoist-era policy decentralization, see Hurst (2004).
9. Restricting a practice known as "foreign supervision" (*yidi jiandu* 异地监督).
10. This situation is by no means unique to China. Poland's journalists similarly exploited cracks in the elite power structure to publish bold articles during various thaws in the communist censorship apparatus. See Curry (1990: 153–159).

11 On the role of leadership in China and elsewhere, see Li and O'Brien (2008), Boin (2001), and Zoller and Fairhurst (2007). On framing, see Tarrow (1998), Zald (1996), Blecher (2002), and Stern (2005).
12 Thomas (2003) discusses this phenomenon in the U.S. among ecologists working in different bureaucracies who still coordinate action.
13 By all accounts, this is how the CCP controlled papers in the Southern Group when they were becoming a political liability. See Kahn (2004) and Esarey (2005).
14 The original Chinese story is no longer available online.
15 For work on how lawyers might shape state policy, see Michelson (2008) and Stern (2013).
16 For example, monetary and fiscal policy in China has been largely determined politically, as opposed to the model of a (relatively) independent central bank, able to act on its own in most Western states. See Chin (2013).
17 For more on this dynamic of co-optation and close relations between social organizations and the state, see Hildebrandt (2013).
18 They tend to concentrate on "misuse" of public power or funds, but misuse is in the eye of the beholder. See Rose-Ackerman (1999) for a full discussion.
19 Jiang Zemin's "three represents" theory, presented in the early 2000s, first encouraged entrepreneurs to join the CCP, and Party officials have tried hard since then to bring the better-off Chinese into the Party's fold.
20 According to official Chinese government figures, China's Gini coefficient – a measure of inequality – is already higher than that of the U.S., at around 0.5. See Whyte (2013).

References

Bandurski, David. 2008. Taxi Strikes in China Highlight Changing Press Controls. Accessed December 15, 2009. http://cmp.hku.hk/2008/11/12/1344/.

Behn, Robert D. 2001. *Rethinking Democratic Accountability*. Washington, DC: Brookings Institution Press.

Blecher, Mark. 2002. "Hegemony and Workers' Politics in China." *The China Quarterly* 170: 283–303.

Boin, Arjen. 2001. *Crafting Public Institutions: Leadership in Two Prison Systems, Explorations in Public Policy*. Boulder, CO: L. Rienner.

Bourdieu, Pierre, and John B. Thompson. 1991. *Language and Symbolic Power*. Cambridge, MA: Harvard University Press.

Brady, Anne-Marie. 2008. *Marketing Dictatorship: Propaganda and Thought Work in Contemporary China, Asia/Pacific/Perspectives*. Lanham, MD: Rowman & Littlefield.

Burstein, Paul, Rachel L. Einwohner, and Jocelyn A. Hollander. 1995. "The Success of Political Movements: A Bargaining Perspective." In *The Politics of Social Protest: Comparative Perspectives on States and Social Movements*, edited by J. Craig Jenkins and Bert Klandermans, 275–295. Minneapolis: University of Minnesota Press.

Canaves, Sky. 2008. "A Bold Media Move on the Psychiatric Detention of Complaining Citizens." *The Wall Street Journal: China Journal [Online]*, Dec. 9, China Journal. Accessed February 18, 2009. http://blogs.wsj.com/chinajournal/2008/12/09/a-bold-media-move-on-the-psychiatric-detention-of-complaining-citizens/?mod=rss_WSJBlog.

Cheng, Li. 2009. "The Chinese Communist Party: Recruiting and Controlling the New Elites." *Journal of Current Chinese Affairs* 38 (3):13–33.

Chin, Gregory T. 2013. "Understanding Currency Policy and Central Banking in China." *The Journal of Asian Studies* 72 (3):519–538.

China Internet Network Information Center (CNNIC). 2014. The 34th Statistical Survey Report on the Internet Development in China (Di 34 Ci Zhongguo Hulianwangluo Fazhan Zhuangkuang Tongji Baodao 第34次中国互联网络发展状况统计报告). CNNIC.
Curry, Jane Leftwich. 1990. *Poland's Journalists: Professionalism and Politics*. Cambridge; New York: Cambridge University Press.
Downs, George W., and David M. Rocke. 1995. *Optimal Imperfection? Domestic Uncertainty and Institutions in International Relations*. Princeton, NJ: Princeton University Press.
Drakulic, Slavenka. 1993. *How We Survived Communism and Even Laughed*. New York: HarperPerennial.
Eckstein, Susan. 1989. "Power and Popular Protest in Latin America." In *Power and Popular Protest: Latin American Social Movements*, edited by Susan Eckstein and Manuel A. Garretón Merino, 1–60. Berkeley: University of California Press.
Egorov, Georgy, Sergei Guriev, and Konstantin Sonin. 2009. "Why Resource-Poor Dictators Allow Freer Media: A Theory and Evidence from Panel Data." *American Political Science Review* 103 (4):645–668.
Esarey, Ashley. 2005. "Cornering the Market: State Strategies for Controlling China's Commercial Media." *Asian Perspective* 29 (4):37–83.
Etzioni, Amitai. 1965. "Organizational Control Structure." In *Handbook of Organizations*, edited by James G. March, chapter 15. Chicago: Rand McNally.
Eyerman, Ron. 1989. "Social Movements: Between History and Sociology." *Theory and Society* 18 (4):531–545.
Fearon, James D. 1997. "Signaling Foreign Policy Interests: Tying Hands Versus Sinking Costs." *The Journal of Conflict Resolution* 41 (1):68–90.
Foucault, Michel. 1977. *Discipline and Punish: The Birth of the Prison*. 1st American ed. New York: Pantheon Books.
Gold, Thomas B. 1986. *State and Society in the Taiwan Miracle*. Armonk, NY: M.E. Sharpe.
Haas, Peter M. 1992. "Epistemic Communities and International Policy Coordination." *International Organization* 46 (1, Knowledge, Power and International Policy):1–35.
Hassid, Jonathan. 2013. "Political Contention on Chinese Micro-Blogs: Motivation and Results." Paper presented at the American Political Science Association Annual Meeing, Chicago, IL, Sep. 1.
Hassid, Jonathan. Forthcoming. "China's Responsiveness to Internet Opinion: A Double-Edged Sword." *Journal of Current Chinese Affairs*.
He Qinglian. 2004. *Media Control in China (Zhongguo Zhengfu Ruhe Kongzhi Meiti* 中国政府如何控制媒体). New York: Human Rights in China.
Hildebrandt, Timothy. 2013. *Social Organizations and the Authoritarian State in China*. Cambridge; New York: Cambridge University Press.
Hirschman, Albert O. 1970. *Exit, Voice, and Loyalty: Responses to Decline in Firms, Organizations, and States*. Cambridge, MA: Harvard University Press.
Hurst, William. 2004. "Understanding Contentious Collective Action by Chinese Laid-Off Workers: The Importance of Regional Political Economy." *Studies in Comparative International Developement* 39 (2):94–120.
Kahn, Joseph. 2004. "Police Raid Chinese Newspaper That Reported New SARS Case." *The New York Times*, Jan. 8. Accessed October 9, 2006. http://query.nytimes.com/gst/fullpage.html?sec=health&res=9D05E6DC1131F93BA35752C0A9629C8B63.
Knight, Peter. 2003. *Conspiracy Theories in American History: An Encyclopedia*. Santa Barbara, CA: ABC-CLIO.

Labaree, Benjamin Woods. 1964. *The Boston Tea Party*. New York: Oxford University Press.

Lawson, Chappell H. 2002. *Building the Fourth Estate: Democratization and the Rise of a Free Press in Mexico*. Berkeley: University of California Press.

Lee, Chin-Chuan, Zhou He, and Yu Huang. 2007. "Party-Market Corporatism, Clientalism and Media in Shanghai." *Harvard International Journal of Press/Politics* 12 (3):21–42.

Li, Lianjiang, and Kevin O'Brien. 2008. "Protest Leadership in Rural China." *China Quarterly* 192:1–23.

Lin, Gang. 2004. "Leadership Transition, Intra-Party Democracy and Institution Building in China." *Asian Survey* 44 (2):255–275.

Lorentzen, Peter L. 2014. "China's Strategic Censorship." *American Journal of Political Science* 58 (2):402–414.

Lü, Xiaobo. 2000. *Cadres and Corruption: The Organizational Involution of the Chinese Communist Party*. Stanford, CA: Stanford University Press.

Mauro, Paolo. 1995. "Corruption and Growth." *The Quarterly Journal of Economics* 110 (3):681–712.

Meyerson, Debra E., and Maureen A. Scully. 1995. "Tempered Radicalism and the Politics of Ambivalence and Change." *Organization Science* 6 (5):585–600.

Michelson, Ethan. 2008. "Dear Lawyer Bao: Everyday Problems, Legal Advice, and State Power in China." *Social Problems* 55 (1):43–71.

Murray, John. 1994. *The Russian Press from Brezhnev to Yeltsin: Behind the Paper Curtain, Studies of Communism in Transition*. Aldershot, Hants, England; Brookfield, VT, USA: E. Elgar.

Ni, Ching-Ching. 2007. "China Slavery Verdicts Anger Victims' Families." *Los Angeles Times*, Jul. 19, The World. http://articles.latimes.com/2007/jul/19/world/fg-china19.

O'Brien, Kevin J. 2003. "Neither Transgressive Nor Contained: Boundary-Spanning Contention in China." *Mobilization* 8 (1):51–64.

O'Brien, Kevin J., and Lianjiang Li. 1999. "Selective Policy Implementation in Rural China." *Comparative Politics* 31 (2):167–186.

Padgett, John F., and Christopher K. Ansell. 1993. "Robust Action and the Rise of the Medici, 1400–1434." *American Journal of Sociology* 98 (6):1259–1319.

Polumbaum, Judy, and Lei Xiong. 2008. *China Ink: The Changing Face of Chinese Journalism*. Lanham, MD: Rowman & Littlefield.

Powell, Robert. 1996. "Uncertainty, Shifting Power, and Appeasment." *American Political Science Review* 90 (4):749–764.

Repnikova, Maria. 2014. "Investigative Journalists' Coping Tactics in a Restrictive Media Environment." In *Chinese Investigative Journalists' Dreams: Autonomy, Agency and Voice*, edited by Marina Svensson, Elin Saether, and Zhi'an Zhang, 113–132. Lanham, MD: Lexington Books.

Rodrigues, Suzana B., and David L. Collinson. 1995. "Having Fun?: Humor as Resistance in Brazil." *Organization Studies* 16:739–768.

Rose-Ackerman, Susan. 1999. *Corruption and Government: Causes, Consequences, and Reform*. London; New York: Cambridge University Press.

Shleifer, Andrei, and Robert W. Vishny. 1993. "Corruption." *The Quarterly Journal of Economics* 108 (3):599–617.

Stern, Rachel E. 2005. "Unpacking Adaptation: The Female Inheritance Movement in Hong Kong." *Mobilization* 10 (3):421–439.

Stern, Rachel E. 2013. *Environmental Litigation in China: A Study in Political Ambivalence, Cambridge Studies in Law and Society*. Cambridge: Cambridge University Press.

Stern, Rachel E., and Jonathan Hassid. 2012. "Amplifying Silence: Uncertainty and Control Parables in Contemporary China." *Comparative Political Studies* 45 (10):1230–1254. doi:10.1177/0010414011434295.

Stockmann, Daniela. 2013. *Media Commercialization and Authoritarian Rule in China, Communication, Society, and Politics Series*. New York: Cambridge University Press.

Sun, Xupei, and Elizabeth C. Michel. 2001. *An Orchestra of Voices: Making the Argument for Greater Speech and Press Freedom in the People's Republic of China*. Westport, CT: Praeger.

Tarrow, Sidney G. 1989. *Democracy and Disorder: Protest and Politics in Italy, 1965–1975*. Oxford: Oxford University Press.

Tarrow, Sidney G. 1998. *Power in Movement: Social Movements and Contentious Politics*. 2nd ed, *Cambridge Studies in Comparative Politics*. Cambridge; New York: Cambridge University Press.

Thomas, Craig W. 2003. *Bureaucratic Landscapes: Interagency Cooperation and the Preservation of Biodiversity, Politics, Science, and the Environment*. Cambridge, MA: MIT Press.

Tilly, Charles. 1995. *Popular Contention in Great Britain, 1758–1834*. Cambridge, MA: Harvard University Press.

Tumber, Howard, and Marina Prentoulis. 2005. "Journalism and the Making of a Profession." In *Making Journalists: Diverse Models, Global Issues*, edited by Hugo de Burgh, 58–74. London; New York: Routledge.

Wallace, Jean E. 1993. "Professional and Organizational Commitment: Compatible or Incompatible?" *Journal of Vocational Behavior* 42:333–349.

Whyte, Martin King. 2013. "Soaring Income Gaps: China in Comparative Perspective." *Daedalus*.

Yu Jianrong and Yu Debao. 2008. "China Civil Society Report: Mass Incidents in China." *Policy Forum Online* 08 (65A).

Zald, Mayer N. 1996. "Culture, Ideology and Strategic Framing." In *Comparative Perspectives on Social Movements: Political Opportunities, Mobilizing Structures, and Cultural Framings*, edited by Doug McAdam, John D. McCarthy and Mayer N. Zald, 261–274. Cambridge; New York: Cambridge University Press.

Zhang Yanlong. 2008. "Confessions of a Propaganda Hitman." *The Economic Observer Online*, Oct. 10, pp 9, Nation. Accessed 12/15/2009. http://www.eeo.com.cn/ens/biz_commentary/2008/10/10/115737.html.

Zhu Zhe. 2007. "More Than 460 Rescued from Brick Kiln Slavery." *China Daily*, Jun. 15. Accessed Feb. 1, 2011. www.chinadaily.com.cn/china/2007–06/15/content_894802.htm.

Zoller, Heather M., and Gail T. Fairhurst. 2007. "Resistance Leadership: The Overlooked Potential in Critical Organization and Leadership Studies." *Human Relations* 60 (9):1331–1360.

Appendices

Appendix A: list of Chinese newspapers analyzed, by province

Newspaper	Province
Anhui Qingnian Bao	Anhui
Anhui Ribao	Anhui
Anhui Shangbao	Anhui
Huaxia Shibao	Beijing
Jiefangjun Bao	Beijing
Renmin Ribao	Beijing
Zhongguo Jingji Shibao	Beijing
Zhongguo Jingying Bao	Beijing
Zhonghua Gongshang Shibao	Beijing
Chongqing Ribao	Chongqing
Fujian Ribao	Fujian
Haixia Daobao	Fujian
Guangzhou Ribao	Guangdong
Nanfang Zhoumo	Guangdong
Yangcheng Wanbao	Guangdong
Jiangsu Jingji Bao	Jiangsu
Xinhua Ribao	Jiangsu
Xinxi Ribao	Jiangxi
Jiefang Ribao	Shanghai
Laodong Bao	Shanghai
Lianhe Shibao	Shanghai
Wenhui Bao	Shanghai
Shanxi Ribao	Shanxi
Sichuan Gongren Ribao	Sichuan
Sichuan Zhengxie Bao	Sichuan
Yunnan Ribao	Yunnan

Appendix B: newspaper rank-order lists

Newspaper sensitivity rank-order list

Newspaper	Mean	Std. error	Rank order
Sichuan Gongren Ribao	0.600	0.039	1
Sichuan Zhengxie Bao	0.289	0.037	2
Renmin Ribao	0.285	0.031	3
Chongqing Ribao	0.220	0.040	4
Anhui Ribao	0.171	0.036	5
Shanxi Ribao	0.115	0.039	6
Jiefangjun Bao	0.110	0.038	7
Lianhe Shibao	0.085	0.037	8
Xinhua Ribao	0.070	0.032	9
Yunnan Ribao	0.066	0.037	10
Fujian Ribao	0.038	0.030	11
Guangzhou Ribao	−0.004	0.036	12
Anhui Shangbao	−0.005	0.052	13
Nanfang Zhoumo	−0.008	0.034	14
Laodong Bao	−0.075	0.059	15
Jiangsu Jingji Bao	−0.082	0.029	16
Yangcheng Wanbao	−0.083	0.042	17
Jiefang Ribao	−0.085	0.038	18
Anhui Qingnian Bao	−0.158	0.036	19
Haixia Daobao	−0.169	0.033	20
Wenhui Bao	−0.195	0.039	21
Xinxi Ribao	−0.198	0.044	22
Huaxia Shibao	−0.215	0.033	23
Zhongguo Jingji Shibao	−0.243	0.034	24
Zhonghua Gongshang Shibao	−0.252	0.033	25
Zhongguo Jingying Bao	−0.294	0.043	26

(ANOVA, $p < .0001$)

Newspaper negative/positive words rank-order list

Newspaper	Mean	Std. error	Rank order
Nanfang Zhoumo	0.674	0.033	1
Anhui Shangbao	0.380	0.051	2
Jiefangjun Bao	0.338	0.037	3
Huaxia Shibao	0.334	0.032	4
Xinxi Ribao	0.222	0.043	5
Zhongguo Jingji Shibao	0.214	0.034	6
Yangcheng Wanbao	0.211	0.041	7
Zhongguo Jingying Bao	0.150	0.043	8
Jiangsu Jingji Bao	0.136	0.028	9
Laodong Bao	0.127	0.058	10
Renmin Ribao	0.078	0.030	11
Sichuan Gongren Ribao	0.068	0.039	12
Zhonghua Gongshang Shibao	0.029	0.032	13
Anhui Qingnian Bao	0.012	0.035	14
Guangzhou Ribao	−0.023	0.035	15
Wenhui Bao	−0.059	0.038	16
Jiefang Ribao	−0.065	0.037	17
Haixia Daobao	−0.077	0.032	18
Xinhua Ribao	−0.113	0.032	19
Shanxi Ribao	−0.242	0.039	20
Chongqing Ribao	−0.266	0.039	21
Anhui Ribao	−0.304	0.035	22
Fujian Ribao	−0.321	0.030	23
Lianhe Shibao	−0.362	0.036	24
Sichuan Zhengxie Bao	−0.432	0.036	25
Yunnan Ribao	−0.466	0.036	26

(ANOVA, $p < .0001$)

Appendices

Newspaper "advocacy journalism" rank-order list

Newspaper	Mean	Std. error	Rank order
Chongqing Ribao	0.699	0.040	1
Nanfang Zhoumo	0.460	0.033	2
Jiefangjun Bao	0.420	0.037	3
Sichuan Zhengxie Bao	0.247	0.036	4
Anhui Qingnian Bao	0.226	0.036	5
Renmin Ribao	0.207	0.031	6
Jiangsu Jingji Bao	0.033	0.028	7
Lianhe Shibao	0.024	0.037	8
Huaxia Shibao	−0.007	0.033	9
Wenhui Bao	−0.010	0.038	10
Zhongguo Jingji Shibao	−0.014	0.034	11
Laodong Bao	−0.044	0.058	12
Anhui Ribao	−0.044	0.035	13
Sichuan Gongren Ribao	−0.045	0.039	14
Yunnan Ribao	−0.074	0.036	15
Xinhua Ribao	−0.074	0.032	16
Shanxi Ribao	−0.081	0.039	17
Jiefang Ribao	−0.102	0.037	18
Zhonghua Gongshang Shibao	−0.155	0.033	19
Fujian Ribao	−0.160	0.030	20
Zhongguo Jingying Bao	−0.174	0.043	21
Xinxi Ribao	−0.198	0.044	22
Yangcheng Wanbao	−0.199	0.042	23
Anhui Shangbao	−0.290	0.051	24
Guangzhou Ribao	−0.317	0.035	25
Haixia Daobao	−0.465	0.032	26

(Higher numbers mean higher measured advocacy journalism; lower numbers mean more "liberal" reporting.)

(ANOVA, $p < .0001$)

Appendix C: list of newspaper topics analyzed

Category	Sub-category (if any)
Agriculture	
Arts	
Blog-sensitive lists	(3): Mingan words, Gaoliang words, and Yanjin words
Business/finance	
Construction/real estate	
Corruption	
Disasters	
Education	
Energy	
Environment	
Family	
Food/consumable goods	
Legal	
Media	
Military	
Politics	(4): Combative, foreign, supportive, and unclear
Science/medicine	
Sentiment	(2): Negative and positive
Sports	(3): General sports, blog-derived sports terms, and sports terms from other sources
Transport	

Appendix D: category means

Newspaper	Agriculture	Arts	Business/finance
Anhui Qingnian Bao	0.001203	0.002320	0.003796
Anhui Ribao	0.006698	0.003154	0.006382
Anhui Shangbao	0.000883	0.000913	0.008550
Chongqing Ribao	0.004303	0.001714	0.005729
Fujian Ribao	0.005480	0.002855	0.006243
Guangzhou Ribao	0.001667	0.001878	0.007116
Haixia Daobao	0.000965	0.001679	0.006978
Huaxia Shibao	0.000919	0.001662	0.007674
Jiangsu Jingji Bao	0.003965	0.001104	0.011583
Jiefang Ribao	0.001377	0.002922	0.008390
Jiefangjun Bao	0.000391	0.001322	0.001019
Laodong Bao	0.000748	0.000566	0.008457
Lianhe Shibao	0.001567	0.003093	0.005445
Nanfang Zhoumo	0.001649	0.001795	0.006674
Renmin Ribao	0.003060	0.002974	0.005282
Shanxi Ribao	0.005569	0.002540	0.006782
Sichuan Gongren Ribao	0.005073	0.001057	0.005530
Sichuan Zhengxie Bao	0.007077	0.001329	0.005375
Wenhui Bao	0.001016	0.002763	0.008788
Xinhua Ribao	0.004058	0.002131	0.007646
Xinxi Ribao	0.002243	0.000848	0.006813
Yangcheng Wanbao	0.001338	0.002537	0.007302
Yunnan Ribao	0.007456	0.003695	0.006457
Zhongguo Jingji Shibao	0.002379	0.001148	0.013471
Zhongguo Jingying Bao	0.000817	0.001495	0.009164
Zhonghua Gongshang Shibao	0.001289	0.001334	0.010727
Category mean	0.002968	0.002018	0.007285

Newspaper	Construction/real estate	Corruption	Disasters
Anhui Qingnian Bao	0.001910	0.001428	0.001087
Anhui Ribao	0.002496	0.002779	0.002355
Anhui Shangbao	0.002976	0.002313	0.001932
Chongqing Ribao	0.003614	0.002070	0.002215
Fujian Ribao	0.002317	0.001687	0.001777
Guangzhou Ribao	0.003423	0.002025	0.001405
Haixia Daobao	0.005020	0.001118	0.001139
Huaxia Shibao	0.003152	0.001147	0.000928
Jiangsu Jingji Bao	0.002647	0.002508	0.000859
Jiefang Ribao	0.002376	0.001532	0.000878

(Continued)

Appendix D: (Continued)

Jiefangjun Bao	0.001141	0.003598	0.000842
Laodong Bao	0.003592	0.001608	0.000897
Lianhe Shibao	0.002149	0.000953	0.000510
Nanfang Zhoumo	0.001585	0.001841	0.000820
Renmin Ribao	0.001307	0.002091	0.001955
Shanxi Ribao	0.003111	0.002491	0.002251
Sichuan Gongren Ribao	0.002177	0.002911	0.003190
Sichuan Zhengxie Bao	0.002308	0.001733	0.000961
Wenhui Bao	0.003070	0.001017	0.000749
Xinhua Ribao	0.004782	0.002156	0.001437
Xinxi Ribao	0.004920	0.001170	0.001252
Yangcheng Wanbao	0.002430	0.001592	0.001018
Yunnan Ribao	0.002720	0.001920	0.002193
Zhongguo Jingji Shibao	0.002188	0.001090	0.000649
Zhongguo Jingying Bao	0.001806	0.001082	0.000349
Zhonghua Gongshang Shibao	0.002354	0.001086	0.000718
Category mean	0.002718	0.001810	0.001312

Newspaper	Education	Energy	Environment
Anhui Qingnian Bao	0.032208	0.000136	0.000833
Anhui Ribao	0.002330	0.000582	0.001245
Anhui Shangbao	0.004019	0.000702	0.000386
Chongqing Ribao	0.003620	0.000477	0.001041
Fujian Ribao	0.003046	0.000462	0.000886
Guangzhou Ribao	0.003529	0.001020	0.000794
Haixia Daobao	0.003947	0.000830	0.000816
Huaxia Shibao	0.002827	0.000674	0.000746
Jiangsu Jingji Bao	0.000999	0.000544	0.001072
Jiefang Ribao	0.003721	0.000643	0.001121
Jiefangjun Bao	0.003954	0.000283	0.000874
Laodong Bao	0.002070	0.000169	0.000562
Lianhe Shibao	0.003591	0.000211	0.000973
Nanfang Zhoumo	0.003530	0.000643	0.000406
Renmin Ribao	0.002055	0.000550	0.000911
Shanxi Ribao	0.002472	0.000748	0.001601
Sichuan Gongren Ribao	0.002439	0.000643	0.000574
Sichuan Zhengxie Bao	0.003636	0.000250	0.001760
Wenhui Bao	0.006168	0.001293	0.001232
Xinhua Ribao	0.004327	0.000606	0.001037
Xinxi Ribao	0.004347	0.000617	0.000821
Yangcheng Wanbao	0.003895	0.000567	0.000668
Yunnan Ribao	0.002727	0.000591	0.001585
Zhongguo Jingji Shibao	0.000650	0.001384	0.000998
Zhongguo Jingying Bao	0.000360	0.000523	0.000653
Zhonghua Gongshang Shibao	0.000818	0.001596	0.000987
Category mean	0.004063	0.000662	0.000966

Newspaper	Family	Food/consumables	Gaoliang ci
Anhui Qingnian Bao	0.000628	0.000421	0.001127
Anhui Ribao	0.000319	0.001433	0.001450
Anhui Shangbao	0.002057	0.001851	0.000581
Chongqing Ribao	0.000274	0.001061	0.001626
Fujian Ribao	0.000540	0.000991	0.001515
Guangzhou Ribao	0.000338	0.001454	0.001417
Haixia Daobao	0.000426	0.001835	0.000711
Huaxia Shibao	0.000267	0.001869	0.000933
Jiangsu Jingji Bao	0.000274	0.002281	0.000767
Jiefang Ribao	0.000412	0.001280	0.001945
Jiefangjun Bao	0.000132	0.000174	0.001930
Laodong Bao	0.000403	0.001190	0.001203
Lianhe Shibao	0.000494	0.000955	0.002874
Nanfang Zhoumo	0.000361	0.000632	0.001720
Renmin Ribao	0.000312	0.000869	0.003482
Shanxi Ribao	0.000269	0.001290	0.001278
Sichuan Gongren Ribao	0.000788	0.000585	0.003076
Sichuan Zhengxie Bao	0.000280	0.000696	0.002852
Wenhui Bao	0.000225	0.001465	0.001218
Xinhua Ribao	0.000582	0.001630	0.001833
Xinxi Ribao	0.001066	0.001892	0.000433
Yangcheng Wanbao	0.000402	0.001950	0.001505
Yunnan Ribao	0.000236	0.001087	0.001479
Zhongguo Jingji Shibao	0.000116	0.001068	0.000711
Zhongguo Jingying Bao	0.000129	0.001630	0.000506
Zhonghua Gongshang Shibao	0.000156	0.001825	0.000681
Category mean	0.000401	0.001293	0.00152481

Newspaper	Legal	Media	Military
Anhui Qingnian Bao	0.002077	0.000952	0.000560
Anhui Ribao	0.003552	0.001192	0.000490
Anhui Shangbao	0.005817	0.000644	0.000325
Chongqing Ribao	0.002938	0.001376	0.000528
Fujian Ribao	0.002799	0.000769	0.000847
Guangzhou Ribao	0.003408	0.000716	0.000475
Haixia Daobao	0.002143	0.001533	0.000388
Huaxia Shibao	0.002056	0.001571	0.000617
Jiangsu Jingji Bao	0.008349	0.000525	0.000324
Jiefang Ribao	0.002496	0.001333	0.000608
Jiefangjun Bao	0.002505	0.000501	0.014930
Laodong Bao	0.007375	0.000684	0.000250
Lianhe Shibao	0.002307	0.001356	0.000485
Nanfang Zhoumo	0.003608	0.001494	0.001015
Renmin Ribao	0.002386	0.002494	0.001900
Shanxi Ribao	0.002699	0.001070	0.000675
Sichuan Gongren Ribao	0.006866	0.000847	0.000537
Sichuan Zhengxie Bao	0.002259	0.001132	0.000797
Wenhui Bao	0.002096	0.001627	0.000484
Xinhua Ribao	0.003190	0.001033	0.000514
Xinxi Ribao	0.002337	0.000669	0.000377
Yangcheng Wanbao	0.002916	0.000977	0.000433
Yunnan Ribao	0.002090	0.001314	0.000623
Zhongguo Jingji Shibao	0.002146	0.001030	0.000628
Zhongguo Jingying Bao	0.001524	0.000949	0.000597
Zhonghua Gongshang Shibao	0.002016	0.000996	0.000650
Category mean	0.003179	0.001141	0.001149

Appendices

Newspaper	Mingang ci	Negative words	Politics (all)
Anhui Qingnian Bao	0.000033	0.026351	0.021326
Anhui Ribao	0.000140	0.020158	0.036998
Anhui Shangbao	0.000007	0.032993	0.015371
Chongqing Ribao	0.000158	0.020714	0.033055
Fujian Ribao	0.000075	0.019673	0.033305
Guangzhou Ribao	0.000066	0.025328	0.026403
Haixia Daobao	0.000128	0.024159	0.018054
Huaxia Shibao	0.000019	0.032424	0.014995
Jiangsu Jingji Bao	0.000036	0.028702	0.025516
Jiefang Ribao	0.000022	0.024671	0.025190
Jiefangjun Bao	0.000103	0.033274	0.039937
Laodong Bao	0.000037	0.028359	0.019025
Lianhe Shibao	0.000038	0.019088	0.048818
Nanfang Zhoumo	0.000178	0.039035	0.024491
Renmin Ribao	0.000292	0.027703	0.036039
Shanxi Ribao	0.000123	0.021360	0.033299
Sichuan Gongren Ribao	0.000072	0.027212	0.031375
Sichuan Zhengxie Bao	0.000106	0.017878	0.063368
Wenhui Bao	0.000083	0.024882	0.022769
Xinhua Ribao	0.000061	0.023789	0.031718
Xinxi Ribao	0.000014	0.030064	0.013105
Yangcheng Wanbao	0.000057	0.029892	0.019834
Yunnan Ribao	0.000056	0.016970	0.034540
Zhongguo Jingji Shibao	0.000020	0.030262	0.022103
Zhongguo Jingying Bao	0.000077	0.028837	0.013792
Zhonghua Gongshang Shibao	0.000100	0.026504	0.019764
Category mean	0.000086	0.025996	0.028490

Newspaper	Politics-combative	Politics-foreign	Politics-supportive
Anhui Qingnian Bao	0.001134	0.000054	0.000036
Anhui Ribao	0.001713	0.000012	0.000080
Anhui Shangbao	0.001661	0.000015	0.000022
Chongqing Ribao	0.002668	0.000133	0.000087
Fujian Ribao	0.001893	0.000089	0.000042
Guangzhou Ribao	0.001518	0.000113	0.000050
Haixia Daobao	0.001591	0.000252	0.000039
Huaxia Shibao	0.001157	0.000538	0.000030
Jiangsu Jingji Bao	0.001477	0.000036	0.000042
Jiefang Ribao	0.001240	0.000521	0.000061
Jiefangjun Bao	0.001278	0.000070	0.000102
Laodong Bao	0.001968	0.000059	0.000005
Lianhe Shibao	0.003103	0.000050	0.000028
Nanfang Zhoumo	0.001863	0.000604	0.000037
Renmin Ribao	0.001785	0.000846	0.000100
Shanxi Ribao	0.001663	0.000032	0.000082
Sichuan Gongren Ribao	0.003891	0.000058	0.000067
Sichuan Zhengxie Bao	0.004057	0.000054	0.000078
Wenhui Bao	0.001321	0.000250	0.000058
Xinhua Ribao	0.001815	0.000061	0.000120
Xinxi Ribao	0.001496	0.000062	0.000010
Yangcheng Wanbao	0.001452	0.000048	0.000051
Yunnan Ribao	0.001613	0.000014	0.000059
Zhongguo Jingji Shibao	0.001346	0.000148	0.000027
Zhongguo Jingying Bao	0.001295	0.000134	0.000025
Zhonghua Gongshang Shibao	0.001169	0.000411	0.000028
Category mean	0.001790	0.000201	0.000055

Newspaper	Politics-unclear	Positive words	Science/medicine
Anhui Qingnian Bao	0.020102	0.068577	0.001766
Anhui Ribao	0.035193	0.069918	0.002113
Anhui Shangbao	0.013672	0.044673	0.002094
Chongqing Ribao	0.030167	0.061239	0.002476
Fujian Ribao	0.031281	0.065386	0.002507
Guangzhou Ribao	0.024722	0.051917	0.002223
Haixia Daobao	0.016173	0.045452	0.001947
Huaxia Shibao	0.013270	0.051743	0.002021
Jiangsu Jingji Bao	0.023962	0.064264	0.002030
Jiefang Ribao	0.023368	0.060893	0.003687
Jiefangjun Bao	0.038487	0.078539	0.002698
Laodong Bao	0.016992	0.055450	0.002102
Lianhe Shibao	0.045637	0.073519	0.002666
Nanfang Zhoumo	0.021986	0.049705	0.002008
Renmin Ribao	0.033309	0.069391	0.002085
Shanxi Ribao	0.031521	0.067363	0.002723
Sichuan Gongren Ribao	0.027359	0.060127	0.002772
Sichuan Zhengxie Bao	0.059180	0.085786	0.002233
Wenhui Bao	0.021140	0.062941	0.002863
Xinhua Ribao	0.029723	0.065441	0.002976
Xinxi Ribao	0.011537	0.048852	0.002326
Yangcheng Wanbao	0.018283	0.049596	0.002475
Yunnan Ribao	0.032855	0.074014	0.002316
Zhongguo Jingji Shibao	0.020581	0.060466	0.002415
Zhongguo Jingying Bao	0.012338	0.054017	0.001888
Zhonghua Gongshang Shibao	0.018155	0.059204	0.002327
Category mean	0.026444	0.062168	0.002366

Newspaper	Sentiment (all)	Sports	Transport
Anhui Qingnian Bao	0.094928	0.001066	0.000661
Anhui Ribao	0.090076	0.001073	0.001524
Anhui Shangbao	0.077666	0.002828	0.002928
Chongqing Ribao	0.081953	0.001673	0.003051
Fujian Ribao	0.085059	0.001334	0.001571
Guangzhou Ribao	0.077245	0.001717	0.003693
Haixia Daobao	0.069611	0.001703	0.003556
Huaxia Shibao	0.084166	0.001512	0.003073
Jiangsu Jingji Bao	0.092966	0.001877	0.001526
Jiefang Ribao	0.085564	0.001236	0.002678
Jiefangjun Bao	0.111813	0.002180	0.000407
Laodong Bao	0.083808	0.001116	0.000843
Lianhe Shibao	0.092607	0.001269	0.001515
Nanfang Zhoumo	0.088740	0.001082	0.001193
Renmin Ribao	0.097093	0.001236	0.000883
Shanxi Ribao	0.088722	0.001520	0.001284
Sichuan Gongren Ribao	0.087339	0.001436	0.001658
Sichuan Zhengxie Bao	0.103664	0.001086	0.000788
Wenhui Bao	0.087823	0.001323	0.002308
Xinhua Ribao	0.089229	0.001134	0.001730
Xinxi Ribao	0.078916	0.001968	0.001844
Yangcheng Wanbao	0.079489	0.001589	0.002103
Yunnan Ribao	0.090984	0.001507	0.001414
Zhongguo Jingji Shibao	0.090728	0.001111	0.002046
Zhongguo Jingying Bao	0.082854	0.001747	0.001580
Zhonghua Gongshang Shibao	0.085708	0.001226	0.001301
Category mean	0.088164	0.001448	0.001806

174 *Appendices*

Newspaper	Yanjin ci
Anhui Qingnian Bao	0.000004
Anhui Ribao	0.000000
Anhui Shangbao	0.000000
Chongqing Ribao	0.000234
Fujian Ribao	0.000022
Guangzhou Ribao	0.000080
Haixia Daobao	0.000001
Huaxia Shibao	0.000007
Jiangsu Jingji Bao	0.000006
Jiefang Ribao	0.000004
Jiefangjun Bao	0.000012
Laodong Bao	0.000009
Lianhe Shibao	0.000003
Nanfang Zhoumo	0.000045
Renmin Ribao	0.000078
Shanxi Ribao	0.000014
Sichuan Gongren Ribao	0.000011
Sichuan Zhengxie Bao	0.000021
Wenhui Bao	0.000020
Xinhua Ribao	0.000017
Xinxi Ribao	0.000010
Yangcheng Wanbao	0.000009
Yunnan Ribao	0.000021
Zhongguo Jingji Shibao	0.000058
Zhongguo Jingying Bao	0.000010
Zhonghua Gongshang Shibao	0.000021
Category mean	0.000028

Index

Note: Page numbers with *t* indicate tables.

ACJA *see* All-China Journalists' Association (ACJA)
advocacy: consequences of 149–50; defined 20
advocate journalist professionals 60–71; characteristics of 26*t*; described 9–10; factors pushing 66–7; informal networks and, power of 66–7; longer-term implications 149–50; market power and 63–6; nationalism and 61–3; overview of 60–1; path dependence and 69–71; pushback and 96–8; role of, as educator 69; short-term consequences 149; tradition and 67–9
All-China Journalists' Association (ACJA) 22–3, 151
All-China Lawyers Association 151
Ambiguities of Domination (Wedeen) 139
American-style journalists 50–7; characteristics of 26*t*; Chinese reality and desires of 51–2; described 9; objectivity limits of 56–7; overview of 50–1; rise of 52–6

Bagdikian, Ben 80
Bandurski, David 19, 34, 37, 94, 140
Beijing Daily 70
Beijing News 7, 10, 25, 51, 149; advocate journalists at 65, 71; background of 113–14; pushback by 74, 94, 96; strike case study 113–16
Beijing *vs.* Chinese media 3–5
Beijing Youth Daily 3
Benson, Rodney 19, 21
Blanchard, Margaret 52
blogging 67
Bourdieu, Pierre 146

Bo Xilai 132
Brady, Anne-Marie 81
Bratkowski, Stefan 145
Burstein, Paul 142

Caijing magazine 51, 54, 87, 92–3, 94, 95, 130, 140, 150
Caixin – China Economics and Finance 51
Caixin Media 61
carfare, as corruption type 41, 44
CCP *see* Chinese Communist Party (CCP)
censorship, of Chinese media: Beijing and 3–5; economic liberalization and 2–3; overview of 1–2; pushback and 7–8; qualitative research limitations 12–14; quantitative research limitations 14–15; self-censorship and 5–7
Central Propaganda Department (CPD) 1, 140; ACJA and 22–3; corruption by 47; editor appointment/removal by 4; self-censorship and 5–7
Chan, Ying 69
Chang, P. H. 53
Chang Ping 74, 75–6
Chen, Chongshan 50
Chen, Feng 120–1
Chen Duxiu 68
Chen Meng 54
Chiang Ching-kuo 152, 153
China Central Television (CCTV) 35
China Commercial Times 46
China Core Newspaper Database 83
China Economic Times 61
China Environment News 31, 131
China Journalism Yearbooks 15, 45, 64, 87
China Management Daily 87
China Media Project 37, 140

Index

China Newsweek 65, 71
China Youth Daily 7, 10, 54, 121; advocate journalists and 60, 61, 62, 63, 64, 71; control of 108–10; Lijiawa coal mine story and 40; open letters background 108; pushback by 74, 76; pushback case study 108–13
Chinese Academy of Social Sciences (CASS) 45; New Research Institute 15
Chinese Communist Party (CCP) 1; see also communist professionals; coercion by 4–5; news workers as throat and tongue of 20; Organization Department 4; Party principle and 22; pushback and 142–4
Chinese Dream 117
Chinese future 152–5
Chinese government cover-ups 46
Chinese journalism: Internet and 128–36; typology of 20t
Chinese journalists 19–27; advocate professionals 60–71; American-style 50–7; characteristics of 26t; Communist professionals 30–7; fieldwork sites for study of 21t; future research for 150–2; introduction to 19–21; methodology used 21–2; professional, making 22–5; pushback and 95–6; workaday reporters 40–8
Chinese media: Beijing vs. 3–5; censorship of (see censorship, of Chinese media); corruption, forms of 41–3; CPD regulation of 2–3; during Cultural Revolution 2; funding for 2; introduction to 1–2; during Mao era 1–2; public service and, commitment to 25
Code of Newspaper Practices 53
Collection of Translated Essays on Mass Media Management (Yu Guoming) 55
Committee to Protect Journalists 4
Communist capitalism model 50
communist professionals 30–7; CCP and 34; characteristics of 26t; described 9; identity of 35–6; overview of 30–3; professionalism of 33–4
Communist Youth League 108, 110–13; see also China Youth Daily; pushback, going beyond
computer-assisted content analysis (CCA) 14; of pushback 81–2
Confucian liberalism model 50
Control 2.0 37, 140

corruption 147–8; causes of media 43–4; definitions of 40; forms of media 41–3; low salaries and 44; profession and 45–6; state 46–7
covert resistance, defined 77
CPD see Central Propaganda Department (CPD)
Crozier, Michel 5
Curry, Jane Leftwich 33, 145

Da Gong Bao 68
Dalai Lama 36
de Burgh, Hugo 9, 76
Deng Xiaoping 2, 152
dictionary construction 83–4
double designation (shuanggui) policy 94

Eckstein, Susan 47
economic determinism, pushback and 78, 80–1
Egorov, Georgy 144
Einwohner, Rachel L. 77
Esarey, Ashley 3, 81, 87
Exporting the First Amendment (Blanchard) 52

Fairhurst, Gail T. 141
Farmer's Daily 34, 35, 44
First, The 32
Fourth Estate 19, 60; see also Chinese journalists
Fox News 23

gatekeepers, news outlets as 134–5
General Administration on Press and Publication (GAPP) 4, 46, 89, 119
Glavlit 143
Goldman, Merle 68
Gong Wen 43–4
Green Journalist Salon 24
grievances, pushback and 120–3
Guangming Daily 2, 25, 113, 114, 116
Guiyang Daily 54
Guriev, Sergei 144

Haas, Peter 146, 150
Hala, Martin 34, 94
Hallin, Daniel C. 52, 66, 80, 87
Harris, Robert 47
He, Zhou 5
Herfindahl-Hirschman Index (HHI) 88
Hollander, Jocelyn A. 77
homophily 13

Huang Yuhao 149
Hu Jintao 14, 152
Hurst, William 121
Hu Shih 68
Hu Shuli 94, 95, 96, 150
Hutchinson, Thomas 145–6
Hu Zhibin 30, 32, 37

individual to professional transformation, four elements of 33
informal networks, power of 66–7
International Organization of Journalists (IOJ) 145
Internet, Chinese journalism and 128–36; article reprints from 134*t*; gatekeepers and, news outlets role as 134–5; isolation and 133–4; overview of 128–33

Jade Bird Group 108–9
Jernow, Allison Liu 50
Jiang Zemin 14
jiduzhe 52
Jie Fang Daily 54
Jin Yongquan 60, 61, 64
journalists *see* Chinese journalists
Judge, Joan 32, 68–9

Kahneman, Daniel 120

Lawson, Chappell H. 80, 153
Lee, Chin-Chuan 9, 32–3, 50, 80
Li, Lianjiang 78
Liang Qichao 67, 69
Li Datong 52, 55, 65, 76, 96, 97, 99, 107, 110, 111–12, 121–2
Liebman, Benjamin 63
Li Erliang 121
Li Liangrong 50–1
Lin, Fen J. 50, 61–2
Lin Biao 98
Lin Zhao 108
Li Qinghua 61
Liu Binyan 30, 69
Liu Di 129
Liu Jianqiang 70
Liu Shaoqi 33
Liu Yong 129, 133
Li Xueqian 108, 112
Li Yang 70–1
Lorentzen, Peter 143–4
Lowe, Will 84
Luo Changping 114

Lü Xun 68
Lu Yuegang 23, 24, 60, 76, 95, 107, 109–12, 121

McAdam, Doug 77, 119, 122
Mancini, Paolo 52, 66, 80, 87
Maoist model of journalism 50
Mao Zedong 36
marketization: political orientation of news and 3–4; pushback and 78
markets, limited power of 63–6
Ma Yunlong 42
media corruption: causes of 43–4; forms of 41–3
Meyerson, Debra E. 75, 149
Modern Express 54
MSN 24
MSNBC 23

National Business Daily 54
National People's Congress (NPC) 24
netizens 32, 129
newspapers analyzed 161; advocacy journalism rank-order list 164; category means 166–74; negative/positive words rank-order list 163; sampling methodology used 82–3; sensitivity rank-order list 162; topics analyzed 165
news professionalism 51
New York Times, The 34, 52, 132
noninstitutionalized tactics 142

objectivity, limits of 56–7
O'Brien, Kevin 78, 84, 121, 142
O'Leary, Rosemary 75
Open Constitution Initiative (*Gongmeng*) 93
Oriental Morning Post 54

paid news 41
paid no-news 43
Party principle 22
path dependence, advocacy and 69–71
Pei, Minxin 80
People's Daily (*Renmin Ribao*) 19, 30, 31, 64, 134; commercialization and 43–4; communist professionals and 35–6; *Overseas Edition* 33
Pierson, Paul 70
play edge ball 75, 76, 94, 118
Polarized Pluralist model 87
political opportunity structures (POS), pushback and 78, 93–5, 118–19
political process theory (PPT) 118–19

178 *Index*

Popping, Roel 83
positive feedback, path dependence and 70
Prentoulis, Marina 25
privileged nonstate actors, pushback and 74–5
professional journalists: communist 33–6; corruption and 45–6; importance of 146–7; making 22–5; objectivity and 23
publication number, obtaining 4
public professions, importance of 146–7
pushback 74–100; advocacy journalism and 96–8; analysis results 90–1*t*, 90–3, 92*t*; causes of 78; CCP allowance of 142–4; Chang Ping and 75–6; Chinese professional journalists example of 95–6; claims made by participants of 76; computer-assisted content analysis of 81–2; context of 77–8, 79*t*; control variables for analysis of 88–9, 89*t*; defined 7, 74; dependent variable construction for analysis of 84–5, 86*t*; dictionary construction for analysis of 83–4; economic determinism example of 78, 80–1; effects of 98–9; examples of 75; forms of 74–5; independent variable construction for analysis of 86–8, 89*t*; introduction to 74; newspaper sampling methodology used in analysis of 82–3, 161–74; political opportunity structures example of 93–5; to resistance 144–6; *vs.* resistance 7–8, 77–8, 79*t*; social movement theory and 141–2; utility of 141
pushback, going beyond 107–23; *Beijing News* strike case study 113–16; *China Youth Daily* case study 108–13; grievances and 120–3; introduction to 107–8; *Southern Weekend* strike case study 116–18; theoretical payoff for 118–20

Qian Gang 19
Qin Benli 69
QQ network 24

radical public opinion 32
reform era 69
rent seeking 43
resistance, defined 77; *see also* pushback
resistance behavior *see* pushback
Rose-Ackerman, Susan 43, 45

SAPPRFT *see* State Administration of Press, Publication, Radio, Film, and Television (SAPPRFT)

Scott, James C. 78
Scully, Maureen A. 75, 149
self-censorship 5–7; defined 5; *Southern Metropolis Daily* and 6–7
Shanghai Times 54
Shen Rufa 32
shut-up fees 41–2
Smyth, Frank 4
Snow, David A. 10, 120
social desirability bias 13
social movement theory: definition of 142; pushback and 141–2
Sonin, Konstantin 144
Southern Metropolis Daily 6–7, 54, 75, 91, 133
Southern Metropolitan News 98
Southern Weekend 3, 7, 10, 30, 51, 54, 87, 93, 123, 131; advocate journalists and 60–1, 62, 64, 69, 70, 71; pushback by 74; strike case study 116–18
spill news 132
State Administration of Press, Publication, Radio, Film, and Television (SAPPRFT) 2, 4, 22, 119, 148
state corruption 46–7
State Council Information Office (SCIO) 2
State Council Internet Office 2
Stewart, Concetta M. 82
Stewart, Potter 152
Stockmann, Daniela 80, 81
Sun Xupei 143
Sun Zhigang case 6–7, 149; pushback and 98

Tan Renwei 133
Tarrow, Sidney G. 77, 119, 122, 142
throat and tongue of CCP, news workers as 20; *see also* communist professionals
Tian, Yan 82
Tilly, Charles 77, 119, 122, 142
Time Weekly 54
Tong, Jingrong 70
transformation from individual to professional, four elements of 33
Tuchman, Gaye 56
Tumber, Howard 25
Tuo Zhen 117
Tversky, Amos 120
21st Century Business Herald 54

uncertainty, study of 139–41
unethical behavior, of workaday reporters 24–5
Unity Times 60
Using News to Influence Today-The Freezing Point Chronicle (Li Datong) 96

"Venus: The Price inside the Wall for the Floating Fragrance outside the Wall" (news article) 61

Wang Chen 33
Wang Zhaoguo 110
Watchdog Journalism and Global Democracy 51
WeChat network 24
Wedeen, Lisa 139
weibo 132, 134; article reprints from 134*t*
Wen Jiabao 132
Wen Wei Po 54
Western journalism theory 34
"Who Is Concerned about Freelance Professionals?" (news article) 60
Wilensky, Harold 23, 24
workaday reporters 40–8; characteristics of 26*t*; described 9; media corruption and, causes of 43–4; media corruption and, forms of 41–3; overview of 40–1; profession, corruption and 45–6; state, corruption and 46–7; unethical behavior of 24–5

Worker's Daily 31, 35
World Association of Newspapers 53

Xiao Qiang 47
Xi Jinping 116–17, 152
Xinhua News Agency 35

Yang, Guobin 129
Yang Bin 7, 74, 94, 113, 114–16, 122
Yangcheng Evening News 93
Yoshikoder 84
Yu Guoming 55

Zhai Minglei 63–4
Zhang Jie 65
Zhang Jinping 65
Zhan Jiang 44, 51
Zhao, Yuezhi 43, 50, 81
Zhao Yong 109–10
Zheng, Yongnian 129, 133
Zhou Zhenglong 129
Zhu Wenna 99
Zipf's Law 83, 85
Zoller, Heather M. 141